Multimodal Analysis in Academic Settings

This volume presents innovative research on the multimodal dimension of discourse specific to academic settings, with a particular focus on the interaction between the verbal and nonverbal in constructing meaning. Contributions by experienced and emerging researchers provide in-depth analyses in both research and teaching contexts, and consider the ways in which multimodal strategies can be leveraged to enhance the effectiveness of academic communication. Contributors employ both quantitative and qualitative analytical methods, and make use of state-of-the-art software for analyzing multimodal features of discourse.

The chapters in the first part of the volume focus on the multimodal features of two key research genres: conference presentations and plenary addresses. In the second part, contributors explore the role of multimodality in the classroom through analyses of both instructors' and students' speech, as well as the use of multimodal materials for more effective learning. The research presented in this volume is particularly relevant within the context of globalized higher education, where participants represent a wide range of linguistic and cultural backgrounds. *Multimodal Analysis in Academic Settings* contributes to an emerging field of research with importance to an increasing number of academics and practitioners worldwide.

Belinda Crawford Camiciottoli is an associate professor in the Department of Philology, Literature and Linguistics at the University of Pisa, Italy.

Inmaculada Fortanet-Gómez is a senior lecturer in the Department of English Language at Universitat Jaume I, Spain.

Routledge Studies in Multimodality

Edited by Kay L. O'Halloran, Curtin University

1 **New Perspectives on Narrative and Multimodality**
Edited by Ruth Page

2 **Multimodal Studies: Exploring Issues and Domains**
Kay L. O'Halloran and Bradley A. Smith

3 **Multimodality, Cognition, and Experimental Literature**
Alison Gibbons

4 **Multimodality in Practice: Investigating Theory-in-practice-through-methodology**
Sigrid Norris

5 **Multimodal Film Analysis: How Films Mean**
John Bateman and Karl-Heinrich Schmidt

6 **Multimodality and Social Semiosis**
Communication, Meaning-Making, and Learning in the Work of Gunther Kress
Edited by Margit Böck and Norbert Pachler

7 **Spoken and Written Discourse in Online Interactions**
A Multimodal Approach
Maria Grazia Sindoni

8 **Critical Multimodal Studies of Popular Discourse**
Edited by Emilia Djonov and Sumin Zhao

9 **Film Discourse Interpretation**
Towards a New Paradigm for Multimodal Film Analysis
Janina Wildfeuer

10 **Multimodal Approaches to Research and Pedagogy**
Recognition, Resources, and Access
Edited by Arlene Archer and Denise Newfield

11 **Multimodal Epistemologies**
Towards an Integrated Framework
Edited by Arianna Maiorani and Christine Christie

12 **Multimodal Analysis in Academic Settings**
From Research to Teaching
Edited by Belinda Crawford Camiciottoli and Inmaculada Fortanet-Gómez

Multimodal Analysis in Academic Settings

From Research to Teaching

Edited by
Belinda Crawford Camiciottoli and Inmaculada Fortanet-Gómez

Routledge
Taylor & Francis Group
LONDON AND NEW YORK

First published 2015 by Routledge

2 Park Square, Milton Park, Abingdon, Oxfordshire OX14 4RN
711 Third Avenue, New York, NY 10017

Routledge is an imprint of the Taylor & Francis Group, an informa business

First issued in paperback 2018

Library of Congress Cataloging-in-Publication Data

Multimodal analysis in academic settings : from research to teaching / Edited by Belinda Crawford Camiciottoli and Inmaculada Fortanet-Gómez.
pages cm. — (Routledge Studies in Multimodality ; #12)
Includes bibliographical references and index.
1. Modality (Linguistics)—Research. 2. Language and languages—Study and teaching (Higher) 3. Grammar, Comparative and general—Modularity. 4. Applied linguistics—Research—Methodology. 5. Multimedia communication. I. Camiciottoli, Belinda Crawford, editor. II. Fortanet-Gómez, Inmaculada, 1962– editor.
P99.4.M6M73 2015
302.2—dc23
2015001697

ISBN: 978-1-138-82710-3 (hbk)
ISBN: 978-1-138-54907-4 (pbk)

Typeset in Sabon
by Apex CoVantage, LLC

Contents

PART II
Classroom Applications

Figures

Tables

Introduction

Inmaculada Fortanet-Gómez and Belinda Crawford Camiciottoli

MULTIMODALITY: DEFINITION AND BACKGROUND

Multimodality is an approach used to understand the contribution of various semiotic resources (e.g., verbal, visual, aural, spatial) in studies of communication. As aptly summarized by Jewitt (2014a, p. 1) "Multimodality approaches representation, communication and interaction as something more than language." The multimodal approach has generated much interest in recent years in an increasing range of domains such as advertising, film, museums and of course linguistic research (O'Halloran & Smith, 2011). Nowadays, it is already assumed among researchers that verbal language analysis is not enough if the aim is to fully understand communication (Baldry, 2000; Kress, 2000, 2003; Jewitt, 2014a). Discourse is multimodal and this fact needs to be recognized in linguistic research.

Most studies that deal with multimodality acknowledge three approaches, according to Jewitt (2014b). The first follows social semiotics with an origin in Hallidayan systemic functional linguistics and the work of Kress and van Leeuwen (2001) and van Leeuwen (2005). Social semiotic multimodality aims to shed light on how people use modal resources in a certain social context (Jewitt, 2014b). The second approach, also based on Halliday's systemic functional grammar (Halliday & Matthiessen, 2014), is closer to discourse analysis, grounded in systemic functional theory (O'Halloran, 2004). Here the objective is to analyze semiotic resources in order to understand their meaning potential and how they function, as well as how they can integrate with each other and how they are interpreted in a given context. The third approach to multimodality, multimodal interactional analysis, was developed by Scollon and Scollon (2003) and combines interactional sociolinguistics, intercultural communication and multimodal semiotics. This approach mainly focuses on the notion of context and situated interaction: how participants in a communicative event express and react to the discourse of others. The three approaches do not have well-defined boundaries and thus have points in common. However, there are differences between them related to the research theories from which they are drawn, the degree of emphasis placed on context, the interrelationship among modes and the extent of the focus on the sign-maker (Jewitt, 2014b).

The rapid development of digital interactive media, involving most social practices and communication media, has also had a clear impact on multimodal research (Hyland, 2009). Apart from multimodality in human-to-human communication, there are also studies which explore the relationship between discourse and technology (cf. Scollon & Levine, 2004; Djonov & Zhao, 2013; Lemke, 2014). Indeed, the study of multimodality often focuses on both human-to-human interaction and human-machine interaction.

As language is inherently multimodal, multimodality is also present in natural language learning. If we observe a child learning a language, we soon realize that s/he starts communicating by reproducing gestures, facial expressions, gaze and sounds. It is only when these modes have been proven successful that children start uttering words with different paralinguistic effects, and later complete information units with their particular pauses, intonation and stress distribution. Close observation of early language learning and later language use has proved that there is usually a relationship between gestures and other modes of expression and meaning (Matthiessen, 2007). For example, extending arms forward can be associated with words such as "inviting" or "going"; a fixed and continuous stare can mean willingness to establish a bond; and certain sounds can mean excitement or joy. These modes of expression may be accompanied by words or produce meaning on their own. The extreme case of this is deaf sign language, which is also multimodal as there are conventional signs and gestures accompanied by expressions that add personal meaning to the signs. However, no words from natural language are needed for this communication (Poveda, Pulido, Morgado, Messina & Hédlová, 2008).

In the preceding paragraphs, we have provided an overview of the notion of multimodality, highlighting its vital role in communication and the different approaches that have been used to understand its contribution to meaning. In the next section, we shift the focus to the level of language and discourse, thus moving closer to the topic of this volume, i.e., academic discourse. More specifically, we look at how multimodal analysis can be applied to analyze written and oral texts in a comprehensive way that takes into account the interplay of multiple semiotic resources.

MULTIMODAL DISCOURSE ANALYSIS: THEORETICAL FOUNDATIONS AND PRINCIPLES

As pointed out in the previous section, most research following the approach of multimodal discourse analysis is based on systemic functional linguistics as developed by Halliday (1994; see also Halliday & Matthiessen, 2014; O'Halloran, 2004). Halliday takes a social semiotic view of communication and distinguishes three metafunctions in human language: *ideational* (representation of the world), *interpersonal* (communication to interact with other human beings) and *textual* (relevance of the context) (Royce & Bowcher, 2007). People construct representations of the world (ideational meaning). At the same time, they relate with other people by means of signs (interpersonal function), which are organized into meaningful texts (textual metafunction).

Matthiessen (2007, p. 1) suggests that semiotic systems can be viewed "from above" and "from below." If one looks at them from above, from the context of culture in which they operate, what can be seen is just a unit. It is like a poster made of a number of puzzle pieces; what is seen from above is the poster, the complete picture, the representation of the world (ideational function). If one looks at the semiotic systems from below, what can be seen is all the modes that interplay to create meaning, like the pieces of a puzzle: text, images, gestures, sounds, music, etc. The pieces are organized as in a text (textual function), but they need to be put together by an individual who finds and transmits the meaning of the puzzle to other people (interpersonal function).

In any communication using a combination of modes, meaning is distributed across all the modes. The relationships between modes are very complex and can vary in time between the moment a communicative event is planned until it is interpreted by a receiver. Iedema (2001) points out the changes a communicative event goes through from its planning to its final outcome. For example, in conference presentations, planning is organized very often in writing, and later the written document becomes an oral performance (usually embedding a number of semiotic modes in itself), which turns again into a written text when it is published in the proceedings of a conference or any other printed version of the paper or lecture presentation. In each of these changes, the communicative event undergoes resemiotization since the modes and their relationships are different. As Iedema (2001, p. 36) states: "It is through this process of resemiotization that the community transposes and reifies its knowledges, techniques and technologies, as well as its interpersonal, social and cultural practices and positionings."

Multimodal research aims to explore how each mode contributes and interacts with the other modes in the same communicative event. For example, Royce (2007, p. 63) examines the relationship between modes in a single text, an article from *The Economist,* and finds that "*intersemiotic complementarity* [. . .] is realized through various linguistic and visual means peculiar to the respective modes." This relationship can occur through intersemiotic sense relations such as repetition or synonymy; through intersemiotic reinforcement of address, attitudinal congruence and attitudinal dissonance (modality) relations; and through compositional relations of information value, visual framing, visual synonymy, etc. (for further explanation see Royce, 1998, 2007). Intersemiotic relationships are varied and different modes may even contradict each other during communication. For example, Querol-Julián and Fortanet-Gómez (2012) suggest that speakers are often unaware of some of the gestures or expressions that accompany their speech, which in some cases may be interpreted as contradictory with the words uttered (also noticed by Jewitt, 2014b). Different semiotic modes may also have more or less prominence. In some instances of multimodal communication, there may be one semiotic resource that can be construed as primary and several secondary ones. For example, in academic lectures the teacher uses primarily spoken language to transmit content, but also gestures and paralinguistic resources to highlight the important parts of the lecture and/or the relationships between the parts, or to interact with the students. On the other hand, in other instances, all modes may be indispensable in order to understand communication. This is the case of films, where it is even possible to focus specifically on a certain gesture or facial expression in order to make it the central element of a certain scene, and where image, sounds or music may be even more important than words (Bateman & Schmidt, 2012; Bateman, 2014).

Multimodal research is complex: In just one communicative event an individual has to choose from a multitude of options in several semiotic systems (O'Halloran, Tan & Smith, 2015, in press). Some researchers have tried to create models that describe multimodal relations based on language systems. Inspired by Martin's (2007) instantiation hierarchy, Tang (2013) proposes a generalized multimodal hierarchy. For these researchers, a system of language consists of all potential meaning that is possible behind all instances of text. Tang clarifies that at the top of the hierarchy there should be the system, consisting of all possible meanings that can be produced with the combination of all semiotic *modes* within a culture. Second in order should be all the *genres* possible in that culture, considering that new genres are continually appearing as new semiotic systems that combine in different ways (e.g., all new genres that have appeared with computer-mediated communication in the last 30 years). *Thematic patterns* come third and can be construed as generic examples, as in the case of classroom lectures. Then, the fourth place is occupied by the multimodal instance, i.e., an actual example of multimodal communication. Finally, at the bottom of the hierarchy is the interpretation made by the receiver, as a communicative act only becomes meaningful when the participants make sense of it. The multimodal instantiation hierarchy is summarized in Figure 0.1.

This model makes an important contribution to multimodal research by clearly articulating the hierarchical relations among instances of communication that exist within a system that encompasses all modes. At the same time, it allows us to conceive of communication as "the integration of language and all modes as one generalized system" (Tang, 2013, p. 24). Thus, the multimodal instantiation hierarchy can shed light on how semiotic modes work together to express local meanings within a particular culture or community.

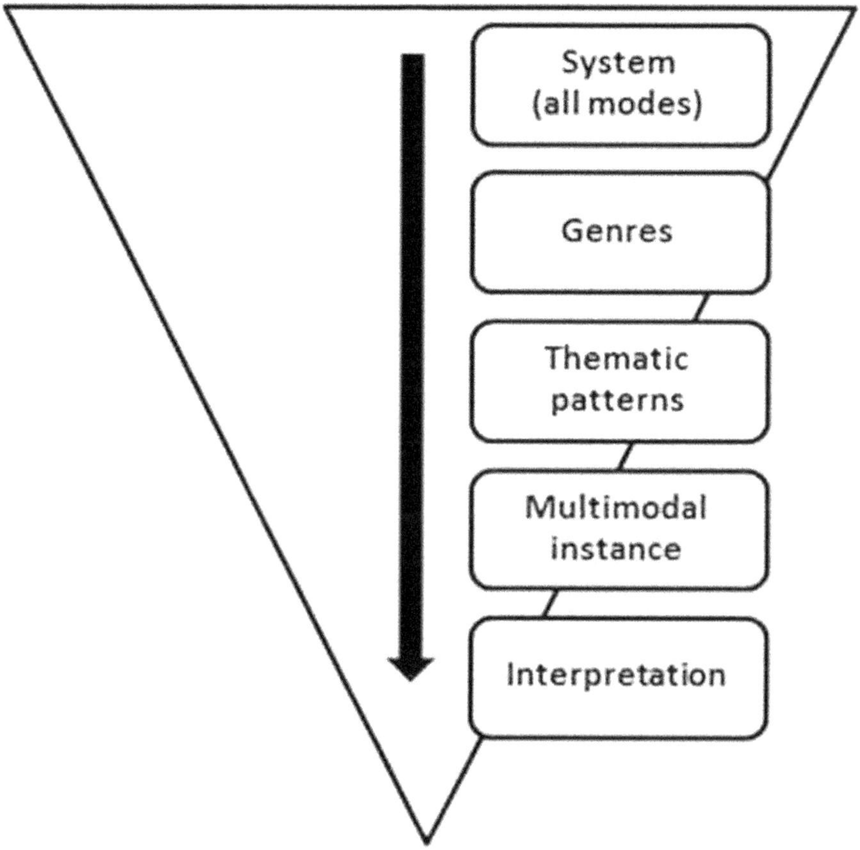

Figure 0.1 Generalized multimodal instantiation hierarchy (Adapted from Tang, 2013)

THE APPLICATION OF MULTIMODAL DISCOURSE ANALYSIS IN ACADEMIC SETTINGS

The aim of the present volume is to contribute to multimodal research by analyzing the discourse of academic settings, focusing specifically on the discourse found in contexts of higher education. The research presented in the various chapters that comprise the volume draws from the three approaches referred to above (social semiotic, systemic functional and interactional analysis) in various ways, e.g., describing the modes speakers can choose from, how speakers choose different modal resources in a communicative event, and how speakers interact with each other by negotiating meaning in certain contexts such as scientific conferences and university classes.

Regarding research settings, many studies that have developed multimodal discourse analysis for conference genres take a particular genre as a basis for the study and one or several multimodal instances as the object of the analysis. Carter-Thomas and Rowley-Jolivet (2003) maintain that genres use several semiotic modes to communicate, which become more or less relevant depending on the nature of the genre and the function they have in each instance. For example, they argue that in conference presentations (CPs), "three main modes are used: language, visual communication and gesture," and that visual communication is even more relevant in science CPs (Carter-Thomas & Rowley-Jolivet, 2003, p. 68). In this genre, the main mode is language, while the other modes are used to reinforce it (gestures are usually limited and visual displays are used as a support to words). However, the three semiotic modes can be used with their appropriate functions at different parts of the speech. Natural language may be more appropriate to indicate time relations, whereas the visual mode is more often used for spatial relations. Gestures can be used for locating items or for animating a static visual. The degree of articulation of a certain mode depends on the communicative needs of a specific discourse community. Audiences at scientific conferences are usually heterogeneous regarding their linguistic background, which makes the combination of modes even more relevant for an understanding of the discourse. Considering the universality of most visual communication, visual support plays a prominent role in scientific conference presentations in order to make communication more effective. The discourse of scientific conferences will be the object of analysis in some of the chapters in this volume (e.g., Chapters 1–5), mainly focusing on the speaker as a sign-maker.

In the classroom, there are two possible ways to look at multimodal research. On the one hand, there are the communication processes that take place between the teacher and the students (or among the students), which are mediated through teaching materials (books, images, websites, etc.). On the other hand, there is the teaching of multimodal discourse, i.e., teaching and learning a language as an ensemble or combination of modes. Students need to acquire skills for understanding and producing texts that combine several modes according to the context and discipline involved, and new pedagogic practices need to be designed in order to raise awareness of multimodality (O'Halloran et al., in press). Research related to teacher-learner interaction stems from the intersection between new literacy studies (Gee, 1996) and multimodality (Street, Pahl & Rowsell, 2014). With reference to literacy, we should mention the important work initiated by the New London Group—ten researchers who met in 1994 to discuss aspects related to the multiplicity of discourses in order to teach them. These discourses belong to culturally and linguistically diverse and increasingly globalized societies, and take a variety of text forms mainly associated with new technologies, including visual images and their relationship to the written word (New London Group, 1996). Most literacy-based studies have focused on written discourse, especially (text)books and educational websites for children and young people (Guzzetti & Bean, 2014; Schamroth Abrams, 2015), while relatively few have looked at spoken academic discourse from a multimodal perspective (cf. Crawford Camiciottoli, 2007). In the area of English for academic purposes (EAP), a key contribution is O'Halloran et al.'s (in press) in-depth analysis of the importance of multimodal approaches in these instructional settings to help learners exploit the affordances of multiple modes and media.

As indicated above, multimodality seems to be especially relevant in the language classroom and this has generated a series of studies that focus on the teaching of multimodal literacies. Even though it is generally assumed that discourse is multimodal, language courses typically teach only verbal resources, often ignoring the nonverbal signals that combine with them in order to convey the complete meaning. Some research (cf. Busà, 2010; Vaarala & Jalkanen, 2010) has demonstrated the effectiveness of introducing several modes in the classroom, paying special attention to the role of multimodality. Busà's (2010) study showed that introducing university English language learners to several modes can be highly effective in raising their awareness of how to enhance English communication by means of a combination of several modes. In this case, the students improved their ability to structure different types of discourse and to communicate in a multimodal way: through the use of language, intonation, gesture and body language.

Vaarala and Jalkanen (2010) discuss new multimodal literacies from the perspective of teaching textual comprehension. They point out that the way of reading and understanding reading is continuously changing nowadays. Texts are more accessible through the Internet and new technologies, and these texts are not printed and linear as they were in the past. Now texts are intertextual and reading is becoming an online activity. As a consequence, the teacher is required to carefully consider the criteria of a good task from a new perspective, for example, designing a task that genuinely encourages interaction. Some of the chapters of this book look at the multimodal nature of university classroom discourse, focusing especially on spoken discourse, as well as on how to teach multimodal discourse to language students.

To wrap up this reflection on multimodal discourse analysis, even though some researchers have traced the concept of multimodality back to the semiotic phenomena pointed out by Saussure (1916) or Barthes (1957) (cited in O'Halloran et al., 2011), multimodality is still a rather recent field of research with a great number of unexplored aspects. As recent research notes (Hyland, 2009; Tang, 2013; Jewitt, 2014a; O'Halloran et al., in press), several questions arise when carrying out research on multimodality: Can we define a semiotic system of image or gesture? How do these systems interact with the system of human language? How do people make meanings by linking text (both written and oral) with images, graphs, equations, gestures, facial expressions and gaze in communication instances? What are the 'affordances' of the several modes to contribute meaning? And here we would add some more: Is it possible to find specific combinations of the several modes with just one meaning in a certain genre (as an aggregated accumulation of many actual multimodal instances)? Moreover, is it possible to teach combinations of modes, when teaching a genre? These are some of the questions that will be addressed in the present volume.

OVERVIEW OF THE VOLUME

The contributions that comprise this volume have been structured into two parts as a way to reflect the two major areas of academic communication: research and instruction. The first part focuses on the multimodal features of two key spoken research genres: plenary addresses and conference presentations. In the second part, the role of multimodality in the classroom is explored through the analysis of genres used by both instructors and students, as well as the application of multimodal materials in the classroom for more effective language learning.

In Part I, the first two chapters focus on multimodal aspects of plenary addresses at academic conferences, representing an important spoken research genre that has not been extensively studied. The plenary lecture is a central component of academic conferences, typically delivered by prestigious invited speakers who make an important contribution to the advancement of knowledge and scientific debate at the conference itself, but also more broadly to the disciplinary discourse community. In Chapter 1, Zuocheng Zhang provides a comprehensive analysis of how plenary speakers express disagreement from the linguistic, interactional, functional and multimodal perspectives. The study highlights the complex interplay between the various communicative modes during the expression of disagreement, as revealed through the use of ELAN (EUDICO—European Distributed Corpora—Linguistic Annotator) multimodal annotation software (Wittenburg, Brugman, Russel, Klassmann & Sloetjes, 2006).[1]

Implications of the study for EAP settings are also discussed, pointing out the need to increase students' awareness of the vital role of disagreement within an academic community of practice and to help them develop strategies to effectively engage in it. Chapter 2, by Noelia Ruiz-Madrid and Inmaculada Fortanet-Gómez, also deals with plenary addresses, but offers an in-depth analysis of their verbal and nonverbal features from a contrastive point of view, i.e., by comparing two plenary lectures: one delivered in English and the other in Spanish. With special attention to how the plenary speakers seek to engage the audience on an interpersonal level during their digressions away from the main topic, the authors analyze simultaneously the verbal message, paralinguistic features and kinesics. Their detailed multimodal analysis brings to the fore some interesting aspects of plenary lectures that would not have been noticed with an analysis based on speech alone, e.g., how the speakers use humor and modesty to evoke empathy among the audience. Interestingly, there were no significant differences in the usage of nonlinguistic resources between the English speaker and the Spanish speaker during digressive episodes, a result which the authors suggest may be linked to the fact that the two speakers have similar profiles as esteemed international scholars. The findings of these two studies on plenary addresses offer new insights into the multimodal dimension of this research genre not only on a descriptive level, but also on a practical one, i.e., by providing valuable knowledge that can help 'aspiring' plenary speakers deliver more effective speeches.

Chapters 3 to 5 deal with different aspects of scientific research presentations given by academics who participate in the regular conference sessions that either follow or precede the plenary addresses discussed above. Each chapter adopts a multimodal analytical approach, although in various ways and from diverse perspectives. Chapter 3, by Miguel Ruiz-Garrido, picks up on the contrastive dimension that was highlighted in Chapter 2 by comparing the use of intensifying adverbs in English vs. Spanish conference presentations. In a dataset made up of two presentations delivered in English and two in Spanish, he found that in both languages linguistic expressions of intensification (e.g., *very/so* and *muy/más*) were usually accompanied by paralinguistic and kinesic resources, which typically served to reinforce their intensifying meanings, although no clear patterns in co-occurrences could be detected. Nonlinguistic features included stress, higher pitch and prolonged syllables, as well as various types of hand, arm, head and body movements. Particularly the latter were used more frequently by the Spanish speakers, which the author suggests could be linked to cultural differences. However, in general, the kinesic movements tended to co-occur both with each other and with the paralinguistic features, forming an interesting mixture of communicative modes used for purposes of intensification. In Chapter 4, Giuliana Diani concentrates on the visual semiotic mode, offering a comprehensive study of visual aids used by presenters to communicate research results during academic conferences. Based on a large corpus of PowerPoint slides projected at international applied linguistics conferences, the methodological approach integrates multimodal and rhetorical analysis, drawing from previous work on visual typologies in academic discourse, as well as structural analysis of research articles, representing the written counterpart of the spoken conference presentation. The findings reveal an interesting multimodal array of slide typologies that incorporate written text, numbers, graphs and images, while also largely following the traditional rhetorical structuring of written research communications (i.e., Introduction-Method-Results-Discussion). However, some interesting differences also emerged. For instance, with respect to the typical 'move' sequence in the macrostructure of research articles, conference slides sometimes exhibited a sequential 'disorder.' This was attributed to the hybrid nature and purpose of conference slides, which function as meaning-making resources for audiences, but also a support system for conference speakers themselves during their oral delivery in a way that is similar to notes. Thus, the analysis shows how conference presenters used PowerPoint slides to blend together the visual and verbal modes into a coherent communicative event, suggesting that the visually supported conference presentation may be construed as a genre in its own right. She concludes by pointing out that developing technologies will likely consolidate the strong contribution and growing importance of the visual mode in the dissemination of scientific knowledge. In Chapter 5, Julia Valeiras Jurado looks at the multimodal aspects of persuasion in conference presentations. She analyzes gestures and head movements (kinesic features) and intonation (paralinguistic features) in order to understand how they function on a rhetorical level to accomplish the aims of the speakers: to present a scientific novelty and to convince the audience that it is valid and valuable. Using a case study approach, she shows how two conference speakers support and reinforce what they consider to be important points in their presentations with gestures, head movements and intonation to communicate a persuasive message. Her analysis is integrated with interviews with the two participants to gain further insights into their verbal and nonverbal behaviors used as persuasive strategies. This feedback showed a keen awareness of their professional role as members of the broader academic community. She also suggests that persuasion in conference presentations is strictly linked to the particular communicative situation in which they take place, as well as the specific values and practices of the disciplinary community.

Part II, dedicated to classroom applications, opens with a conceptual chapter by Christine Räisänen (Chapter 6) that acts as a bridge between research and instruction. For this reason, it has been strategically placed at the beginning of this section. Although she refers to the conference presentation as an academic speech genre, her focus is on teaching and learning this genre, with particular reference to novice presenters (PhD students) as learners who are undergoing the challenging process of being enculturated into the discursive and social practices of the professional academic community. She brings a fresh and broadened perspective to multimodality by looking at material aspects of the setting (e.g., the organization of space, lighting, technical props) that all come into play during a presentation and can significantly contribute to its success or failure. In fact, conference presentations are viewed here through a sociomaterial lens, arguing for the need to problematize the role played by materials in terms of their affordances and/or constraints for both speakers' and audiences' affect and meaning-making. Drawing from a large number of conference presentations in various fields, she constructs a 'vignette' from her extensive experience that allows us not only to empathize with novice presenters, but also to better understand the difficulties that they may encounter in relation to materials. She concludes with some practical suggestions to enhance awareness of the crucial role of materials when teaching and learning how to deliver conference presentations.

The next two chapters offer multimodal analyses of two classroom genres. In Chapter 7, Belinda Crawford Camiciottoli focuses on academic lectures, with particular reference to how university professors elaborate explanations for a student audience. Using text-mining techniques and ELAN multimodal annotation software (Wittenburg et al., 2006), she analyzes explanatory episodes in a dataset compiled from Yale University OpenCourseWare lectures from the disciplinary area of humanities, and identifies linguistic expressions of explanation, as well as accompanying nonverbal signals (i.e., prosodic stress, direction of gaze and gestures). The analysis revealed that these humanities lecturers preferred complex argumentative forms over simpler explanatory devices (e.g., exemplification) on the verbal level, and used nonverbal signals in a synergistic way to facilitate and reinforce comprehension. Chapter 8, by Juan Carlos Palmer-Silveira, provides an in-depth look at the nonverbal dimension of student presentations in the context of a business communication course, with particular attention to how physical space, head movements, hand/arm gestures and eye contact were exploited by learners to convey an effective message during a company presentation. The author tracks the progress of three students who were learning to use body language more effectively by observing their video-recorded presentations. He also makes a series of useful recommendations for teaching nonverbal communication skills in the classroom as a way to help students learn to deliver better presentations.

The last two chapters of Part II present practice-oriented models for exploiting multimodal resources and multimodal transcription in the context of language teaching. Chapter 9, by Mari Carmen Campoy-Cubillo and Mercedes Querol-Julián, offers a new theoretically grounded framework for the multimodal assessment of listening comprehension skills in foreign language teaching. With respect to traditional forms of listening assessment that emphasize mainly audio input, the multimodal listening tasks that the authors propose are designed to measure students' ability to identify, interpret and evaluate both verbal and nonverbal information in the same kind of authentically multimodal input that they experience in real-life communicative situations. Thus, multimodal listening comprehension must be seen as a complex assessment that requires learners to successfully process various semiotic modes, and calls upon teachers to have a clear understanding of multimodality and how to incorporate it in their classroom activities. In Chapter 10, Silvia Bruti concludes by making the case for using film clips as important multimodal resources in the foreign language classroom. She demonstrates their pedagogical validity in the teaching of pragmatic features of conversational interaction, specifically the conversational routines of greeting and leave-taking. Through a detailed multimodal analysis of two film clips from the Berkeley Language Center's film clip database (Library of Foreign Language Film Clips—LFLFC), she shows how multimodal transcription of film dialogue can offer insights into the interplay of linguistic and nonlinguistic elements during conversational interaction, while also suggesting ways to exploit multimodal transcription as a learning activity to teach conversational routines from a holistic perspective.

Using both traditional and innovative analytical techniques, the various contributions to this volume have considerably enhanced our understanding of how multimodal resources may be exploited to reinforce and integrate meanings in spoken academic discourse. Indeed, the fine-tuned analyses undertaken from a variety of perspectives have highlighted the subtle yet fundamental role of the nonverbal message in spoken academic communication. The emerging insights are useful to help novice academic communicators learn how to support their linguistic abilities with nonverbal behaviors, either when presenting their research results at conferences or when teaching in the classroom. Moreover, they may also be used in the context of language learning in order to enhance students' comprehension when attending classes taught in foreign languages, when performing presentations in class or when asked to use multimodal audiovisual materials, which are becoming increasingly common in both undergraduate and graduate courses.

NOTE

1. ELAN was developed at the Max Planck Institute for Psycholinguistics, the Language Archive, Nijmegen, the Netherlands. It is freely available at http://tla.mpi.nl/tools/tla-tools/elan/.

REFERENCES

Baldry, A. (Ed.) (2000). *Multimodality and multimediality in the distance learning age*. Campobasso: Palladino Editoriale.
Barthes, R. (1957). *Mythologies*. Paris: Seuil.
Bateman, J. (2014). Looking for what counts in film analysis: A programme of empirical research. In D. Machin (Ed.), *Visual communication* (pp. 301–329). Berlin: De Gruyter Mouton.
Bateman, J., & Schmidt, K.-H. (2012). *Multimodal film analysis: How films mean*. London: Routledge.
Busà, M. G. (2010). Sounding natural: Improving oral presentation skills. *Language Value, 2*(1), 51–67.
Carter-Thomas, S. & Rowley-Jolivet, E. (2003). Analysing the scientific conference presentation (CP), A methodological overview of a multimodal genre. *ASp, 39–40*, 59–72.
Crawford Camiciottoli, B. (2007). *The language of business studies lectures. A corpus-assisted analysis*. Amsterdam: John Benjamins.
Djonov, E., & Zhao, S. (Eds.). (2013). *Critical multimodal studies of popular discourse*. London: Routledge.
Gee, J. P. (1996). *Social linguistics: Ideology in discourses*. London: Taylor & Francis.
Guzzetti, B. J., & Bean, T. (2014). *Adolescent literacies and the gendered self: (Re)constructing identities through multimodal literacy practices*. London: Routledge.
Halliday, M.A.K. (1994). *An introduction to functional grammar* (2nd edition). London: Edward Arnold.
Halliday, M.A.K., & Matthiessen, C.M.I.M. (2014). *Halliday's introduction to functional grammar* (4th edition). London: Routledge.

Hyland, K. (2009). *Academic discourse: English in a global context.* London: Continuum.
Iedema, R. (2001). Resemiotization. *Semiotica, 137*(1/4), 23–39.
Jewitt, C. (Ed.) (2014a). *The Routledge handbook of multimodal analysis.* (2nd edition) London: Routledge.
Jewitt, C. (2014b). Different approaches to multimodality. In C. Jewitt (Ed.), *The Routledge handbook of multimodal analysis* (2nd edition) (pp. 28–39). London: Routledge.
Kress, G. (2000). Multimodality. In B. Cope, & M. Kalanzis (Eds.), *Multiliteracies: Literacy learning and the design of social futures* (pp. 182–202). London: Routledge.
Kress, G. (2003). *Literacy in the new media age.* London: Routledge.
Kress, G., & van Leeuwen, T. (2001). *Multimodal discourse: The modes and media of contemporary communication.* London: Edward Arnold.
Lemke, J. (2014) Multimodality, identity and time. In C. Jewitt (Ed.), *The Routledge handbook of multimodal analysis* (2nd edition) (pp. 140–150). London: Routledge.
Martin, J.R. (2007). Genre, ideology and intertextuality: A systemic functional perspective. *Linguistics and the Human Sciences, 2*(2), 275.
Matthiessen, C.M.I.M. (2007). The multimodal page: A systemic functional exploration. In T.D. Royce, & W.L. Bowcher (Eds.), *New directions in the analysis of multimodal discourse* (pp. 1–14). Mahwah, NJ: Lawrence Erlbaum Associates, Inc.
New London Group. (1996). A pedagogy of multiliteracies: Designing social futures. *Harvard Educational Review, 66*(1), 60–92.
O'Halloran, K.L. (Ed.) (2004). *Multimodal discourse analysis: Systemic functional perspectives.* London: Continuum.
O'Halloran, K.L., & Smith, B.A. (2011). *Multimodal studies: Exploring issues and domains.* London: Routledge.
O'Halloran, K.L., Tan, S., & Smith, B.A. (in press). Multimodal approaches to English for academic purposes. In K. Hyland, & P. Shaw (Eds.), *The Routledge handbook of English for academic purposes.* London & New York: Routledge.
Poveda, D., Pulido, L., Morgado, M., Messina, C. & Hédlová, Z. (2008). Storytelling with sign language interpretation as a multimodal literacy vent: Implications for deaf and hearing children. *Language and Education, 22*(4), 320–342.
Querol-Julián, M., & Fortanet-Gómez, I. (2012). Multimodal evaluation in academic discussion sessions: How do presenters act and react? *English for Specific Purposes, 31*(4), 271–283.
Royce, T. (1998). *Visual-verbal intersemiotic complementarity in* The Economist *magazine* (Unpublished doctoral dissertation). University of Reading, United Kingdom. Retrieved from http://www.isfla.org/Systemics/Print/Theses/RoyceThesis/.
Royce T.D. (2007). Intersemiotic complementarity: A framework for multimodal discourse analysis. In T.D. Royce, & W.L. Bowcher (Eds.), *New directions in the analysis of multimodal discourse* (pp. 63–109). Mahwah, NJ: Lawrence Erlbaum Associates, Inc.
Royce, T.D., & Bowcher, W.L. (Eds.). (2007). *New directions in the analysis of multimodal discourse.* Mahwah, NJ: Lawrence Erlbaum Associates, Inc.
Saussure, F. (1916). *Cours de linguistique générale.* Lausanne: Payot.
Schamroth Abrams, S. (2015). *Integrating virtual and traditional learning in 6–12 classrooms: A layered literacies approach to multimodal meaning making.* London: Routledge.
Scollon, R., & Levine, P. (Eds.). (2004). *Multimodal discourse analysis as the confluence of discourse and technology.* Washington, DC: Georgetown University Press.

Scollon, R., & Scollon, S. (2003). *Discourses in place: Language in the material world*. New York: Routledge.

Street, B., Pahl, K., & Rowsell, J. (2014). Multimodality and new literacy studies. In C. Jewitt (Ed.), *The Routledge handbook of multimodal analysis* (pp. 181–200). London: Routledge.

Tang, K.-S. (2013). Instantiation of multimodal semiotic systems in science classroom discourse. *Language Sciences, 37*, 22–35.

Vaarala, H., & Jalkanen, J. (2010). Changing spaces, expanding mindsets: Towards L2 literacies on a multimodal reading comprehension course. *Language Value*, 2(1), 68–99.

van Leeuwen, T. (2005). *Introducing social semiotics*. London: Routledge.

Wittenburg, P., Brugman, H., Russel, A., Klassmann, A., & Sloetjes, H. (2006). ELAN: A professional framework for multimodality research. Proceedings of LREC 2006, Fifth International Conference on Language Resources and Evaluation. Retrieved from http://www.lrec-conf.org/proceedings/lrec2006/pdf/153_pdf.pdf.

Part I

Research Communications

1 Disagreements in Plenary Addresses as Multimodal Action

Zuocheng Zhang

1.1 INTRODUCTION

Disagreement has been discussed extensively in pragmatics. It is typically treated as a face-threatening speech act that needs mitigation. For example, Stalpers (1995) identifies ten strategies that may be used to mitigate disagreements. Her research is valuable in that it demonstrates the use of pauses, hedging expressions, modal verbs, token agreement and indirect speech acts in performing disagreements and illustrates their use both prior to and during the expression of the disagreement. However, this set of strategies does not reflect the complexity of disagreement in real-life communication. As Sifianou (2012, p. 1553) argues, disagreements are "complex, multidirectional and multifunctional acts" because of the context of the social interaction under question, face dynamics and multiple functions that are relevant to specific disagreements. Current research in multimodal discourse analysis also points to the interplay between various social semiotic resources in mediating social interaction: For example, Norris's (2007) study of a public speech illuminates the variety of meaning-making resources or communicative modes such as spoken language, posture and gaze, and their complementary roles for conveying multiple messages and performing multiple identities. It is thus important to examine how actions such as disagreements are performed by investigating the various possible resources that are mobilized including linguistic and paralinguistic resources. By building on research in multimodal discourse analysis—in particular, Norris's (2004) multimodal interaction analysis—this chapter explores how disagreements are accomplished by plenary speakers at academic conferences, with the focus on their use of multimodal meaning-making devices to achieve their communicative goals, and discusses how such insights may contribute to teaching English for academic purposes.

1.2 LITERATURE REVIEW

As an important research process genre, academic presentations have received growing attention since Shalom (1993). This is reflected in the expanding research that has drawn on multimodal discourse analysis (Rowley-Jolivet, 2002; Rendle-Short, 2005; Morton, 2009; Tardy, 2005, 2009; Querol-Julián & Fortanet-Gómez, 2012; Zhang & Wang, 2014). These studies have shed valuable light on language and other meaning-making resources in performing academic presentations. For example, Rowley-Jolivet's (2002) study of visuals in 90 presentations at five international conferences in three different fields reveals multiple functions of such meaning-making resources, including structuring the discourse and expressing logical relations. Multimodal resources are also found to interact with each other in making meaning. A good case in point is Querol-Julián and Fortanet-Gómez's (2012) multimodal study of the Q&A session following the paper presentation. They identify interesting uses of language, paralanguage and kinesic features in expressing evaluative meaning in the speech event. For example, these different semiotic resources may co-express attitudes as when the presenter nodded and uttered *yes* simultaneously. They may also complement each other as when the presenter smiled while expressing a negative affect.

However, little has been written about the handling of pivotal actions such as disagreements in such activities. Disagreements are understandably important to academic presentations. This derives from the multiple roles of academics including "disciplinary servant" and "originator" (Hyland, 2004, p. 108). The latter role is particularly true of senior academics such as plenary speakers at academic conferences. As experts on the topic they are speaking to, plenary speakers are expected to respond to uncertainties in their discipline (Woodward-Kron, 2002) and articulate their original views, which may distinguish them from others who may be present or absent at the conference venue, hence disagreements. Disagreements may therefore play a "constructive" (Sifianou, 2012, p. 1560) role in the academic context.

There has been much discussion of disagreement in the literature with a focus on its nature as a potentially face-threatening speech act that should be mitigated (Mulholland, 1991; Stalpers, 1995). Although this focus has much validity, it should be noted that a speech act such as disagreement does not necessarily perform one single function in the whole discourse. Instead, it may perform different functions subject to the context. This has been pointed out by Sifianou (2012) in her discussion of the multifunctionality feature of disagreements. On a larger scale, Bhatia (2002, pp. 51–52) outlines several identities that

> professionals may be required to give expression to simultaneously in the *same* piece of discourse: professional identities as members of a particular disciplinary community, organizational identities as members of specific organizations or institutions, social identities, as valued members of social groups, and of course individual identities as indications of self-expression. [Italics added for emphasis]

This position also resonates with Charles's (1996) study of business discourses. According to Charles, business negotiators are, by their professional status, buyers or sellers that are enacted through different language and business strategies. They also play situationally adopted roles such as friendly business partners with social and personal concerns, and are individuals with idiosyncratic behavior in their interaction with each other. The negotiation discourse that may be produced is subject to the interplay between these different roles. Considering the multiple roles the same piece of discourse performs in a situated interaction, it is compelling to investigate how they are achieved in the discourse.

Sociocultural linguistic research provides a clue. Of high relevance is Bucholtz and Hall's (2005) discussion of indexicality as "the mechanism whereby identity is constituted" (p. 593) and the range of indexing operations:

> Disparate indexical processes of labeling, implicature, stance taking, style marking, and code choice work to construct identities, both micro and macro, as well as those somewhere in between.
>
> (p. 598)

Identities as social constructs are therefore accomplished via indexing devices including language and other semiotic resources. When we explore a social action and its multiple meanings, the devices that are employed provide the objects of observation and interpretation. Norris's (2007) study may be used to illustrate the synchronized performance of multiple identities in the same discourse through multiple indexing devices. In her analysis of an official meeting with diverse participants, including Hispanic/Latino Americans, other minority group individuals and white Americans, she shows how the speaker, a Mexican American, took on the identity of the white majority group and meanwhile constructed her Mexican identity. She was able to achieve her foregrounded majority identity by "controlling her use of spoken language" and present her Mexican identity "through other modes" such as hand gestures and facial expressions (p. 669). When plenary speakers are performing disagreements at academic conferences, how they navigate the professional, organizational, social and personal spaces to respond to the exigency of academic conference situations may be explored with reference to multiple meaning-making or indexing devices.

Academic presenters have a range of resources at their disposal. Norris (2004) proposes nine communicative modes including spoken language, proxemics, gesture, head movement, posture, gaze, layout, print and music. These communicative modes mediate the interaction as social action in the sense that these modes, loaded with meaning-making potential, enable the interaction to proceed in culturally and situationally recognizable ways, hence multimodal interaction as mediated discourse (Scollon, 2001). As each mode has its meaning-making potential, it is interesting to examine how the modes are drawn on by social actors such as academic presenters to perform social actions, for example, disagreements.

Four types of disagreements are identified in academic presentations (Zhang & Zhu, 2014), namely: 1) disagreement with a specific person who is named; 2) disagreement with a specific phenomenon; 3) disagreement with hypothetical/possible views held by the audience; and 4) disagreement in the guise of a suggestion for improving a practice or situation. Following Brown and Levinson (1987), the first type of disagreement appears to be the most imposing and confronting as the speaker names a specific individual to disagree with in public and is thus worth a specially close examination. This chapter aims to explore the use of spoken language and other communicative modes by plenary speakers in handling the action of disagreement with the following three questions to answer:

1. What kinds of disagreements are enacted in plenary speeches?
2. What are the linguistic strategies plenary speakers use in expressing disagreements?
3. How do different communicative modes interplay with each other in enacting disagreements in plenary speeches?

1.3 PLENARY CONFERENCE DATA

1.3.1 Data Sources

This chapter draws on the plenary speeches of two internationally renowned scholars in the field of applied linguistics on topics of their expertise at two international conferences in China. Paul Nation, the world's leading researcher in the field of vocabulary teaching, was invited to address a plenary session at an international conference on English writing teaching and research in China in 2006. He spoke about writing from the perspective of vocabulary with three focal points: 1) how much vocabulary learners need to know in order to write; 2) how writing fits into a whole language course; and 3) how writing can help learners to learn vocabulary. In the process of delivering the second point, Nation presented his four-strand language lesson framework, which includes meaning-focused input, language-focused input, meaning-focused output and fluency development, and critiqued an applied linguist highly regarded for his research in second language acquisition. He prepared handouts for the audience and invited questions from the audience after he had covered the first two points. Nation answered a number of questions from four conference participants before moving on to his last point. His presentation finished without a Q&A session because of time constraints. The whole speech lasted 46:26 minutes.

Helen Spencer-Oatey is an internationally renowned expert on intercultural communication and language education research. Her studies of cross-cultural pragmatics and rapport management are widely cited. She sets the example of focusing on the cooperative and collaborative behavior of intercultural communicators to achieve their communicative goals rather than breakdowns in intercultural communication. She was invited to speak at the first international conference on intercultural business communication in China in 2010. Her talk, entitled "Understanding intercultural competence for business: Insights from the eChina-UK programme," consisted of a brief introduction, a review of research on intercultural competence, research in business discourse, insights from an international project she directed and suggestions for future research. Her talk was assisted with the use of PowerPoint slides and finished with a Q&A session in which she responded to several questions from the audience. As her slides show, her aims in the speech were three-fold: to critically review conceptualizations of intercultural competence in different disciplines including communication studies and business and management studies; to outline insights from the analysis of business discourse; and to argue for a new approach to conceptualizing intercultural competence. The speech was 49:51 minutes long.

1.3.2 Coding Scheme

The two plenary speakers' speeches were video-recorded and transcribed for this study by using ELAN, a computer-assisted annotation tool developed by the Max Planck Institute for Psycholinguistics, the Language Archive, Nijmegen, the Netherlands.[1] ELAN has been widely used in annotating video and/or audio data (Wittenburg et al., 2006). As ELAN allows annotations to be made with great precision on multiple tiers on the same screen, observations of co-occurrence of the multiple communicative modes within a specified time period may be made. This advantageous feature of the software makes it possible to scrutinize the use of multiple communicative modes in a social interaction over time and, more importantly, the interplay between them at any one specific time, which suits the purpose of this study. The statistics that may be generated by using the software are also useful for corpus linguistic research. Researchers need to devise a set of codes that represent features of the social interaction they want to investigate. The coding scheme for annotating the data for this study was adapted from Zhang and Zhu (2014), which itself was designed on the basis of Norris's (2004) communicative modes. The coding scheme is summarized in Table 1.1.

The annotation process can be described as follows. The videos of the two plenary speeches were watched several times to get familiar with the content and to identify the segments of disagreement according to the working definition specified earlier, that is, voicing a different view from someone else or about a certain practice or phenomenon (also see Section 1.2). Each identified segment was transcribed against the video at least twice. The linguistic utterances were transcribed verbatim. The comma in the transcript indicates a perceptible pause and the full stop indicates the completion of a sentence. The paralinguistic features such as pauses, stresses, intonation and other communicative modes were annotated through ELAN following the coding scheme. The annotations were checked at least twice to ensure

Table 1.1 Coding scheme

Modes	Codes
Spoken Language	[S-] Speech; [PIF] Intonation Fall; [PIR] Intonation Rise; [PIRF] Intonation Rise & Fall; [PIFR] Intonation Fall & Rise; [PPS] Pause Short; [PPL] Pause Long; [PTS] Slow Tempo; [PTF] Fast Tempo; [PSt] Stress; [PS] Silence; [PVU] Volume Up; [PVD] Volume Down
Hand Movement	[HNI] Hand Iconic; [HNM] Hand Metaphoric; [HNDe] Hand Deictic; [HNB] Hand Beats/underliners; [HNP] Hand Up; [HND] Hand Down; [HNC] Hand Cross; [HNH] Hand Home Position; [HNS] Hand Shaking; [HNF] Hand Fist
Head Movement	[HDU] Head Up; [HDD] Head Down; [HDN] Head Nod; [HDS] Head Shaking; [HDMA] Head Moving Around; [HDT] Head Tilting
Facial Expression	[FFS] Face Smile; [FFSe] Face Serious; [FFA] Face Angry; [FFL] Face Laugh; [FFr] Frown
Posture	[POF] Forward; [POB] Backward; [POH] Home Position; [SHS] Shoulder Shrug
Gaze	[EGA] Gaze at the audience; [EGH] Gaze at the handout; [EGW] Gaze at the watch; [EGT] Gaze at the table; [EGC] Gaze at the computer; [EGB] Gaze at the book; [EGHa] Gaze at the hand

accuracy. The individuals cited by the plenary speakers during their presentations have been anonymized [by using author 1/2/3/4] in this chapter.

1.4 RESULTS AND DISCUSSION

A number of salient features can be observed in the two plenary speakers' conduct in the disagreements. This section presents the types of disagreements that were identified in the plenary speeches and the linguistic strategies that were employed in performing the disagreements. The complicated interplay between the communicative modes is illustrated with examples of disagreements with specific individuals. These results are then discussed with reference to the nature and roles of disagreements in academic presentations, multimodal mitigating strategies for performing them, professional identities and a system of choices in meaning-making.

1.4.1 Types of Disagreements in the Plenary Speeches

Twenty-eight and 40 instances of disagreement were identified in Nation's and Spencer-Oatey's plenary speech, respectively. These disagreements were

Table 1.2 Types of disagreements in the two plenary speeches

Types	Nation	Spencer-Oatey
Type 1	9	4
Type 2	13	32
Type 3	2	0
Type 4	4	4
Total	28	40

grouped into four types following Zhang and Zhu (2014). It should be noted that the categorization of the disagreements is not always clear-cut as will be shown in the following subsections. Generally, the co-text of the specific utterance was considered to determine its type. The results are summarized in Table 1.2.

1.4.1.1 Type 1 Disagreements

Type 1 disagreements involve named individuals with whom the speaker does not share a certain view. Utterances 1–5 are examples of the first type of disagreement in Nation's speech in which he voiced his difference in opinion with a specific individual.

(example 1) but I don't agree with that at all

(example 2) I never taught writing in the United States, I taught teachers in the United States

(example 3) there is no reason why teaching in one country should be greatly different from teaching in another in terms of opportunities for learning

(example 4) so when she is around I don't speak

(example 5) you have to count what happens outside the class, but you have to be realistic about what happens outside the class

The first disagreement is concerned with another international scholar whose theory Nation did not accept. Examples (2) and (3) are Nation's responses to a conference participant who related to Nation's experience and queried the applicability of his approach to teaching English writing in the United States of America and China. Example (4) is his anecdote of being corrected by his wife when he was learning to speak her native language to illustrate the importance of not correcting students when they are doing fluency activities. The last example, (5), is Nation's disagreement with a conference participant who reported difficulty in controlling out-of-class activities when measuring the time for each of the four strands of her language course, which followed Nation's language course framework.

The next four examples (6–9) are from Spencer-Oatey's speech when she was presenting a brief review of the conceptual frameworks for intercultural competence in the literature. The four examples are all concerned with specific individuals. While the first three examples are straightforward disagreements with the individuals' works, the last example, (9), takes issue with the use of the term "knowledge blocks" in another scholar's research.

(example 6) so if you read [author1]'s work, for example, there's very very little or no mention at all of work in communication studies
(example 7) [author2]'s books I cannot find one authentic example in the whole hum any of his books
(example 8) [author3], a few examples, but they are all made-up ones, they are not authentic language
(example 9) knowledge blocks mean you cannot understand it, but I don't think hum I don't think she means hum that

What is striking about these disagreements is that both plenary speakers were direct in making them through polarized expressions. In Nation's speech, for example, he voiced his total disagreement with the international scholar's guiding principle for language lessons by saying "but I don't agree with that at all"—example (1). Similarly, Spencer-Oatey noted the "very very little or no mention at all of work in communication studies" in the foreign language education expert [author1]'s work—example (6).

1.4.1.2 Type 2 Disagreements

Type 2 disagreements are directed at specific phenomena the speakers did not agree with. They are the largest in number in the data. This may not be surprising as making comments on current practices is a default practice in plenary speeches. Utterances (10) to (18) are some examples from both Nation and Spencer-Oatey. The first four examples are Nation's views on what meaning-focused input means (only 2% of unknown words in the reading material), fluency development as one of four essential strands of a language course, and the traditional teaching methods such as grammar translation. These issues are still debated in applied linguistics and Nation clearly indicated his stance regarding them. In examples (14) to (18), Spencer-Oatey critiqued practices in intercultural communication research such as the lack of exchange between researchers in different disciplines, inauthenticity of data, conceptualization in business discourse studies, and orientation to communication breakdowns rather than strategies for achieving success in communication.

(example 10) if there is more than one unknown word in every 50 words then you do not have meaning-focused input
(example 11) if the teacher is always explaining this to the learners and the learners are concentrating on the language, on the

grammar and on the vocabulary instead of the meaning, it is not meaning-focused input

(example 12) now the fourth strand of the course is one that is often neglected

(example 13) you don't have to throw away the traditional ways of teaching, you just have to make sure they are there in the right proportion

(example 14) so people working in different areas hum a bit unfortunately I feel, are not usually speaking to each other and hum not reading each other's works

(example 15) I find that a problem because if you only look at hum made-up examples when you come to real interaction it's not like that, it's much more complicated

(example 16) if I now turn to business discourse, we'll see another extreme which hum is also problematic hum to a certain extent

(example 17) there was no mention in any of them, not in one article about intercultural competence of any of the frameworks within communication studies, within foreign language education, within business, none of them

(example 18) strategies for building rapport, again quite rare, much more emphasis on what's gone wrong, less focus on what we can do what strategies we could use hum to hum to build rapport

Similar to their use of language in Type 1 disagreements, the two plenary speakers used polarized statements to indicate their position regarding the practices in their field, for example, "there is," "do not," "it's not." There is, however, a higher level of hedging in Spencer-Oatey's disagreements, as in her use of expressions such as "a bit," "could," and comparative structures.

It can also be seen through these examples that the plenary speakers illustrated or recast their disagreements to a considerable extent. Examples (10) and (11) are both about meaning-focused input. Example (17) is a specific case of example (16). This partly explains the large number of disagreements in Table 1.2. It is also an indication of the speakers' expertise in discussing various aspects and nuances of an issue or phenomenon in their relevant field.

1.4.1.3 Type 3 Disagreements

Type 3 disagreements concern the speaker's reaction to their audience's potentially adverse views. This type of disagreement is not common in the two plenary speeches. No instance was found in Spencer-Oatey's speech. The following examples are taken from Nation.

(example 19) I like grammar translation

(example 20) grammar translation is an excellent way of teaching language

Nation made these two utterances when he was introducing his third strand of a language course, i.e., language-focused input. Although grammar translation is often criticized for its focus on form in language teaching, it was mentioned by Nation as a viable type of activity in a language course. Considering that communicative language teaching is the prevailing methodology, which Nation later invoked in his speech, these two utterances can be seen as his proactive action towards possible queries or even rejection by the audience. It is interesting to note his evaluative language (Martin & Rose, 2003) for such disagreements—for example, affect as in "I like" and appreciation as in "excellent."

1.4.1.4 *Type 4 Disagreements*

Type 4 disagreements are those in the guise of suggestions for improving a practice or situation. Eight such disagreements were found in the two plenary speeches. Examples (21–26) are reproduced below.

(example 21) if you don't have a good balance then try and get that balance

(example 22) Chinese teachers should have some psychotherapy so that they don't worry about other people's mistakes during the fluency part of the course

(example 23) we have to live with that problem until we can find a good computer-based solution to that problem

(example 24) we very much need more work including hum what are the dimensions of stylistic variation, so a lot more work will be useful in this area

(example 25) only when we've got that will we have a clearer understanding of what we need to aim at in our teaching and development courses

(example 26) and so you know reading in a [prepared generalized] I don't think that's the way[2]

In example (21), Nation was commenting on the need to have a balanced language course with 25% of the time for each of the four strands as elaborated in his speech. Example (22) is his response to a conference participant's query about Chinese teachers' inclination to correcting students' language mistakes. The next example, (23), is his reply to another conference participant's concern with the handling of phrases in the study of lexical profiles, which at the time only covered lexical items. Examples (24) and (25) are Spencer-Oatey's suggestions for future research in intercultural communication. Example (26) is her advice to a conference participant who asked her to recommend ways of addressing the oversimplification and stereotyping of communication in publications. All these utterances take the form of advice or suggestion, which is actually the two plenary speakers' way of expressing their disagreement with certain current practices in language teaching and intercultural communication. As such, these disagreements are characterized by the softening of the tone through the use of modals such as "will," "can," as well as "I don't think"; conditional structures such as "if . . . then . . ." and "only when . . . will . . ."; and verbs expressing tentativeness such as "try."

1.4.2 Linguistic Strategies for Expressing Disagreement

It can be observed from the four types of disagreement that the plenary speakers made very careful use of the spoken language mode and followed several linguistic strategies. This is particularly true of Type 1 and Type 2 disagreements. For example, Nation had chosen the diction of "differ" when he was referring directly to the international scholar [author4], but changed the object to "that" ([author4]'s theory) when he used the word "don't agree"—example (1). Following Scollon, Scollon, and Jones (2012, p. 52), this is a linguistic strategy of independence in the sense that the speaker and the hearer are "dissociated" from the discourse. In other words, it was not [author4] as a person who was taken issue with but his theory. He also indicated that his position is evidence-based by evoking research as support, as he said that "research does not agree with that either." In doing this, he hedged his claim with the expression "I would argue," which signals his caution against overstatement given the magnitude of and diversity in research in applied linguistics. Nation was also adopting Stalpers's (1995) A3 mitigating strategy: showing some agreement before expressing a disagreement. Before he articulated his disagreement, he identified one strand in his framework that is shared by [author4]'s theory, commenting that "[author4] would be very happy to see meaning-focused input as one of the essential elements of language learning." Similar to his above use of the hedging expression "I would argue," the modal verb "would" in this comment also indicates the speaker's effort to avoid sounding somewhat presumptuous about someone else's reaction.

Spencer-Oatey chose an existential process (Halliday, 1994), that is, "there's very very little or no mention at all of work in communication studies," rather than a possible material process to critique [author1]'s work—example (6). This choice of the existential process has the effect of dissociation (Scollon et al., 2012). Note that this disagreement came after a criticism of the practice in research for intercultural competence in general. In this co-text, the impact of singling out an individual to disagree with may become less confronting. As such, this strategy is a valuable addition to Stalpers's (1995) list of ten mitigating strategies. Spencer-Oatey also followed up her disagreement with the argument in favor of taking an interdisciplinary approach, which is exactly her approach to defining and researching intercultural competence for business communication. Following up a critique of research practices in general with a specific case to target and supporting a disagreement with an argument are two patterns in Spencer-Oatey's discourse of disagreement. In effect, the potential imposition in the social action of disagreement is cushioned.

It is worth thinking about the rationale for such choices. All these features of language use are understandable when the nature of the action itself is considered. It seems that for both plenary speakers, disagreement with their academic peers of international standing is face-threatening and the possible impact of the face threat needs to be mitigated. Linguistic choices are among their strategies for achieving the purpose.

1.4.3 Interplay Between Communicative Modes

The spoken language mode and other communicative modes interplayed in interesting ways in the plenary speakers' enactment of the disagreements. This section provides an illustration of such interplays by focusing on the Type 1 disagreements expressed by Nation and Spencer-Oatey when they were introducing their own theory in their plenary speeches. Nation's disagreement, starting at 11:40 during his 46:26-minute speech, is transcribed as follows:

> So [author4] would be very happy to see meaning-focused input as one of the essential elements of language learning. *But I differ from him,* and I think there're three other essential elements, he thinks that's the only one. *But I don't agree with that at all. And I, I would argue research doesn't agree with that either.*

Spencer-Oatey's disagreement began at 11:45 during her 49:51-minute speech and is transcribed below.

> So people working in different areas hum a bit unfortunately I feel, are not usually speaking to each other and hum not reading each other's works. *So if you read [author1]'s work, for example, there's very very little or no mention at all of work in communication studies.* And similarly in communication studies, there's very little mention hum of foreign language education, and applied linguistics, has no mention at all, hum completely ignored. And I think that's a great shame because we learn things from different disciplines. And hum each discipline will often bring a slightly different perspective and it's really very unfortunate to stick within a single discipline. Something like hum intercultural communication hum is almost by definition multidisciplinary.

The italicized parts in the transcripts above are the direct disagreements with [author4] and [author1], i.e. Type 1 disagreements, and were analyzed to illustrate how they were accomplished by the two plenary speakers.

Both plenary speakers articulated explicit and direct disagreements. They were explicit about what distinguishes their own theory from that of other academics they disagreed with. In Nation's case, he advocated four strands of language lessons, which are different from the single strand in [author4]'s theory. Spencer-Oatey called for interdisciplinary studies of intercultural competence, which was not the approach commonly taken in the literature she reviewed. These disagreements were expressed via direct spoken language, for example, polarized statements such as "I don't agree . . ." and "I differ . . ."

The two plenary speakers enlisted a range of communicative modes in their speech that interplayed in complex ways. While some of the modes expressed the same meaning as spoken language, other modes and spoken language seem to complement each other. Figures 1.1 and 1.2 present the annotations of the disagreeing actions where various communicative modes were employed together. Generally, head movement, prosodic features such as stress, and hand movement expressed the same meaning as spoken language. For example, as the three annotation tiers of Hand Movement, Head Movement and Prosody in Figure 1.1 show, Nation made a dismissing gesture with his right hand ([HNM]) while he was articulating the word "differ" and nodded his head ([HDN] when uttering the word "three." He also slowed down ([PTS]) and put stress ([PSt]) on the word "three," which is the new information in the clause. These communicative modes co-articulated the meaning expressed by spoken language.

Facial expressions, gaze and posture played significant roles in the two plenary speakers' disagreements. As can be seen in the relevant annotation tiers in Figure 1.1 representing these communicative modes, the facial expression of smile ([FFS]) was displayed when Nation suggested [author4]'s possible acceptance of meaning-focused input until he began to utter his disagreement starting with "But I differ from him." His facial expression became clearly serious ([FFSe]) when he was articulating "But I don't agree with that at all." His gaze ([EGA]) at the audience is also worth noting. Apart from gazing in the direction of the audience, which seems to signal the beginning of a new sentence (e.g., "so [author4] would be very happy to . . .," "But I differ from him," and "But I don't agree with that at all"), the other instances of his gaze are what can be described as a powerful "demand gaze" (Kress & van Leeuwen, 2006, p. 118). For example, when he was saying "I would argue," he cast his gaze at the audience as if requesting the audience to align with his position. It is also interesting to observe that he shrugged ([SHS]) twice, once when he was articulating "I think" and the second time when articulating "I would argue." As shrugging indicates doubt or indifference and came shortly before voicing his own view, it seems reasonable to read this posture as an indication of self-depreciation, which could have a mitigating effect on the incoming disagreement.

Similar to Nation, Spencer-Oatey used prosodic features such as stress ([PSt]) to highlight key/new information, for example, stress on "unfortunately" and "would not read." Although she also used facial expressions including a smile ([FFS]), her use of it is of a different kind. As is shown in the annotations of Figure 1.2, her facial expression was consistently neutral in this part of her presentation until the disagreement was uttered. As a smile is an indication of "social affinity" (Kress & van Leeuwen, 2006, p. 118), the use of this facial expression may be a way to tone down the disagreeing action being performed by language.

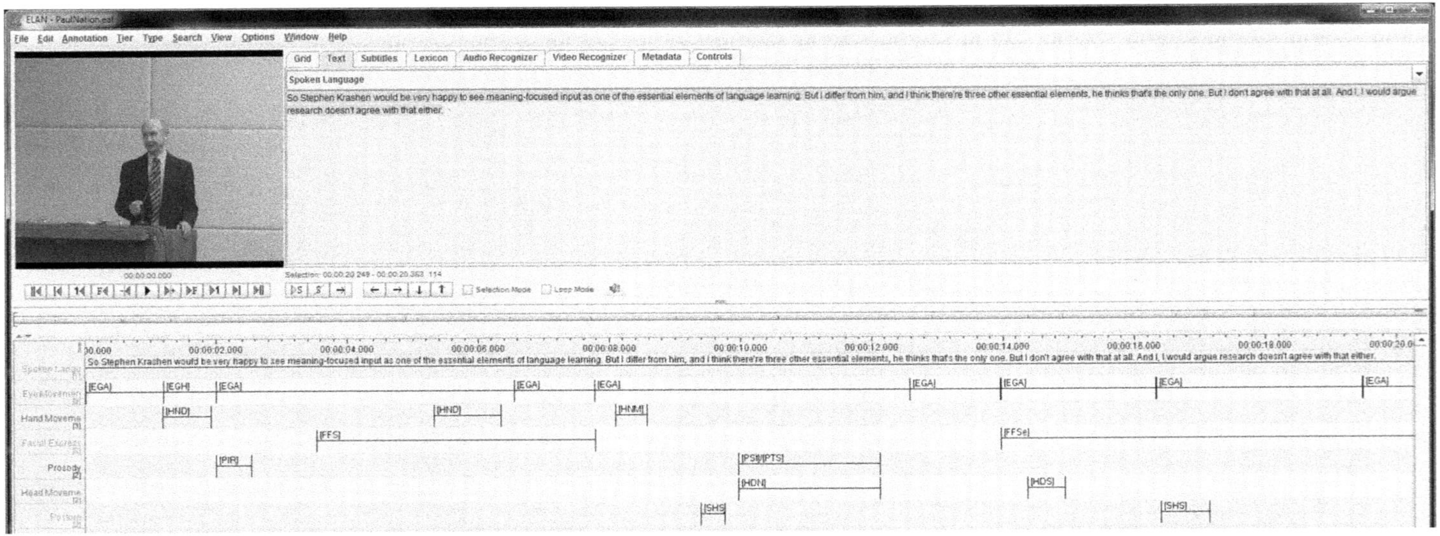

Figure 1.1 Nation's use of communicative modes in his disagreement

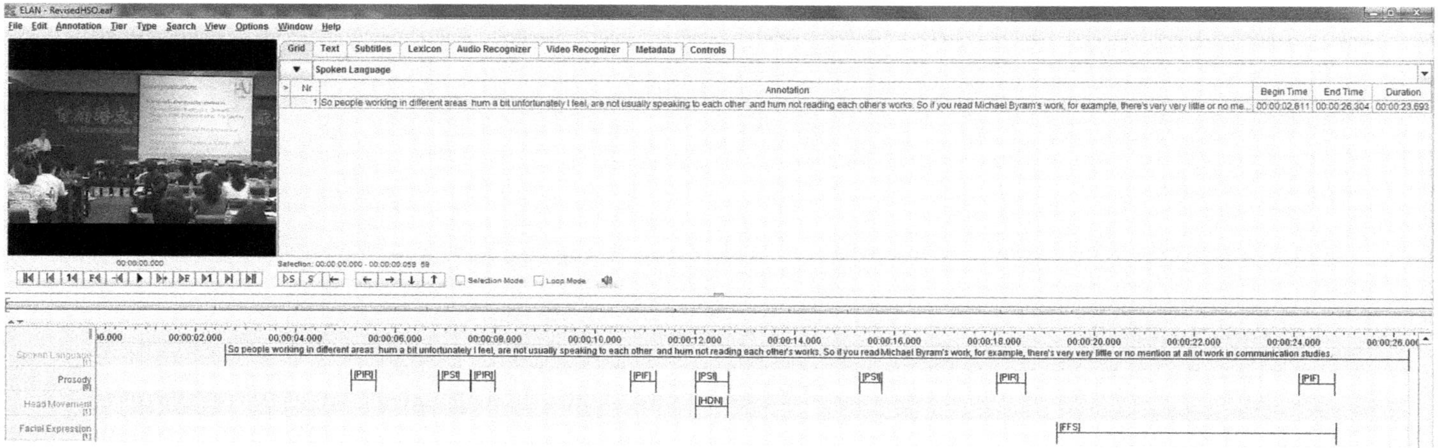

Figure 1.2 Spencer-Oatey's use of communicative modes in her disagreement

1.5 DISCUSSION

This chapter illustrates that disagreement is an essential element of plenary speeches. This arises out of the tension between showing membership in the community of practice (Lave & Wenger, 1991) in academia, that is, as fellow academics, and projecting the professional identity of originator (Hyland, 2004). In the two academic presentations, Nation and Spencer-Oatey articulated disagreements with other researchers when they were introducing their core concepts, that is, the four-strand language lesson and intercultural competence, respectively. Their disagreements align with and legitimate their status as plenary speakers and originators of knowledge. However, they are also members of the research community where collegiality is valued. Such tension means that disagreements cannot be performed at will. The two plenary speakers exemplify that disagreements are handled with great care, as in the way they made careful linguistic choices at the lexical, syntactic and discoursal levels; followed the practice of evidence-based research; and avoided sounding presumptuous.

Disagreements at plenary speeches are complicated multimodal actions. This study corroborates the argument for the simultaneous performance of multiple identities in the same piece of discourse (Bhatia, 2002; Norris, 2007). It demonstrates that plenary speakers perform multiple identities in the same action of presentation via different communicative modes. The spoken language mode constructs knowledge enabling the speaker to perform status-bound behavior, that is, providing original insights and understandings, while other communicative modes are used to accommodate social and personal concerns. The various communicative modes and their meaning potential as sociocultural tools (Engeström, 1999) mediate the apparently individual actions such as academic presentations. For Nation and Spencer-Oatey, constructing the professional identity of originator by textualizing differences from other researchers, as in the assertive statements such as "I don't agree" and "there is no mention" would be a head-on confrontation. While spoken language and some other communicative modes serve to (co-)articulate their disagreements, spoken language and others such as smile, gaze and posture enable the speakers to project another façade of their identity, i.e., collegial members of the academic community or likable individuals. Being experts both on their topics and on multiple communicative modes, and drawing on these identity-indexing resources (Bucholtz & Hall, 2005), they were able to achieve their multiple identities in a seamless manner. By viewing multimodal actions as mediated by communicative modes, their constituting elements such as the speaking, doing, and speaking/doing as discussed in Gu (2006) are integrated for scrutiny. It should be noted that organizational identities, which are not the focus of this chapter and are only mentioned in passing, were also performed via the indexing mechanism. For example, Spencer-Oatey's use of her university logo as the background of her PowerPoint slides and the name of her university and her university email as part of her presentation of her affiliation pointed to her organizational identity as staff of the university. Such organizational identities may have also consolidated the legitimacy of the plenary speakers' disagreements with their academic peers.

When the disagreements described in this chapter are put back into the whole speech event of academic presentation, a striking similarity to research articles can be observed. Although the disagreements were distributed across the whole speech event of the plenary addresses, they were concentrated in the early sections of the event. For example, the two disagreements focused on in Section 1.4.3 both occurred in the early sections of the plenary speeches, that is, when the two speakers were presenting their theoretical constructs, i.e., four-strand language lesson and intercultural competence, respectively. These were the key constructs the two speakers built on and elaborated in their whole presentation. By expressing the two disagreements, the speakers demonstrated their originality and justified the space for their speech at the academic conferences. The disagreements are thus comparable to the move of "establishing a niche," in particular the rhetorical steps of "counter-claiming" or "indicating a gap" in introductions of research articles as discussed by Swales (1990, p. 141). As such, some types of disagreements are not merely a kind of speech act, but represent critical moments in the whole speech event of plenary address.

Disagreements in academic presentations are face-threatening and are typically mitigated. Although the results based on the two plenary speeches do not warrant anything definitive, they do suggest that the different types of disagreements mobilize different meaning-making resources. For example, Type 1 and Type 2 disagreements and their syntactically polarized realizations seem to match; Types 3 and 4 disagreements take the form of indirect realizations as in the greater use of modals and affect. These results only make sense when we examine the various aspects of face involved and the corresponding mitigating strategies for each type of disagreement. Take Type 1 for example. The speakers addressed their positive face (to affirm their ability to participate in the academic exchanges in their default originator role) and their hearers' negative face (not to be imposed a criticism on). This was achieved by the speakers' use of "multimodal mitigating strategies" (Zhang & Li, 2014, p. 147), including the linguistic strategies of independence and the nonverbal communicative modes. In Type 4, the speakers' positive face (fulfilling the expectation of giving an expert talk on their topic) and the hearers' negative face (not to feel impeded by a suggested course of action) were at stake. The speakers adopted the indirect speech act to address both face concerns. This chapter therefore supports the politeness theory (Brown & Levinson, 1987) and meanwhile highlights the need to consider face for both the speaker and the audience in the study of disagreements in academic settings.

Some idiosyncrasy can be noted about the two plenary speakers both in the number of disagreements they expressed and in the use of the communicative modes. For example, Nation tends to use more polarized statements, while hedgings and the general to specific pattern of presentation seem to be more often used in Spencer-Oatey's disagreements. Such differences between the two plenary speakers may derive from the specific nature of their speech event. Nation's plenary speech resembles a lecture in which the expert researcher and teacher presents research-based solutions to classroom teaching problems. For Spencer-Oatey, as indicated in her statement of aims, the plenary speech is the vehicle of arguing for an innovative and interdisciplinary approach to intercultural competence. The goals of the apparently identical events thus differ, which may account for some of the multimodal strategies each speaker employed. Some use of the communicative modes is probably a result of personal speech habit, for example, the use of "hum" as a filled pause by Spencer-Oatey. Such individual features may be taken as resources that index personal identities of the speakers (Bhatia, 2002).

It does not follow from this, however, that each individual speaker's communicative modes are random. Rather, there seems to be a system of choices for each speaker. Most notable is the choice system of facial expressions. For Nation, the choice between serious looking [FFSe] and smile [FFS] is meaningful. It allows him to indicate his attempt to mitigate the impact of his verbal disagreement. More specifically, the serious-looking face signals the speaker's awareness of the possible face threat to his academic peer and represents a mitigating gesture. For Spencer-Oatey, there also appears to be a choice system regarding facial expressions, despite the different value attached to each choice. For her, a neutral-looking face and a smile constitute the system, and the smile was used to show social affinity when she was uttering the disagreement. The choice system of multiple communicative modes provides the basis for multiple identities in discourse production and consumption. This chapter has illustrated the complexity involved in the interplay between the communicative modes in the process. It is therefore necessary to identify the system of choices for each participant and include it in the analysis of multimodal actions so that the actions may be accurately described. To enhance descriptive accuracy, wherever possible, the participants may be interviewed on their choice systems and the value of specific choices that is assigned to each. Such interviews or play-back sessions where the researcher and the study participant review the multimodal actions and the researcher's interpretations should be productive, as has been increasingly used in qualitative research and demonstrated in Querol-Julián and Fortanet-Gómez's (2012) study of multimodal evaluation in academic discussion sessions.

1.6 CONCLUSIONS AND IMPLICATIONS

This chapter has demonstrated that disagreements are indispensable in the professional genre of academic presentations, in particular plenary speeches, where speakers handle the tension between their status-bound role of originator, member of a collegial academic community of practice, organizational identity as a member of their organization or institution, and/or individual identity. Disagreements are multimodal actions and are mediated by a configuration of communicative modes. These findings have important implications for teaching English for academic purposes (EAP).

EAP students need to be aware that disagreements are not always negative. In academic presentations and other professional discourses such as business negotiations, disagreements are the inherent or obligatory element because of the nature of the discourse genre. They may actually play a constructive role in these professional contexts. By viewing disagreement in a positive light, students may feel comfortable exploring ways of managing them. This metaknowledge of disagreements is particularly important to students from lingua-cultures where public display of disagreement is dispreferred. Meanwhile, apart from appreciating the potential of disagreements to enhance the speaker's professional face at academic presentations, students also need to understand that such actions do pose a face threat for both the speaker and their audience. They threaten the speaker's positive face as collegial members and likable individuals as they do to the positive face of the audience, in particular the colleagues they openly disagree with. Recognizing these two aspects of disagreements and face, students are more fully informed of the complexity of the multimodal action in the genre of academic presentations. When a genre-based pedagogy for teaching academic English is used, this awareness-raising exercise contributes to building the context or understanding the exigency of the rhetorical situation. Students may also be guided to draw a parallel between academic presentations and other academic genres such as research articles to broaden their understanding of specific multimodal actions in academic discourse and enhance their metaknowledge of them.

The multimodal strategies for handling disagreements at academic presentations that are modeled by the plenary speakers are useful for EAP students. Of particular relevance are the linguistic strategies involving the variety of choices at lexical, syntactic and discoursal levels. Students can be taught to compare the different choices of words and the expressive effect of diction. At the syntactic level, an existential process in the form of a "there be" structure not only introduces the new entities, but also somewhat dissociates the hearer from the discourse that transmits a negative message. Other forms that may achieve the same effect, such as the passive structure "be verb + ed," are also useful for inclusion in the discussion. At the discoursal level, the deductive structure, that is, beginning with some general premises or statements and then stating the disagreement as exemplified by Spencer-Oatey when critiquing her academic peer's approach to intercultural competence, is a useful addition to the pool of linguistic strategies for mitigating face threat. It should be emphasized that these lexical, syntactic and discoursal choices seem to co-occur for effectiveness when they are deployed.

EAP students need to be taught to read nonverbal communicative modes in multimodal actions such as academic presentations. Communicative modes such as posture, head movement, hand movement, gaze, proxemics and music are mediating tools that have meaning potentials as does spoken language. The use of such meaning-making resources is, however, often overlooked in EAP teaching. As this chapter has shown, these resources are extremely important in the performance of more social and personal identities of plenary speakers, such as collegial members of academia. While some of the nonverbal resources, for example, head movements, hand movements and posture, have meanings that are quite often readily accessible, other resources may require careful observation. To fully understand this, students need to learn how to examine the choice system, which may differ from individual to individual. The use of video clips demonstrating changes in facial expressions corresponding to different interactional contexts, for example, can be valuable. Video and audio annotating tools such as ELAN provide a range of such screenshots that can be used for this purpose. These screenshots also display the sequence or co-occurrence of the multimodal resources, which is useful information for student viewers. Students may even be guided to diagram the choice system in a graphic display.

Finally, an integral understanding of multimodal action is needed to promote sensitivity to the multiple messages that are transmitted in the same action or discourse. Thanks to computer software and increasing sophistication of semiotic theories, research in multimodal discourse analysis has been able to uncover the use of various meaning-making resources and thus their multiple purposes, functions and impact in human interaction. As was illustrated in this chapter, the synchronized performance of disagreements at academic presentations is accomplishable when senior academics like plenary speakers enlist multiple meaning-making resources. The subtlety of the multidimensional interaction may be overlooked unless due attention is paid to the distinct but simultaneous employment of the multimodal resources. While it is unrealistic to expect students to imitate the two exemplary speakers, they can be taught to be sensitive to their own choice systems and the meaning potentials the choices in the system may realize. This sensitivity is essential for students in EAP settings in their socialization into the community of practice within academia and should be incorporated into their EAP units of study, in particular in lessons targeting spoken interaction.

ACKNOWLEDGMENTS

I would like to thank the two plenary speakers for their generous support for using their videos in this chapter.

NOTES

1. ELAN can be downloaded for free from http://tla.mpi.nl/tools/tla-tools/elan/.
2. The two words in brackets are an approximation since the utterance was not clear.

REFERENCES

Bhatia, V.K. (2002). Professional discourse: Towards a multi-dimensional approach and shared practice. In C.N. Candlin (Ed.), *Research and practice in professional discourse* (pp. 39–60). Hong Kong: City University of Hong Kong Press.
Brown, P., & Levinson, S.C. (1987). *Politeness: Some universals in language usage.* Cambridge: Cambridge University Press.
Bucholtz, M., & Hall, K. (2005). Identity and interaction: A sociocultural linguistic approach. *Discourse Studies, 7*(4–5), 585–614.
Charles, M. (1996). Business negotiations: Interdependence between discourse and the business relationship. *English for Specific Purposes, 15*(1), 19–36.
Engeström, Y. (1999). Activity theory and individual and social transformation. In Y. Engeström, R. Miettinen, & R.-L. Punamäki (Eds.), *Perspectives on activity theory* (pp. 19–38). Cambridge: Cambridge University Press.
Gu, Y. (2006). Multimodal text analysis: A corpus linguistic approach to situated discourse. *Text & Talk, 26*(2), 127–167.
Halliday, M.A.K. (1994). *An introduction to functional grammar* (2nd edition). London: Edward Arnold.
Hyland, K. (2004). A convincing argument: Corpus analysis and academic persuasion. In U. Connor, & T.A. Upton (Eds.), *Discourse in the professions: Perspectives from corpus linguistics* (pp. 87–112). Amsterdam: John Benjamins.
Kress, G., & van Leeuwen, T. (2006). *Reading images: The grammar of visual design* (2nd edition). London: Routledge.
Lave, J., & Wenger, E. (1991). *Situated learning: Legitimate peripheral participation.* Cambridge: Cambridge University Press.
Martin, J.R., & Rose, D. (2003). *Working with discourse: Meaning beyond the clause.* London: Continuum.
Morton, J. (2009). Genre and disciplinary competence: A case study of contextualization in an academic speech genre. *English for Specific Purposes, 28*(4), 217–229.
Mulholland, J. (1991). *The language of negotiation: A handbook of practical strategies for improving communication.* London: Routledge.
Norris, S. (2004). *Analyzing multimodal interaction: A methodological framework.* London: Routledge.
Norris, S. (2007). The micropolitics of personal national and ethnicity identity. *Discourse and Society, 18*(5), 653–674.
Querol-Julián, M., & Fortanet-Gómez, I. (2012). Multimodal evaluation in academic discussion sessions: How do presenters act and react? *English for Specific Purposes, 31*(4), 271–283.
Rendle-Short, J. (2005). Managing the transitions between talk and silence in the academic monologue. *Research on Language and Social Interaction, 38*(2), 179–218.
Rowley-Jolivet, E. (2002). Visual discourse in scientific conference papers: A genre-based study. *English for Specific Purposes, 21*(1), 19–40.
Scollon, R. (2001). *Mediated discourse: The nexus of practice.* London: Routledge.
Scollon, R., Scollon, S.W., & Jones, R.H. (2012). *Intercultural communication: A discourse approach* (3rd edition). Malden, MA: Wiley-Blackwell.
Shalom, C. (1993). Established and evolving spoken research process genres: Plenary lecture and poster session discussions at academic conferences. *English for Specific Purposes, 12*(1), 37–50.
Sifianou, M. (2012). Disagreements, face and politeness. *Journal of Pragmatics, 44*(12), 1554–1564.
Stalpers, J. (1995). The expression of disagreement. In K. Ehlich, & J. Wagner (Eds.), *The discourse of business negotiation* (pp. 275–290). Berlin: Mouton de Gruyter.

Swales, J. M. (1990). *Genre analysis: English in academic and research settings.* New York: Cambridge University Press.

Tardy, C. M. (2005). Expressions of disciplinarity and individuality in a multimodal genre. *Computers and Composition, 22*(3), 319–336.

Tardy, C. M. (2009). *Building genre knowledge.* West Lafayette, IN: Parlor Press.

Wittenburg, P., Brugman, H., Russel, A., Klassmann, A., & Sloetjes, H. (2006). ELAN: A professional framework for multimodality research. *Proceedings of LREC 2006, Fifth International Conference on Language Resources and Evaluation.* Retrieved from http://www.lrec-conf.org/proceedings/lrec2006/pdf/153_pdf.pdf.

Woodward-Kron, R. (2002). Academic discourses and their discourses of learning: Participants, texts and social practices. In C. N. Candlin (Ed.), *Research and practice in professional discourse* (pp. 499–548). Hong Kong: City University of Hong Kong Press.

Zhang, Z. C., & Li, X. F. (2014). moni shangwutanpan zhong butongyijian de biaoda (Disagreements in simulated business negotiations). In Z. C. Zhang, J. Y. Xing, et al. (Eds.), *Multimodal study of situated discourses* (pp. 124–150). Guangzhou: World Publishing Corporation.

Zhang, Z. C., & Wang, X. (2014). xueshuhuiyi zhuzhiyanjiangzhe zhuanyeshenfen goujian de duomotai shijiao (Plenary speakers' construction of professional identities: A multimodal perspective). In Z. C. Zhang, J. Y. Xing, et al. (Eds.), *Multimodal study of situated discourses* (pp. 83–105). Guangzhou: World Publishing Corporation.

Zhang, Z. C., & Zhu, M. H. (2014). biaodabutong guanjianpianduan de yuliaoku fenxi (Disagreements in academic presentations: A corpus linguistics approach). In Z. C. Zhang, & J. Y. Xing, et al. (Eds.), *Multimodal study of situated discourses* (pp. 162–177). Guangzhou: World Publishing Corporation.

2 Contrastive Multimodal Analysis
Conference Plenary Lectures in English and in Spanish

Noelia Ruiz-Madrid and Inmaculada Fortanet-Gómez

2.1 INTRODUCTION

Much of the research carried out up to now on academic spoken discourse has been based on classroom lectures or conference paper presentations (Deroey & Taverniers, 2012; Flowerdew, 1994; Fortanet & Räisänen, 2006; Heino, Tervonen & Tommola, 2002; Strodt-Lopez, 1991, just to name a few). However, with particular reference to the latter, scarce attention has been paid to the plenary lecture as a distinct genre, even if it has been included in analyses of conferences as macrogeneric events. To our knowledge, there is just one article (Hood & Forey, 2005) that deals with plenary conference presentations, though the analysis is limited to the introduction of the study. Shalom (2002) divides conference genres into research process genres (paper presentation, poster session, plenary lecture and the book of abstracts), and social genres (coffee breaks, outings, lunch and conference dinner). Plenary lectures share with all the other conference genres many of the characteristics that define them, such as a) dynamism, b) situatedness, c) form and content, and d) community ownership, as described by Berkenkotter and Huckin (1995) for written genres, and applied by Shalom (2002) to conference genres. More specifically, a) dynamism means that conference genres are not static, but evolve as they are used; b) situatedness refers to the relevance of context in understanding and building the speech events that form the genre; c) the form of the genre is related to the content (e.g., the use of formulae, or certain types of visuals common with certain contents); and finally d) ownership involves a discourse community's need to share a common discourse based upon discipline-specific conventions. However, the plenary lecture can also be distinguished by certain characteristics. First of all, plenary speakers are not selected through the process followed for the other participants (call for proposals, peer review, etc.). They are instead invited by the organizers among the most influential researchers in the field. These speakers hold the highest status in the conference, which is highlighted by the time allotted to them, usually one hour, and the time slot of the presentations, usually at the beginning and at the end of the conference. On the other hand, plenary lectures are not strictly subject to the same constraints as the rest of the speech events in the conference. Speakers are supposed to present research in a more general way and provide a more global view on the research field as a specific contextualization for the conference. The plenary speaker is an authority in the field, so it is common for the other presenters to make reference to his or her lecture in their presentations.

The reasons why this genre has not received attention up to now are varied. The objective of much of the research carried out in recent years seems to respond to the need to provide guidelines to new researchers who want to participate in conferences (Ventola et al., 2002). As plenary speakers are generally senior researchers, this does not seem to apply to them. Moreover, this genre does not usually follow an established structure, as can be found in paper or poster presentations, which may have also discouraged research on it.

The lack of attention devoted to plenary lectures was one of the reasons why we selected this genre for our research. As a point of departure, we tried to find points in common with other genres that have already been analyzed, such as the paper presentation. Carter-Thomas and Rowley-Jolivet (2003) analyzed conference presentations following three different approaches:

1. The rhetorical approach, which identifies recurrent moves;
2. The microscopic syntactic approach, which analyzes the syntactic choices made by the speakers;
3. The multimodal approach, in which language, visual communication and gestures are jointly analyzed.

This particular study offers a comprehensive analysis of conference presentations, which involves various semiotic systems and shows how the relationship among them adds a particular pragmatic value to the linguistic message conveyed. We will use Carter-Thomas and Rowley-Jolivet's (2003) study as a basis for our research, comparing some of the results obtained for our dataset with their findings.

2.1.1 Structure of Conference Papers

Up to now, there have been no attempts to describe the structure of conference plenary lectures. However, some researchers have noticed recurrent patterns in paper presentations. Ventola (2002) provides the generic structure of the conference paper and its discussion as follows:

1. Introduction of the speaker by the chair
2. Thanking chair for the introduction
3. Contextualizing the paper
4. The paper and its generic structure (e.g., Introduction, Materials and Methods, Results, Discussion and Conclusion) (IMRDC)
5. Thanking the audience

2.1.2 Asides

Some research suggests that university lecturers often try to make their lectures more comprehensible by using asides. According to Strodt-Lopez (1991, p. 121), "[a]nalytically, an aside is an episode of discourse with a distinct topic framework which occurs between discourse episodes having the same topic framework." Asides are connected semantically, pragmatically and formally to the surrounding and global discourse by means of key words. Strodt-Lopez (1991) analyzed the functions of asides, especially their interactive function, relating the topic to everyday frames. Some researchers have used other terms when referring to the same communicative resource. Pons and Estellés (2009, p. 922) refer to 'digression,' when "the theme of the adjacent utterances [. . .] is shifted," a definition that is very close to that of asides. In this paper, we will consider both terms, 'aside' and 'digression,' as synonyms. Pons and Estellés (2009) classify digressions into three types:

1. Utterance-based digressions: There is some content relationship between the main topic and the digression.
2. Interaction-based digressions: The digression is related to contextual or situational factors.
3. Inserted sequences, connective and clarificatory speech acts, which are situated halfway between the other two types.

Though it is not specifically applied to academic spoken discourse, this classification may be useful to describe asides in plenary lectures. Strodt-Lopez's (1991) research takes an innovative perspective, since in addition to language, paralanguage is also considered. She transcribes asides together with intonation units and pauses. Also relevant for our research is the delimitation of asides. Strodt-Lopez uses paratones, the equivalent of paragraphs in written text, to structure discourse units and to delimit asides. These units begin with introductory expressions and with phonological prominence, a rise in pitch, and end with low pitch and volume, and a pause. She also describes types of asides, including disjunction markers, such as "by the way" as starters of asides, as well as three different ways to terminate asides: 'pat-ending expressions' (e.g., "this is the issue"), a promise to return to the main issue, and a short summary of the aside and its relation to the main issue. The resumption of the main lecture is often marked by three discourse markers: "anyway," "but" and "so," plus a repetition of previous discourse. Pons and Estellés (2009) also found digressive markers in their analysis of Spanish conversation to start digressions, such as "por cierto"*(by the way)* and to end them, such as "volviendo al tema" *(coming back to that).*

The objective of the present study is to analyze asides in plenary lectures taking a multimodal approach, which will start from a linguistic analysis and will move on to the paralinguistic and kinesic resources that accompany and complement language. We attempt to establish a structure for the two invited lectures, taking as a point of departure Ventola's (2002) generic stages. Then, we describe asides and locate them within that structure. For this analysis, we adapted previous studies by Strodt-Lopez (1991) and Pons and Estellés (2009).

2.2 METHOD

In order to fulfill the objective of the research, we selected two plenary lectures given at conferences in linguistics: one in Spanish and the other in English. The first one was delivered by Dr. José Manuel Blecua, at the Congreso ASELE 2012 in Girona and is available online.[1] This is the annual international conference of the Asociación para la Enseñanza del Español como Lengua Extranjera (ASELE) which, in this edition, had as a theme multilingualism and the teaching of Spanish as a foreign language in multicultural contexts. The audience was formed by members of this association from over 50 countries, mainly university lecturers and researchers on Spanish as a foreign language. The title of the lecture was "Multilingüismo y creación literaria," and its duration was 60:36.

The second lecture was delivered by Professor David Crystal at the 47th Annual International IATEFL Conference & Exhibition in 2013 in Liverpool and is also available online.[2] IATEFL is the International Association of Teachers of English as a Foreign Language. The audience was formed by members from over 100 countries, mainly university lecturers and researchers on English as a foreign language. The title of the lecture was "The world in which we live in: Beatles, blends and blogs," and its duration was 59:53.

In these two texts, we identified asides following the parameters established by Strodt-Lopez (1991): a) paralinguistic elements (high/low pitch and pauses), and b) disjunction or digression beginning and end markers. Then, we classified the asides, adapting Pons and Estellés's (2009) taxonomy.

After analyzing the asides in both lectures, we followed a three-step analysis, in line with Carter-Thomas and Rowley-Jolivet (2003):

1. We established the macrostructure of the lectures and located the previously identified asides (the rhetorical approach);
2. We distinguished language elements that were reflected in the asides, as well as terms that were used to embed the aside in its context (the linguistic approach);
3. We selected a few particularly rich aside sequences in which language, visual communication and gestures were jointly analyzed, while also considering how these three dimensions interact (the multimodal approach).

As a multimodal approach requires an extremely high level of detail, we have selected one aside from each lecture where both verbal and nonverbal resources are used in order to carry out this particular component of our analysis.

2.3 RESULTS AND DISCUSSION

2.3.1 Asides

We found 25 asides in Professor Crystal's lecture and 39 in Professor Blecua's, ranging from 2 to 358 words. These asides were classified using the following taxonomy, based on Pons and Estellés (2009) scheme:

1. Context-based digressions:
   - 1a. University/city (space) context
   - 1b. Lecture context (e.g., reference to slides, handouts, etc.)
   - 1c. Relation between topics in lecture and 'real life' for speaker or audience
2. Utterance-based digressions: Clarifications
3. Addressing the audience directly

It must be mentioned that sometimes it is difficult to include an aside in a specific category or subcategory since some asides can have different functions. In these cases, we have selected what we consider their main function. For instance, in example (1), there are two parts. In the first one, the speaker makes a reference to photocopies within the lecture context (subcategory 1b). In the second part, he asks the audience for patience (category 3). There is just one aside, since the discourse is only broken once, but it has two parts and two functions. In this case, the predominant function from our point of view is addressing the audience directly, which is reinforced by a higher pitch in the speaker's voice.

(example 1) Bueno, entonces y vamos ya a las dos últimas fotocopias . . . ¿Pueden aguantar un poquito más todavía?
(Well, then and let's go to the last two photocopies. . . . Can you hold on a little bit more?)

As for the number and characteristics of the asides in the first category, for subcategory 1a, there are just a few relating the lecture to the university and city context (Crystal: 2 and Blecua: 1 [see example 2]). They occur mainly at the beginning of the lecture as an introduction and first contact between lecturer and audience. The function of these asides is establishing rapport, and they are quite long as seen in example (2), in which the speaker refers back to his first time in the conference venue and his special relationship with it, since he was one of the first persons teaching there.

(example 2) No les tengo que decir que para mí volver a esta casa es volver a algo mío porque vine aquí antes de que existiera. Vine aquí antes de que existiera. . . . Quizá hará cuarenta años, treinta y tantos. Precisamente porque acababa de nacer el colegio y veníamos a dar clase y yo vine con un gran amigo al que admiraba mucho, era un Maestro, un Catedrático de Latín que se llamaba Eduardo Valenti.

(Needless to say that for me, coming back to this place means coming back to my place, since I came here before this university had been created. I came here before it existed. . . . It might be forty, thirty something years ago. It was precisely because the college had just been created and we came to teach and I came with a very good friend I admired a lot, he was a professor, a professor of Latin whose name was Eduardo Valenti.)

The second subcategory of asides is used to refer to the visuals in the lecture (1b), usually in the form of short instructions scattered throughout the lecture. These asides are the most frequent in both lectures (Crystal: 8 and Blecua: 14) as seen in example (3):

(example 3) Can you go back to the previous slide, Hilary, for a second? Right. . . . Thank you. . . .

The third subcategory of asides (1c) is also quite frequent (Crystal: 6 and Blecua: 8), and the function of these asides is to make the lecture more relevant and interesting for the audience by creating a common space, as shown in example (4), in which Blecua mentions that he has taught part of the audience for a long time and how much he admires them for having become brilliant teachers now.

(example 4) Bueno, después he venido muchas veces y algunas de las personas que están aquí pues han sido alumnos míos de toda la vida, los quiero muchísimo y son unos maestros sapientísimos.

(Well, after that I have come many times and some of the people who are here have been my students along my life, I love them so much and they are the wisest professors.)

Category 2 is not so large (Crystal: 4 and Blecua: 3). The function of these asides is to clarify something explained by the speaker on the topic of the lecture, see example (5):

(example 5) I should add here, by the way, for those of you who know that there are some regional dialects in English where

"Why weren't I taught it?" would be perfectly normal, but this lecturer does not use that dialect.

Category 3 is the one that shows the most discrepancy between the two speakers. There are many asides in this group in Blecua's lecture (13), while the number is quite smaller in Crystal's lecture (5). We consider this as an individual trait of Blecua's discourse, though further study of his other lectures would be necessary to corroborate this interpretation. Blecua uses this resource more often in order to involve the audience as seen in example (1), in which he addresses the audience directly. As will be seen below, the asides in this category have very distinctive characteristics and are the ones that seem to interact more directly with the audience.

Regarding the use of digression markers, they are not very common in any of the categories. Crystal uses two of them at the beginning of an aside, "well," and "by the way" (which follows a starting phrase, "I should add here"). Then, he also uses six end digression markers. He repeats twice "but" and "so," both of them already noticed by Strodt-Lopez (1991). The other two, only used once, are "right," and a pat-ending expression to indicate resuming the main topic, "so back to my point." Blecua makes a wider use of beginning digression markers. He uses "entonces" *(then)* three times, and "bueno" *(well* or *good)* five times; he uses once both "bueno, entonces" and once "pues" *(then)*. However, he makes scarce use of end digression markers, only four times and once for every marker: "pero" *(but)*, "bueno," "entonces" and a 'pat-ending expression,' "como les digo" *(as I am telling you)*. Following this classification of asides, we will move now to the three-step analysis as previously described.

2.3.2 Structure of the Lectures and Location of Asides

For the macrostructure of both lectures, we adapted the generic structure presented by Ventola (2002) for the conference presentation, even if there are significant differences. For example, it is interesting to see how in these two lectures the generic structure is not based on the IMRDC, as presented by Ventola (2002). In fact, there is no description of research. Many similarities can be found between both lectures and one of them is the structure. Indeed, there does not seem to be a clear argument thread in the discourse; rather, the topics of the lectures (i.e., syntactic blends in Crystal's lecture and the use of multilingual voices in Blecua's lecture) are illustrated by means of examples selected by the speaker, based on lyrics of Beatles' songs and on literature works in Spanish, respectively. The examples, visualized for the audience by means of slides or a handout, are described and explained with frequent expressions of evaluation, and are sometimes related to theoretical concepts, especially by Crystal. There are no conclusions at the end, and neither of these lectures is followed by a question and answer session. It would be necessary to complement this analysis with a larger dataset to understand whether this is a general trend, either in applied linguistics plenary lectures, or in plenary lectures in general. The resulting two-part structure of these lectures is:

1. Introduction: thanking the chair for the introduction and the conference organization for their invitation, while making explicit the relationship of the speaker with the organizers, the place or the institution of the conference venue.
2. Body of the lecture: analysis of examples (presentation of the example, analysis, evaluation, conclusion).

The beginning and the end of both lectures are very similar, characterized by an extensive introduction with acknowledgments for the organizers and an explanation of their relationship with the place of the conference. Hood and Forey (2005, p. 294) also point out the prominence of the introduction or "set-up stage" in plenary lectures. The end in both lectures is marked by a climax, with a special example selected by both lecturers, and a surprising end that provokes laughter from the audience.

Regarding the location of the asides, we cannot say there is a concentration of asides in any part of the lectures; only the first subcategory of asides (1a) is mainly placed at the beginning of the lecture where the asides are used to establish a rapport with the audience. The asides in the second and third subcategories appear intermittently throughout the lecture. Those in the second subcategory (1b) are used as markers to indicate a change from one example or one slide to the next, or to relate the several parts of the lecture, with a discourse structuring function. The third subcategory (1c) is more related to the content and contextualizes the examples provided by each lecturer. Only in the case of Blecua, these asides are mainly placed at the beginning in the introduction. The asides that clarify the content are used to explain the examples in the core part of the lectures, while those addressing the audience directly can be found anywhere in the speech.

2.3.3 Linguistic Analysis of Asides

Here we will just describe the general language features found in the asides. A more microscopic approach will be made together with the multimodal approach of one aside from each lecture in the next subsection.

In general terms, longer asides are used to relate the lecture and the lecturer to the context, either physically to the place where the conference is located, or in a more abstract way by means of references to a common social space. It is frequent in subcategories 1a and 1c to find narratives using first person singular and past tense through which speakers explain their own experiences. In example (6), Crystal explains his relationship with the city of Liverpool, where he spent part of his childhood and his teenage years.

(example 6) Welcome to my town—well, sort of. **I wasn't** born in Liverpool, so **I** can't claim to be a real scouser, but my family **moved** here in 1951 when **I** was 10 and I **had** all my secondary schooling here in the pool just a couple of miles north of where we are right now, and the accent you are listening to still has echoes of those teenage years. And **I** have the happiest of memories of being in this place at that time for this **was** the 1950s.

There is also some convergence in form with the asides in subcategory 1b, which are used to refer to the visual support, and those in category 3 in which the speaker addresses the audience directly. There is a frequent use of questions, indicating requests to assistants, and imperatives in subcategory 1b in order to ask or direct somebody or the audience to move to the right visual, or to draw their attention to a certain part of it. In category 3, asides are used to call the attention of the audience and to interact directly with them. We can see asides in both categories in example (7).

(example 7) **Can you go** back to the previous slide, Hilary, for a second? Right, . . . Thank you, onto the next slide. Okay, but **listen. Look at** the lines here.

In this example, Crystal uses a polite question to ask his assistant to change the slide. He then thanks her and asks to move to the next slide using an elliptical phrase that omits the verb. In the next two sentences, he uses imperatives, directing the audience to listen to the lyrics of the song and look at the lines on the slide.

As mentioned above, digressive markers are not very frequent. In the aside in example (8), from category 3, Blecua uses a digressive marker to start ("bueno") *(well)* and another one to resume the main theme of the lecture ("entonces") *(then)*. He addresses the audience with the formal second person plural form of the verb, and two sentences with subordinate clauses that indirectly ask the audience to perform actions.

(example 8) **bueno,** si lo **leen sabrán** que hubo un concurso al final, y a ver quién ganó el premio. Cuando **averigüen** quién ganó el premio **verán** que se lo merecía. **Entonces, . . .**

(well, if you read it you will learn that there was finally a contest and you can guess who won the prize. When you guess who won the prize you'll see he deserved it. Then, . . .)

Finally, in the asides in category 2, we find first or third person pronouns. These are thus the least interactional, just trying to clarify what has just been explained as in example (4). This example starts with a first person to introduce the aside by means of a phrase ("I should add there") and a digression marker ("by the way"). The audience or part of the audience ("those of you who . . .") is addressed somewhat indirectly and given the explanation in the third person. At the end, the speaker refers to himself in the third person, something he does several times during the lecture.

2.3.4 Multimodal Analysis of Asides

Following previous studies that have dealt with multimodal discourse analysis (Querol-Julián, 2010; Fortanet-Gómez & Ruiz-Madrid, 2014; Querol-Julián & Fortanet-Gómez, 2014), we distinguished:

1. Four types of kinesics: *gestures* (Kendon, 2004; McNeill, 1992), *head movement* (Goodwin & Goodwin, 1987; Kendon, 2002; McClave, 2000), *facial expression* (Ekman & Friesen, 1969; Kendon, 1981) and *gaze* (Argyle et al., 1981; Kendon, 1967);
2. Four types of gestures (McNeill, 1992): *iconic* when there is a formal relationship with the semantic content of speech; *metaphoric* when the relationship is pictorial but the gestures present abstract ideas; *beats* when the same gesture is used regardless of the content showing the word or phrase as significant; and *deictic* when the gesture points out something concrete or abstract;
3. The functions that kinesics accomplish in the discourse (Bavelas et al., 1989; Kendon, 2004; McNeill, 1992; Morris, 1977): *referential* function when the kinesic feature represents any aspect of the content of the utterance; *cohesive* when kinesics link part of the discourse; *interactive* when kinesics are used to maintain interaction rather than convey meaning; and *pragmatic* when kinesics add actual meaning to the communicative value of the utterance;
4. How they all interact with the speech (Kendon, 2004; McNeill, 1992; Schegloff, 1987): showing semantic or pragmatic synchrony, adding meaning and going beyond the utterance.

As for paralanguage, we identified three types: *two voice qualities* and *one voice differentiator* (Poyatos 2002), as well as the functions they accomplish in the discourse. In this particular case, the analysis of paralinguistic elements was narrowed to the role intonation plays in the discourse following Brazil's (1997) approach to Discourse Intonation (DI). According to Brazil, speakers make intonation choices depending on their perception of the understandings they share with their hearers and the purpose of their talk. DI provides a tool for analyzing and interpreting speakers' significant intonation context-referred choices within four systems as shown in Table 2.1.

As illustrated in Table 2.1, speakers make a choice of five *tones*, each one with a different meaning. In this sense, Cauldwell (2002) summarizes the interpretation of the choices as follows: a low key tone adds meaning that could be paraphrased as 'this discourse unit has an equitable relationship

Table 2.1 Choices in the intonation systems (Brazil, 1997, p. vii)

System	Choices
Prominence	prominent/non-prominent syllables
Tone	rise-fall, fall, level, rise, fall-rise
Key	high, mid, low
Termination	high, mid, low

with what has gone before,' and high key tone adds 'this discourse unit is not related to what has preceded,' or 'this tone is discourse-initial.' Low termination tone also adds meaning such as 'this is discourse-final,' and high termination tone adds 'this is something I want you to reflect and give judgment on.' We agree with Querol-Julián (2010), who suggests that although DI seems to disregard the attitudinal aspects of intonation, it is possible to interpret some attitudinal function, since the key system enables the speaker to show feelings or anticipate feelings in their hearers, as is the case in the present study.

In order to carry out this analysis, one rich aside sequence from each lecture was selected. In each one, language, visual communication and gestures were jointly analyzed to understand how the linguistic expression co-occurs with kinesics and paralanguage, as well as to provide new insights into asides and the generic nature of invited plenary lectures. Some asides are long and complex. In order to facilitate the analysis, we have divided them into moves by applying Strodt-Lopez's definition of paratones, which are marked by phonological prominence and digression markers to define the beginning and the end of these asides as well as the moves.

The first example belongs to Crystal's conference. It was taken from the very beginning of his plenary, where the speaker thanks the organization of the conference for their invitation. In this context-based aside (subcategory 1c) the speaker resorts to a personal narrative in which linguistic, paralinguistic and kinesic resources co-occur to achieve a direct and intensive interaction with the audience. It seems that he wants to break the ice and create a friendly atmosphere for the whole speech. Hood and Forey (2005) also considered this as one of the components of the introduction of plenary lectures when the speaker makes an effort to establish interaction with the audience.

Table 2.2 summarizes the three-level analysis of example (10) including 1) the structure of the aside and its relation to the structure of the lecture, 2) the linguistic analysis and 3) the multimodal analysis (paralinguistic elements and kinesics). We have divided this aside into four different moves.

As shown in Table 2.2, in this example the speaker begins with a narrative passage to initiate his discourse. He likely knows that the audience's expectations are high, since he is a well-known linguist, and the academics in the room are probably looking forward to listening to him. Narratives are often present in invited lectures and they represent one of the most common discourse strategies for plenary lecturers to pave the way for the rest of the

Table 2.2 Three-level analysis of Aside 1 (example 9)

Aside 1: Context-based, the speaker refers to his own life (example 9)	
	Relation to the structure of the lecture: Thank you section
Well, thank you for **that.** [Laughter]	Move 1) Linking the aside with previous discourse. Linguistic analysis: • discourse marker ("well") as a starter of aside. • demonstrative pronoun ("that") with an anaphoric function, making reference to the presenter's previous discourse. Multimodal analysis: • paralinguistic elements: high key (i.e., discourse-initial function) and laughs. • kinesics: the speaker steps backwards from the lectern.
Oh, dear. Never **trust** Wikipedia, of course. **I mean** the things you read there. **I learn** something new about myself every time **I look** at Wikipedia. [Laughter] **You** never know what somebody is going to say.	Move 2) Introduction of the aside: the speaker refers to the chair's mention of him in Wikipedia to give cohesion to the lecture and to interact with the audience. Linguistic analysis: • discourse marker, "oh, dear," informal expression used as digression marker to signal beginning of move. • imperative ("never trust"). • 1st person singular (e.g., "I mean") • 2nd person ("you") to interact directly with the audience. Multimodal analysis: • paralinguistic elements: rising and falling intonation. • kinesics: head movements to emphasize significant discourse.
I mean for a while, a few years ago, just for a day or two, a) they **knighted me.** For a while I was Sir David Crystal according to Wikipedia and it only lasted a short time, but it was nice while it lasted.	Move 3) Extension of the aside: narrative on different topics: a) Sir David Crystal; b) number of children; c) number of wives. Linguistic analysis: • 1st person singular (e.g., "I mean") and simple past and time expressions (e.g., "a few years ago").

(*Continued*)

Table 2.2 (Continued)

Aside 1: Context-based, the speaker refers to his own life (example 9)	
b) I've had **different numbers of children on Wikipedia** [Laughter], c) varying **numbers of wives**	Multimodal analysis: • paralinguistic elements: rising and falling intonation, slow speech rhythm. • kinesics: head movements + intensive gaze to emphasize significant discourse.
you never know what's going to turn up	Move 4) End of the aside: pat-ending expression. Linguistic analysis: • 2nd person ("you") as an undetermined person, though also used as direct reference to the audience. Multimodal analysis: • paralinguistic elements: rising and falling intonation. • kinesics: head movements to emphasize significant discourse.
So, well good morning	Move 5) Resumption of main topic. Linguistic analysis: • discourse marker (e.g., "so") to note the end of the aside, use of the expression "well, good morning" to link to the chairwoman's discourse (she said good morning at the very beginning). Multimodal analysis: • paralinguistic elements: rising intonation. • kinesics: arm and hand movements to emphasize significant discourse; use of pauses.

speech. In this case, Crystal produces a context-based digression that focuses on his real life, perhaps as a strategy to attract the audience's attention.

For more insight into the pragmatic value of this aside, we should look closer at the co-occurrence of the linguistic, paralinguistic and kinesic features that Crystal uses to convey the final message. In this sense, it is interesting to highlight how intonation and head movements help Crystal to emphasize specific words or utterances in Move 3. In this move, Crystal extends the aside by talking about different topics, among which is the anecdote about having become Sir for some days according to Wikipedia. He uses the first person singular and simple past tense ("knighted," "was," "lasted"), which are common in narratives. The intonation he uses is neutral when saying "they knighted me," but he wants to emphasize this anecdote and therefore he adopts a more ironic and humoristic approach. In order to do so, he uses linguistic features to rephrase the same idea ("I was Sir David Crystal") and paralinguistic features, since he makes intentional pauses in between each word (see [P] in Figure 2.1), thus establishing a slow rhythm as when inviting people to listen carefully to what he is saying. However, in this particular example, the kinesic features seem to play a fundamental role, since Crystal makes repetitive head movements (up-down) when pronouncing every word as shown in Figure 2.1. These beat gestures have a parsing function that adds an implicit punctuation to discourse. Moreover, they are accompanied by an intensive gaze at the audience. Argyle et al. (1981) note that one of the functions of gaze is to communicate interpersonal attitudes, although the signal sent also depends on the facial expression accompanying the gaze. In Argyle's words, "It might be suggested that the intensity of the attitude communicated is a joint product of the length of gaze and the intensity of the expression" (Argyle et al., 1981, p. 20). One can deduce from Crystal's intonation, gestures and gaze that his intention is to interact with the audience by creating a shared understanding of his ironic approach to this anecdote. He accomplishes this by means of an intense and significant interaction, which combines a slow speech rhythm, repetitive gestures and an intensive gaze.

Paralinguistic dimension			[P]		[P]		[P]	
Linguistic dimension	I	was		Sir		David		Crystal
Kinesics				Head movement/beat (up-down)  		Head movement/beat (up-down)  		Head movement/beat (up-down)  
	Intense gaze at the audience → 							

Figure 2.1 Head movement and gaze coexpressed with "I was Sir David Crystal" (Crystal)

The second aside we will analyze comes from Blecua's lecture. We have selected this aside because of its similarities with Crystal's aside. Indeed, it is a context-based aside (subcategory 1c) in which Blecua, by means of a narrative, seeks intensive interaction with the audience to break the ice. It is placed at the beginning of the conference and it belongs to the part where lecturers thank chairs for their introduction.

Table 2.3 summarizes the three-level analysis of this example including 1) move structure of the aside, 2) the linguistic analysis and 3) the multimodal analysis.

In this, the speaker uses a narrative passage to initiate his plenary. As in the example from Crystal's lecture, Blecua knows that the audience's expectations are high and probably feels the need to describe the context in which he has prepared his lecture. Basically, this digressive narrative seems to attempt to mitigate or lower the audience's high expectations regarding his speech.

To better understand the pragmatic dimension of this aside, we can analyze the co-occurrence of linguistic, paralinguistic and kinesic features that Blecua uses to convey the final message. In this sense, particularly interesting in this aside is the use Blecua makes of laughter to create a favorable atmosphere. We can find a clear example in Move 3 of Aside 2 in which the aside is expanded. In this section of the aside, the speaker wants to reinforce the fact that, despite the difficulties described in the previous move, he has prepared a lecture on the topic proposed by the organization. In order to do that, he uses the first person singular ("yo") *(I)* and confirms that he is going to present his lecture by using an immediate future verbal tense ("voy a hacer") *(I am going to do)*. These linguistic resources co-occur with paralinguistic elements such as rising intonation and a head movement (head backwards) to emphasize the link to previous discourse and ("entonces") *(then)*. He also makes hand movements that accompany the first person singular ("yo he preparado") *(I have prepared)*, thus reinforcing the final message *(the lecture is ready and I have prepared it despite the difficulties)*. Moreover, the speaker uses his gaze to co-express some of the utterances or expressions. For instance, in the case of "modestamente," he emphasizes the meaning of this word (i.e., modestly) by looking down and lowering his head. Again, he tries to provoke a receptive and positive atmosphere among the audience.

To conclude the multimodal analysis of this second aside, we would like to highlight the way it ends. Move 4 (i.e., resumption of the main lecture) is linguistically based on repetition through which the speaker links the aside to the thread of the main topic. He repeats utterances, e.g., "yo voy a hacer una reflexión" *(I am going to make a reflection)* and words, e.g., "Multilingüismo" *(multilingualism)*, "literatura" *(literature)*, "español para extranjeros" *(Spanish as a foreign language)*. In order to emphasize this discourse, the topic words are pronounced with a rising intonation, accompanied by head movements with a parsing function and an intensive

Table 2.3 Three-level analysis of Aside 2 (example 10)

Aside 2: Context-based, the speaker refers to his own life (example 10)	
	Relation to the structure of the lecture: Thank you section
Pues cuando pensábamos hacer **eso** me comunicó Beatriz que el Congreso anterior había sido sobre problemas de recursos electrónicos y que cambiara el tema y que este año era Multilingüismo y yo trabajé en el multilingüismo hace muchos años, con Claudio Guillén, y tenía una conferencia que **no sé dónde está,** claro, como es lógico. *When we thought about doing that Beatriz told me that the previous conference had been about web resources and that I should change the topic. This year was about multilingualism and I worked on multilingualism many years ago, with Claudio Guillem, and I had a lecture, which I do not know where it is, obviously. (Our translation)*	Move 1) Linking the aside with previous discourse. Linguistic analysis: • discourse marker (i.e., "pues") as a starter of aside and a demonstrative pronoun (i.e., "eso") with an anaphoric function, making reference to previous discourse. Use of 1st person singular. Multimodal analysis: • paralinguistic elements: high key (i.e., emphasizing) in key words (e.g., "problemas de recursos," "multilingüismo"). • kinesics: head movement (e.g., "no se dónde está"), laugh (e.g., "es lógico").
Entonces pensé que podría fabricar una cosa rápidamente, **lo que pasa es que estos días** pues he tenido mil cosas, a) desde los 70 años de Ariel, b) la Gramática dichosa que han citado elogiosamente, c) y **tantas cosas** que han surgido **hasta ayer,** que tuve que presentar el manual de Fundeu del uso del español en la red. *Then I thought I could rapidly elaborate something, but these days I have been very busy, since I had so many things to do,* *a) from the 70th anniversary of Ariel* *b) to the Grammar you have praised so much* *c) and so many things that have come up until yesterday, when I had to present the manual of Fundeu about the use of the Spanish language on the web.* (Our translation)	Move 2) Introduction of the aside: causal discourse marker (i.e., "entonces"). The speaker needs to justify the lecture he is about to present and gives reasons for that (i.e., extensive digressions). Linguistic analysis: • 1st person singular (i.e., "pensé," "podría,"), past simple (e.g. "pensé") and present perfect (e.g.," he tenido") to reinforce the link between the inconveniences from the past that have affected the elaboration of his plenary lecture. Multimodal analysis: • paralinguistic elements: falling and rising intonation (e.g., "hasta ayer"). • kinesics: head movements (e.g., "la Gramática dichosa") + gaze (e.g., "lo que pasa es que estos dias," "tantas cosas") to emphasize significant discourse.

(*Continued*)

Table 2.3 (Continued)

Aside 2: Context-based, the speaker refers to his own life (example 10)	
Entonces, a) **yo** he preparado **modestamente** unas fotocopias, b) y voy a hacer una, c) como **dicen ustedes** a propósito de la gramática, d) **que me hace mucha gracia,** e) voy a hacer una reflexión, igual que hacen **ustedes** reflexiones gramaticales *So,* *a) I have modestly prepared some photocopies* *b) and I am going to make a . . .* *c) as you say . . . because of the grammar . . .* *d) that makes me laugh* *e) I am going to make a reflection, in the same way you make grammatical reflections.* (Our translation)	Move 3) Extension of the aside: discourse marker with an explicative function (i.e., "entonces"), introduction of other asides within this aside: a) photocopies, b) reflection, c) as you say about grammar, d) which is funny for me. Linguistic analysis: • 1st person singular (e.g., "yo") and immediate future (e.g., "voy a hacer"), 2nd person plural (e.g., "ustedes") to engage the audience in a direct but highly formal way. Multimodal analysis: • paralinguistic elements: falling and rising intonation (e.g., "entonces"). • kinesics: head movements (e.g., "entonces") + hand movement (e.g., "yo he preparado") + gaze (e.g., "entonces," "modestamente") + laughter (e.g., "que me hace mucha gracia," "una reflexión") to emphasize significant discourse.
yo voy a hacer **una reflexión** sobre el **multilingüismo, la literatura y ciertas zonas de la literatura** que están relacionadas con la enseñanza del español para extranjeros. *I am going to make a reflection on multilingualism, literature and some areas from literature that are related to Spanish as a foreign language teaching.* (Our translation)	Move 4) End of the aside: repeated utterance as a resumption of main lecture. This is reinforced with a gesture as 'pat-ending expression' (putting his glasses on). Linguistic analysis: • 1st person singular (e.g., "yo") and immediate future (e.g., "voy a hacer"). Multimodal analysis: • paralinguistic elements: falling and rising (e.g., "multilingüismo," "literatura," "ciertas zonas"). • kinesics: head movements (e.g., "que están relacionadas") + gaze ("ciertas zonas de la literatura") + laughter (e.g., "reflexión") + gestures (i.e., putting his glasses on) to emphasize significant discourse.

Paralinguistic dimension	Rising intonation + laughter
Linguistic dimension	yo voy a hacer una reflexión sobre el multilingüismo, [PAUSE] la literatura, [PAUSE] PAUSE]y ciertas zonas de la literatura, que están relacionadas con la enseñanza del español para extranjeros.
Kinesics	Head movements + intensive gaze  gesture (glasses on)  (Pat-ending expression)

Figure 2.2 Coexpression of paralinguistic, linguistic and kinesic elements in Move 4 (Blecua)

gaze at the audience. However, the most interesting aspect in the multimodal analysis of this move is the pat-ending expression used to mark the end of the aside and the return to the main topic. In this case, the speaker does not resort to a linguistic resource, but rather a gesture: he stops and puts on his glasses. This signals to the audience the end of the aside, as shown in Figure 2.2.

2.4 CONCLUSION

In this chapter, we have looked at the role of asides in plenary lectures from a multimodal perspective, which includes a detailed analysis of linguistic, paralinguistic and kinesic resources that afford a comprehensive understanding of discourse. Though this can be considered a preliminary study whose results need to be corroborated with additional sources of data, we think there is enough evidence to state that discourse analysis cannot be complete unless there is a joint study of verbal and nonverbal behaviors.

Concerning genre definition, the results showed that plenary lectures do not follow an IMRDC structure as presented by Ventola (2002). Indeed, there is no description of research, no specific conclusions at the end and no Q&A session. The beginning and the end of the two lectures that were analyzed are very similar, with an extensive introduction with acknowledgments for the organizers, as well as an explanation of their relationship with the conference venue. The end in both lectures is marked by a climax, with a special and surprising example selected by each lecturer, which provokes the laughter of the audience.

Regarding the in-depth study of the two asides selected, our joint analysis of verbal and nonverbal elements following the three-level analysis adapted from Carter-Thomas and Rowley-Jolivet (2003) confirms the validity of this analytical framework. It has allowed us to apply a multimodal approach to better understand the role of asides and their final communicative aim in the genre of plenary lectures. Results showed that context-based asides are mainly found at the beginning of the lecture. The rest of the categories can be located anywhere throughout the whole lecture. These context-based asides are signaled by a discourse marker, include first person singular pronouns or first person singular verb forms when referring to the speaker, and imperatives and second person plural pronouns when interacting with the audience. This extensive use of personal pronouns is typical of nonscientific language and closer to spontaneous spoken discourse (Morell, 2007), which can be considered one of the objectives of plenary speakers. More specifically, the speakers seem to aim to sound natural and spontaneous in order to create empathy with the audience and to bond with members of the discourse community, as is clearly evident in both examples analyzed.

Plenary speakers are invited and are usually allotted more time for their lectures and therefore may feel freer to include digressions, anecdotes and humor, thus using more organizing clues than is usual in paper presentations. However, we agree with Webber (2005, p.173) when she refers to this specific trait of plenary lectures as "very complex material since the speaker may be one of the few experts in the field and only a handful of experts in the audience may be able to follow the speaker's argument adequately." It is at this point when a multimodal approach proves to be necessary and effective for a comprehensive understanding of the whole message as shown in the analysis of Aside 1 (Figure 2.1) in which kinesics and paralinguistic elements play a fundamental role in understanding Crystal's communicative goal.

As for the differences between English and Spanish plenary lectures, it is important to underline that this chapter presents the analysis of examples from only two lecturers. It would be therefore necessary to extend this research using a larger dataset in order to corroborate our results and determine whether they reflect a general trend in both Spanish and English applied linguistics plenary lectures. However, from the results we can draw some tentative conclusions. We can say that there do not seem to be significant differences in the linguistic, paralinguistic and kinesic resources used in both languages by these two speakers when constructing digressions. It is important to mention that this might be because of the similar profile of both plenary speakers. In fact, both are highly renowned researchers with a long experience in the field and numerous plenary lectures in their careers.

Though the results in this chapter can only be considered preliminary because of the limitations of the dataset, some of them are in line with those obtained by previous researchers such as Hood and Forey (2005), for example, the use of humor as well as verbal and nonverbal resources when thanking the organization for the invitation or referring to the conference venue. On a practical level, the findings of this study can be very useful in the context of training courses for new researchers, providing support for the need to pay careful attention to both verbal and nonverbal features for a complete understanding of conference lectures.

ACKNOWLEDGMENTS

We would like to thank Professor David Crystal and Professor José Manuel Blecua for their collaboration in this research and their permission to use the recordings and show their images in this chapter. This study has been developed as part of a research project funded by the Ministry of Science and Innovation of Spain (ref. FFI2011–24269).

NOTES

1. Available at http://diobma.udg.edu/handle/10256.1/2692. Creative Commons Licence [http://creativecommons.org/licenses/by-nc-sa/3.0/es/deed.en] (17/10/2014).
2. Available at http://iatefl.britishcouncil.org/2013/sessions/2013–04–09/plenary-session-david-crystal (17/10/2014).

REFERENCES

Argyle M., Ingham, R., Alkema, F., & McCallin, M. (1981). The different functions of gaze. In A. Kendon (Ed.), *Nonverbal communication, interaction and gesture* (pp. 283–295). Paris: Mouton.

Bavelas, J.B., Hagen, D., Lane, L., & Lawrie, D.A. (1989, May). *Interactive gestures and a systems theory of conversation.* Paper presented at the annual meeting of the International Communication Association, San Francisco.

Berkenkotter, C., & Huckin, T.N. (1995). *Genre knowledge in disciplinary communities.* Hillsdale, NJ: Lawrence Erlbaum Associates, Inc.

Brazil, D. (1997). *The communicative value of intonation in English.* Cambridge: Cambridge University Press.

Carter-Thomas, S. & Rowley-Jolivet, E. (2003). Analysing the scientific conference presentation (CP): A methodological overview of a multimodal genre. *ASp, 39–40,* 59–72. Retrieved from http://asp.revues.org/1295.

Cauldwell, R. (2002). *Streaming speech: Listening and pronunciation for advanced learners of English.* Birmingham, UK: Speechinaction.

Deroey, K.L.B., & Taverniers, M. (2012). "Ignore that 'cause it's totally irrelevant": Marking lesser relevance in lectures. *Journal of Pragmatics, 44*(14), 2085–2099.
Ekman P., & Friesen, W. V. (1969). The repertoire of nonverbal behavioural categories: Origins, usage and coding. *Semiotica, 1*(1), 49–98.
Flowerdew, J. (1994). Research of relevance to second language lecture comprehension: An overview. In J. Flowerdew (Ed.), *Academic listening: Research perspectives* (pp. 7–29). Cambridge: Cambridge University Press.
Fortanet, I., & Räisänen, C. (2006, June). *Do genres have body language? Nonverbal communication in conference paper presentations.* Paper presentation at Conference in Honor of John Swales. University of Michigan, Ann Arbor.
Fortanet-Gómez I., & Ruiz-Madrid, M.N. (2014). Multimodality for comprehensive communication in the classroom: Questions in guest lectures. *Ibérica, 28*(Fall), 203–224.
Goodwin C., & Goodwin, M.H. (1987). Concurrent operations on talk: Notes on the interactive organizations of assessments. *IPRA Papers in Pragmatics, 1*(1), 1–54.
Heino, A., Tervonen, E., & Tommola, J. (2002). Metadiscourse in academic conference presentations. In E. Ventola, C. Shalom, & S. Thompson (Eds.), *The language of conferencing* (pp. 127–146). Frankfurt: Peter Lang.
Hood, S. & Forey, G. (2005) Introducing a conference paper: Getting interpersonal with your audience. *Journal of English for Academic Purposes, 4*(4), 291–306.
Kendon, A. (1967). Some functions of gaze direction in social interaction. *Acta Psychologica, 26*(1), 22–63.
Kendon, A. (1981). Some functions of the face in kissing round. In A. Kendon (Ed.), *Nonverbal communication, interaction and gesture* (pp. 321–356). Paris: Mouton.
Kendon, A. (2002). Some uses of head shake. *Gesture, 2*(2), 147–183.
Kendon, A. (2004). *Gesture. Visible action as utterance.* Cambridge: Cambridge University Press.
McClave, E.Z. (2000). Linguistic functions of head movements in the context of speech. *Journal of Pragmatics,* 32(7), 855–878.
McNeill, D. (1992). *Hand and mind: What gestures reveal about thought.* Chicago: The University of Chicago Press.
Morell, T. (2007). What enhances EFL students' participation in lecture discourse? Student, lecturer and discourse perspectives. *Journal of English for Academic Purposes, 6*(3), 227–237.
Morris, D. (1977). *Manwatching: A field of guide to human behaviour.* London: Jonathan Cape.
Pons, S., & Estellés, M. (2009). Expressing digression linguistically: Do digressive markers exist? *Journal of Pragmatics, 41*(5), 921–936.
Poyatos, F. (2002). *Nonverbal communication across disciplines: Volume II. Paralanguage, kinesics, silence, personal and environmental interaction.* Amsterdam: John Benjamins.
Querol-Julián, M. (2010). Multimodality in discussion sessions: Corpus compilation and pedagogical use. *Language Value, 2*(1), 1–26.
Querol-Julián, M., & Fortanet-Gómez, I. (2014). Evaluation in discussion sessions of conference presentations: Theoretical foundations for a multimodal analysis. *Kalbotyra, 66*: 77–98.
Schegloff, E.A. (1987). Analyzing single episodes of interaction: An exercise in conversation analysis. *Social Psychology Quarterly, 50*(2), 101–114.
Shalom, C. (2002). The academic conference: A forum of enacting genre knowledge. In E. Ventola, C. Shalom, & S. Thompson (Eds.), *The language of conferencing* (pp. 51–68). Frankfurt: Peter Lang.
Strodt-Lopez, B. (1991). Tying it all in: Asides in university lectures. *Applied Linguistics, 12*(2), 117–140.

Ventola, E. (2002). Why and what kind of focus on conference presentations? In E. Ventola, C. Shalom, & S. Thompson (Eds.), *The language of conferencing* (pp. 15–50). Frankfurt: Peter Lang.

Ventola, E., Shalom, C., & Thompson S. (Eds.), (2002). *The language of conferencing*. Frankfurt: Peter Lang.

Webber, P. (2005). Interactive features in medical conferences monologues. *English for Specific Purposes*, *24*(2), 157–181.

3 Intensifying Adverbs in Academic Spoken Discourse

A Contrastive Study Between English and Spanish

Miguel F. Ruiz-Garrido

3.1 INTRODUCTION

Over the last few decades, English has reached its role of lingua franca in many settings, including the academic world. English for academic purposes (EAP) has become one of the main areas of teaching and research within the field of applied linguistics. However, academic written discourse has been the main objective for a long time (Björkman, 2011; Mauranen, Pérez-Llantada & Swales, 2010). As Mauranen et al. (2010) summarize, the reasons for focusing on writing over speaking are three: a) mostly written language is assessed in higher education, b) it is easier for EAP instructors and researchers to access written materials and c) most EAP courses and workshops focus on written discourse. In spite of this, over a decade ago, the focus began to shift from written discourse to spoken discourse in EAP (Diani, 2008), thanks to the appearance of major spoken corpora of academic English, such as MICASE (Michigan Corpus of Academic Spoken English), which has become one of the leading and best-known corpora of spoken academic English.

The study of such spoken corpora has shed some light on the features of academic spoken discourse. These corpora have been a continuous source of reference in the recent publications of prestigious journals such as the *Journal of English for Academic Purposes, English for Specific Purposes* or the *Journal of Pragmatics,* among others. Nevertheless, most of this research has been conducted by analyzing the written transcripts of the lectures, conference papers or any other academic event that had been recorded and transcribed. Only recently have new elements come into play: gestures, intonation or the role of the slides, which represent an important component of spoken academic communication.

3.2 SPOKEN ACADEMIC DISCOURSE

Several authors have explained the main features of the conference presentation (hereinafter CP) in comparison to some other spoken academic genres, such as lectures, or genres within the field of written academic discourse (cf. Räisänen, 1999; Rowley-Jolivet, 2002; Ruiz-Garrido & Fortanet-Gómez, 2008). With particular reference to CPs, their main features can be summarized as follows:

- "The CP is, even if semi-prepared and/or rehearsed, a live event in real-time. Speakers have to adapt the high-density informational content to this constraint" (Carter-Thomas & Rowley-Jolivet, 2003, p. 60). Even though they are oral events, many times conference presentations are written first and then delivered orally.
- Whereas the purpose of scientific research communication is informative and rhetorical/persuasive, regardless of the media, this fact has a direct effect on the audience. In a conference presentation, the audience is physically close and, therefore, "it is necessary to set up a feeling of connivance. Too detached a monologue would be ill-suited to the communicative context and appropriate interpersonal strategies are important" (Carter-Thomas & Rowley-Jolivet, 2003, p. 60).
- Finally, the use of semiotic modes in conference presentations is required so that the audience can perfectly follow the oral and visual information.

An interesting contribution to establish differences in scientific discourse or genres was offered by Gilbert and Mulkay (1984), later on supported and re-expressed in other works (Swales & Burke, 2003; Wulff, Swales & Keller, 2009; Querol-Julián, 2011). These authors refer to a dual concept of classifying scientific discourse as *empiricist repertoire* (objective, impersonal style, such as in a research paper) or *contingent repertoire* (more personal style, showing insights and beliefs, such as in confidential interviews with researchers). Wulff et al. (2009) propose a continuum from empiricist to contingent repertoires, including examples like formal research papers (on the empiricist end), moving to reviews, conference presentations, post-presentation discussions, personal remarks addressed to speakers and personal remarks about third parties at conferences (on the contingent end). Based on this as well as on previous literature, they point out that the CP genre seems to include more contingent elements than their equivalent written productions (Wulff et al., 2009).

This kind of continuum is also considered by Spanish researchers when describing Spanish spoken academic discourse. Sanz Álava (2007) refers to a continuum between spoken and written academic discourse. She also adds the idea of different levels of formality between one end and the other, describing daily conversation as spoken and informal, and an opinion article as written and formal. However, she argues that there are certain spoken events that look like a written text, but also the other way around, thus promoting the idea of the continuum within the different spoken academic events.

Swales and Burke (2003) also summarize various features of academic speech according to previous research. They state that speakers, mainly in conference presentations, apologize and admit mistakes (Rowley-Jolivet, 1999), heavily hedge their discourse (Poos & Simpson, 2000) and frequently signpost the discourse by means of discourse markers (Swales & Malcewski, 2001). In addition, they may be more informal (at least in the US), using phonological reductions (e.g., *gonna* rather than *going to*), filled pauses or 'vague' words (e.g., *thing*). Other authors have analyzed additional features of academic speech, including the frequent use of first person pronouns, active verb forms, sequencing words, repetition or episodes of humor and self-irony, among others (cf. Hyland, 2009; Ruiz-Garrido & Fortanet-Gómez, 2008). In sum, Swales and Burke (2003, p. 2) conclude by saying that "it looks . . . as though academic speech turns out to be much 'more like' ordinary conversation than academic prose" (but not exactly alike, as they explain later).

With particular reference to CPs, Hyland (2009) explains that a conference presentation may be delivered according to a range of presentation styles. He refers to the three styles Dudley-Evans and Johns (1981) established for delivering lectures, which are also applicable to conference presentations:

1. *reading style:* when the presenter reads from notes
2. *conversational style:* when the presenter adopts a more informal, conversation-like delivery
3. *rhetorical style:* when the presenter is more expansive and performance-oriented

Our hypothesis is that nowadays each of these styles may not be strictly applied in isolation, but that finding a combination of two or three of them is actually a better possibility. In fact, Hyland (2009, p. 83) also adds that there is "a trend towards a more interactive pattern as the speaker shapes the message to connect with the immediate context." One way of shaping the message could be done by highlighting certain expressions, as the following section will explain.

3.3 INTENSIFICATION AND INTENSIFYING ADVERBS

From a communicative viewpoint, intensification is related to the emphasis a speaker/writer wants/needs to place upon certain linguistic items (e.g., words, phrases, clauses). Partington (1993) explains that intensification is

> a direct indication of a speaker's desire to use and exploit the expression of hyperbole. In other words, s/he tells the listener that what is being

> said is sincerely vouched for. The importance of intensification in the communicative process is that it is a vehicle for impressing, praising, persuading, insulting, and generally influencing the listener's reception of the message.
>
> (p. 178)

This idea seems to have been accepted by other later works. Lorenz (1999, p. 24) also states that intensification "expresses an 'interpersonal' message in what might otherwise be taken to be purely 'ideational' statement." Similarly, Swales and Burke (2003) add that there is some kind of rhetorical effect produced by intensification.

According to previous studies, intensification in English or Spanish (the two languages the present study focuses on) can be carried out in different ways. Albelda Marco (2005) provides a complete summary of how this pragmatic category (as she defines it following Briz Gómez 1997, 1998) functions from the semantic and rhetorical perspectives, and how it can be implemented in discourse by means of a wide variety of resources (i.e., morphological, lexical, syntactic, semantic and phonetic). In Albelda Marco (2005) and the works she refers to, the use of adverbs as modifiers of adjectives is considered to be one of the main resources of intensification, and they will also be the focus of this chapter. For example, in the expression *"la verdad es que soy muy conservadora" (the truth is that I am very conservative),* the adverb *muy (very)* is reinforcing the truthfulness of the statement (taken from Albelda Marco, 2005, p. 305).

In relation to the concept of intensifying adverbs, there have been numerous terms and classifications that have been used, which may lead to some confusion. Probably one of the most important grammar books in the English language (Quirk, Greenbaum, Leech & Svartvik, 1985; Biber, Johansson, Leech, Conrad & Finnegan, 1999) use the terms in a slightly different manner. Quirk et al. (1985)—following previous work by Bolinger (1972) or Quirk and Greenbaum (1973), but also Spanish authors like Portero Muñoz (1997)—classify intensifiers (most of them adverbs) into *emphasizers, amplifiers (maximizers* and *boosters)* and *minimizers (compromisers, diminishers, minimizers* and *approximators).* Biber et al. (1999) instead refer to these features as adverbs of degree and divide them into *amplifiers* or *intensifiers* and *diminishers* or *downtoners.* The former increase intensity, some modify gradable adjectives and "indicate degrees on a scale," and some "indicate an endpoint on a scale" (Biber et al., 1999, pp. 554–555), whereas the latter just "scale down the effect of the modified item" (Biber et al., 1999, p. 555). Hyland (2000) identifies amplifiers or intensifiers as *boosters,* while diminishers are usually referred to as *hedges* or *minimizers,* following Quirk et al.'s (1985) terminology. Following previous research (Querol-Julián & Fortanet-Gómez, 2012), in this analysis we will use Biber et al.'s classification when referring to linguistic expressions of intensification.

3.4 INTENSIFICATION IN SPOKEN DISCOURSE

As Xiao and Tao (2007, p. 242) explain, intensifiers "have been studied for decades and have attracted interest from a number of linguistic fields." Initial studies concentrated on their structural and semantic properties (e.g., Bolinger, 1972; Jespersen, 1922; Mustanoja, 1960; Quirk et al., 1985; Stoffel 1901). This research has contributed to the taxonomy and description of intensifiers in English. Some authors have studied gender bias in the use of intensifying adverbs in male vs. female speech (Drescher, 2003; Jeon & Choe, 2009; Lakoff, 1973, 1975, 1990; Stenström, 1999; Tagliamonte & Roberts, 2005; Xiao & Tao, 2007, among others). Although these studies are not conclusive, we can see how some of them make use of spoken academic discourse and demonstrate specific frequencies in the use of certain adverbs. For example, Jeon and Choe (2009) used the ICE-GB (International Corpus of English-Great Britain) for their research on intensifiers and found *very* to be the most frequent intensifying adverb, regardless of male or female authorship, with *so, more* or *too* also appearing among the forms commonly used. Drescher (2003) analyzed the TOEFL 2000 Spoken and Written Academic Language (T2K-SWAL) corpus, and also found intensifiers like *very, absolutely, really* or *so* as the most common ones in relative terms.

However, the literature shows us that research on intensifiers is very often linked to the study of evaluation. Biber et al. (1999) consider adverbs of degree (our concern in this chapter) as premodifying stance adverbs (stance adverb + adjective or noun phrase), one of the existing grammatical devices used to express stance (e.g., in the sentence "*Well that's not really a weird name*" (p. 874), the stance adverbial *really* is used to soften disagreement). Furthermore, they also explain that in conversation, "stance meaning can be conveyed through a number of nonlinguistic means, . . . and paralinguistic devices . . ." (Biber et al., 1999, p. 967). They conclude that speakers always tend to express a "covert stance" when utterances are delivered.

Diani (2008, p. 297), referring to previous research on the role of emphasizers (or 'emphatics' in those studies) in academic discourse (Bondi, 2008 and Silver, 2006), concludes that they "play an essential role in academic discourse, allowing the researcher to convey judgments and situate her/his positions in relation to knowledge and truth claims." In a later work on pragmatic force modifiers on lectures from the British Academic Spoken English corpus (BASE), such as *really* or *actually,* Lin (2010) explains the function of intensifiers as modifying:

- non-controversial and widely acknowledged facts which play a central part in the speech,
- lecturers' subjective opinions in favour of their main arguments, and
- third party viewpoints.

(p. 1180)

The author also claims that these intensifiers try to signpost key points, achieve a rhetorical effect, or create a lively and dramatic effect, respectively. We agree with her that these intensifiers have an inherent emphatic meaning, which imply a high personal involvement and, consequently, a feeling of closeness with the audience.

There are also other studies that show the possibility of combining intensifying adverbs and positive adjectives to comment on a negative situation in order to express irony or sarcasm (Kreuz & Roberts, 1995, cited in Crawford Camiciottoli, 2012, p. 203). These occurrences often involve the use of hyperbole (e.g., the comment *What an absolutely fantastic day!* to refer to bad weather), highlighting a further use of intensifiers with evaluative functions.

Some authors have analyzed the MICASE in order to study the use of intensifiers in academic speech. Swales and Burke (2003) compared evaluative adjectives in the MICASE with a corpus of written research articles. They found that evaluative adjectives were sometimes preceded by adverbs like *very* (one of the most frequent), and that intensifiers preceding adjectives were used four times as frequently in spoken academic discourse as compared to the research articles. Thus, they conclude that "MICASE data shows a much greater affinity to casual speech as opposed to formal prose" (Swales and Burke, 2003, p. 16).

Recski (2004) also used the MICASE, comparing it to the ICLE (International Corpus of Learner English), showing that the most common boosters in both corpora were *very, so* and *too,* as well as *really* in the MICASE results; in both corpora the adverb accounting for the highest percentage was *very*. According to the author, the fact that there were many more boosters than amplifiers in his results may mean that "boosters seem to be more 'multipurpose' (they combine with a wider range of words) and more 'abundant' (used in more examples) than the maximizers" (Recski, 2004, p. 220).

Regarding spoken Spanish and the analysis of intensifiers, to our knowledge all the studies have dealt with colloquial and daily oral discourse (e.g., Albelda Marco, 2005; Briz Gómez, 1997, 1998; Portero Muñoz, 1997). Because conference presentations may be seen as a genre that falls somewhere in between written and oral, or formal and informal, these studies are valuable and useful for our purposes. Additionally, Spanish authors also support the evaluative dimension of intensification. Vergara Heidke (2012, p. 164) proposes the idea of "enhancement" and enumerates various aspects that define this concept, such as:

- the high number of resources available to intensify any item: written features (bold, size, color and so on), oral features (pauses, intonation, vowel length increase, silence and so on), lexical elements (superlatives, intensifiers) and syntactic structures (repetitions, enumerations)
- the diverse functions these resources may fulfill (expressive, referential, conative)

- the different effects they may cause (feelings, emotions, better remembering)
- the possible occurrence of nonconscious or nonvoluntary performances of enhancing (pauses caused by distraction or hesitation)

As we can appreciate from the above description, intensifiers in spoken discourse cannot be isolated from the context in which they are produced. Vergara Heidke's conceptualization accounts not only for the words that express intensification, but also for how they are uttered by paying attention to paralinguistic or oral resources. However, other resources such as gestures or facial expression have been disregarded. To our knowledge, no previous research has focused on the various multimodal resources used for intensifying adverbs in spoken conference presentations. The fact that intensifying adverbs and the whole phrase in which they appear have an intrinsic emphasizing value in themselves does not necessarily mean that they occur in isolation. In other words, they may or may not occur together with other nonlinguistic elements. The aim of this chapter is to contribute to research on academic spoken discourse from a multimodal standpoint, with particular reference to the use of intensifying adverbs in conference presentations in English and Spanish. We will try to identify the most common intensifiers that modify the adjectives that speakers use in their presentations, paying special attention to the paralinguistic and kinesic resources used to add more emphasis to the linguistic meaning of intensifying adverbs. Our research questions are the following:

1. Which intensifying expressions are used most frequently by English vs. Spanish conference speakers?
2. Which nonlinguistic resources (paralinguistic and kinesic) do speakers use to reinforce the linguistic expression of intensification?
3. What are the functions of the nonlinguistic resources used by the speakers?
4. How are nonlinguistic resources used to convey or support meaning according to the speakers' purposes?

3.5 METHODOLOGY

The present study is part of a wider project that aims to explore linguistic and nonlinguistic features (kinesics and paralanguage) in a set of spoken academic events. The data selected for analysis belongs to a corpus called MASC (Multimodal Academic Spoken Language Corpus), compiled by the Group for Research on Academic and Professional English (GRAPE) at Universitat Jaume I. From this source, two subcorpora were utilized. First, we used the JSCC (John Swales Conference Corpus), compiled by GRAPE members and transcribed in collaboration with the English Language

Institute (ELI) at the University of Michigan. This corpus was recorded in 2006 and its transcripts are available at the TalkBank archive.[1] The whole conference consisted of presentations delivered by a group of invited speakers, all experts in their areas of interest within the field of applied linguistics. The JSCC contains 23 transcribed presentations with an average length of about 20 minutes, and the corresponding question and answer session of about 10 minutes, though we do not deal with the latter here. For this current study, the conference presentation transcript was analyzed, as well as the corresponding video recordings, as will be explained in further detail.

The second source is a subcorpus of Spanish conference presentations. Two of them were selected and the video recordings and their transcripts were analyzed. Both presentations were delivered at the AELFE (Asociación Europea de Lenguas para Fines Específicos, an academic association specialized in languages for specific purposes) conference held in Valencia in 2011 and also dealt with topics within applied linguistics. The average length was also about 20 minutes, and the question and answer session was also disregarded for our purposes.

As there were only two presentations in Spanish delivered by female lecturers, we decided to restrict the parallel analysis of English presentations to two also delivered by female speakers in order to minimize or avoid any possible difference between male and female speech, as mentioned above. Therefore, from the JSCC subcorpus, two presentations given by female speakers were selected at random. In addition, since the contrastive analysis needs to be based on a quantitatively balanced dataset, presentations over 20 minutes or too long in their number of words were discarded. The final dataset made up of four presentations is illustrated in Table 3.1, where *Eng* stands for English language and *Sp* for Spanish language.

In the following paragraphs, we describe the physical settings in which the four conference presentations took place, along with key features of the

Table 3.1 Dataset used for the study

Topic	Code	Word count	Duration
Corporate mission statements	Eng1	2783	21:88
The concept of genre and its evolution from a diachronic perspective	Eng2	2716	13:18
Verbal forms in civil engineering research articles in Spanish and English	Sp1	2122	15:97
Terminology within the popularized scientific discourse	Sp2	1911	19:05

speakers' delivery style, as observed from the video recordings. The two English-speaking presenters are standing up and speaking from a podium. The screen is behind them to their left, and they use overhead transparencies. The first speaker (Eng1) stands behind the podium, so only face and hand/arm movements could be seen and analyzed. She tends to use a reading style in delivering her presentation. Speaker Eng2 also starts speaking standing behind the podium, but turns back to look at the screen from time to time, and also leaves the podium and moves a bit with notes in her hands; she reads the first part of her presentation, but she tries not to stick only to the written text in the second part, especially when she moves from the podium to the screen and vice versa. In this second case, we had more opportunities to analyze her body language, although sometimes we could only see her back.

As for the Spanish speakers, both of them are sitting down, behind a desk and a desktop (positioned at their right without hiding the speakers) and the screen is behind them to their left (as in the English presentations), although they used projected PowerPoint slides instead of transparencies. Therefore, none of them stand up or move around, so we could analyze only the movements of the upper part of their bodies. Speaker Sp1 employs her right hand to use the mouse and show the slides. She tends not to read and instead looks at the audience, although she sometimes looks at the computer screen or even at the screen where the slides are projected. Even if she looks at the screen, she always tries to sound natural, looking at the audience, and accompanying her speech with arm and hand movements most of the time. Speaker Sp2 also uses her right hand to show the slides. Unlike the previous Spanish speaker, she has her written version of the presentation close to her and follows or uses it from time to time in a regular manner. She also looks sometimes at the computer screen and sometimes at the audience. She combines a strong reliance on the written paper and on the slides with looking at the audience, seeking approval or checking their understanding from time to time. When doing the latter, she accompanies her speech with arm and hand movements as well.

Once the dataset was selected, a wordlist of each presentation was generated by means of the text analysis software WordSmith Tools 5.0 (Scott, 2008). These lists show all of the words used in each presentation ranked according to frequency, so that the most frequent single-word adverbs could be identified manually, and then compared to previous research (especially Biber et al., 1999). Our lists showed the following results from more to less frequent:

- English: so, more, very, quite, really, still, rather, too, exactly, right, pretty, real, relatively
- Spanish: más, muy, también, qué, siempre, ya, mucho, solo, muchas, efectivamente, tan, demasiado

Then, the emerging adverbs were studied in their context of usage to check whether their function was actually to modify an adjective (alone or preceding a noun) or something else, like a clause or a noun. We selected only those adverbs that belong to the category and function under analysis (i.e., adverbs modifying adjectives) and could be compared and contrasted in English and Spanish. Thus, the adverbs we finally selected for comparison were *very, more* and *so* in English and *muy, más* and *tan* in Spanish. These items were then marked in the transcripts in order to analyze co-occurring nonlinguistic features. As the dataset and the number of items to analyze was limited in size, the paralinguistic and kinesic analysis was performed manually, using the video recordings to observe nonlinguistic behaviors that occurred together with linguistic expressions of intensification.

Regarding the analysis of the nonlinguistic resources, and following previous research on multimodality and spoken academic discourse (e.g., Querol-Julián, 2011 or Querol-Julián & Fortanet-Gómez, 2012), it is typically necessary to narrow down the nonverbal resources that will be investigated. However, in the present research we decided to first identify the most frequent ones across the whole dataset and then analyze how they were used by the four speakers. We expected to check both kinesic features (hand, head and even body movements) and paralinguistic ones (such as pitch, silence or syllabic duration). To do so, all the samples were watched by two different researchers who agreed, first, on whether there was a nonlinguistic resource used when uttering the adverb and the adjective, and second, on the kind of nonlinguistic resources used for every occurrence. When disagreements happened (just a few times), the analysis of a third researcher was solicited and final agreement was reached.

3.6 RESULTS AND DISCUSSION

3.6.1 Analysis of Intensifying Adverbs

Table 3.2 illustrates the adverbs that emerged from the elaboration of the dataset with WordSmith Tools (Scott, 2008), as described above. Several of the adverbs from the wordlists shown previously could have been valid for our study since they can modify an adjective (e.g., *quite, pretty,* or *qué, demasiado*). However, not all occurrences were chosen as they did not always meet this requirement that we previously established (i.e., adverb modifying an adjective). All in all, the selection was reduced to 50 occurrences of *so, very* and *more* as the most frequent adverbs in the English-delivered presentations, and their closest equivalents *tan, muy* and *más* in the Spanish texts.[2] On the few occasions when two adverbs were used—e.g., *very very* (twice) or *muy muy* (once)—they were counted as a single occurrence as it is the expression that must be taken into account and not the isolated word. Similarly, we did not make any distinction in the use of *más* as a comparative or superlative form.

Table 3.2 Most frequent single-word adverbs

Adverbs	Total occurrences	Selected occurrences	Distribution of selected occurrences			
			Eng1	Eng2	Sp1	Sp2
so	4	3	2	1		
very	8	7	0	7		
more	20	6	3	3		
tan	2	2			1	1
muy	20	16			14	2
más	22	16			8	8
	76	50	5	11	23	11

The first results show that even though the present study is based on a very limited number of texts, the findings of earlier works on the use of certain adverbs of degree are confirmed. For example, Biber et al. (1999) found that *very, so, too* and some others are quite common intensifying adverbs in academic prose (and some of them also appear in conversation). Swales and Burke (2003) include in their list of the most common adverbs in MICASE *very* and the doubled intensifier *very very*. Similarly, also using MICASE, Recski (2004) noted the presence of the adverbs *very, really, so* and *too,* Diani (2008) the adverb *really* and Tao (2007) the adverb *absolutely*. In Spanish, there is no research to our knowledge on frequent adverbs appearing in academic spoken discourse, but the studies done on intensification and colloquial Spanish found that, in line with previous studies for English, *muy (very)* and a great variety of other possible adverbs can be used as intensifiers (see Albelda Marco, 2005).

It is also interesting to observe in Table 3.2 two other findings: a) the Spanish speakers used more adverbs of degree than the English speakers (68% vs. 32%), and b) the frequency of usage seems to depend on the individual speaker delivering the speech and their personal style. In the English-delivered presentations, Eng1 contains 5 occurrences and Eng2 11, whereas in the Spanish texts, Sp1 contains 23 occurrences and Sp2 11, thus revealing considerable variation between speakers of the same language.

In the methodology section, we explained the style used by each of the speakers when delivering their conference presentations. Our results show that the speakers who tend to sound more natural, by not sticking only to their papers and trying to create a more direct connection with the audience, also tend to use a higher number of adverbs of degree. In our case, speakers Eng2 and Sp1 tried to deliver their presentations in a more informal way, not very close to a *reading style* (in an imaginary continuum) in comparison with the other two speakers who were always behind the podium using their notes (Eng1) or had their notes on the table and followed them regularly (Sp2).

3.6.2 Analysis of Nonlinguistic Resources

Once the occurrences of intensifying adverbs had been identified, we moved to another important issue: whether these adverbs, apart from their own value as words that emphasize what they modify, may be highlighted by means of kinesic or paralinguistic resources.

Table 3.3 shows the co-occurrence of intensifying adverbs and the adjectives they modified with nonlinguistic resources. At first sight, no common pattern seems to exist between English speakers and Spanish speakers, or even when comparing speakers of the same language. Only half of the occurrences of intensifying expressions found previously (25 out of 50) were additionally intensified by means of nonlinguistic resources, despite their intrinsic intensifying value. Among the 16 occurrences contained in the English-speaking conference papers, 7 received a further emphasis (44%) by means of nonlinguistic resources, in comparison to 18 occurrences out of 34 in the Spanish presentations (53%). Moreover, in the English presentations, speaker Eng1 showed an additional emphasis on 2 occasions (out of 5) and speaker Eng2 did so 5 times (out of 11). Similarly, Sp1 used nonlinguistic resources 11 times (out of 23), whereas Sp2 made use of these resources 7 times out of 11. Therefore,

Table 3.3 Distribution of intensifying adverbs and adjectives modified with nonlinguistic resources

Adverb	Eng1	Eng2	Total occurrences	Adverb reinforced	Adjective reinforced
so	2	1	3	1	0
very	0	7	7	2	1
more	3	3	6	3	0
Items reinforced nonlinguistically				6	1
Adverb	**Sp1**	**Sp2**	**Total occurrences**	**Adverb reinforced**	**Adjective reinforced**
tan	1	1	2	1	0
muy	14	2	16	5	4
más	8	8	16	3	5
Items reinforced nonlinguistically				9	9

it seems that speakers who include more degree adverbs in their speech also make greater use of accompanying nonlinguistic resources, regardless of the language used, although this hypothesis would need to be corroborated with a larger dataset.

At this point, before discussing more in-depth the nonlinguistic resources used by the different speakers, an observation is required. Among the intensifying adverbs that were not reinforced by means of kinesic or paralinguistic behaviors, there are a few that deserve our attention. In 4 instances, 1 from Eng2 and 3 from Sp1, the use of intensifying adverbs (*very, muy* and *más*—twice each) is accompanied by a decreasing pitch or a low volume, so that the speaker does not reinforce the adjective, and perhaps even produces the opposite effect. This occurred in the following examples.

(example 1) all this stage is a fact. it's **very persuasive.** ok so let's (Eng2)
(example 2) miniestudio, no es un estudio **muy grande,** se basó en la (Sp1)
ministudy, it is not a ***very large*** *study, it was based on the*
(example 3) verbos en inglés nos resultó **más sencilla.** El sistema verbal (Sp1)
verbs in English were ***very easy.*** *The verbal system*
(example 4) con la pasiva refleja es **muy elevado.** Yyyy donde hay (Sp1)
with the passive by means of reflexive verbs is ***very high.*** *Aaand where there are*[3]
(example 5) sino un poco **más suavizadas,** y en español (Sp1)
but a bit ***more softened,*** *and in Spanish*

There could be several reasons not to make the most of the intensifiers in these samples. The English example (1) sounds more like an additional comment as the speaker is somehow repeating an idea previously said; it seems that the speaker does not want to sound repetitive, even though what she utters is a good summary of the previous statement. In the Spanish examples (3, 4 and 5), the stressed words appear at the end of the utterances (before a stop or a comma) and this is where the pitch lowers (see Boquete Martín, 2011). In example (2), the speaker seems to avoid emphasizing the negative idea that the phrase expresses ("not a very large study"). All in all, these items, regardless of their position in the utterance, could have been uttered in a different way (i.e., to emphasize the phrase), but the speaker's decision was to lower their voice and produce a contradiction between the words uttered and the paralinguistic resources accompanying them.

Table 3.3 also shows that, among the intensifying adverbs and adjectives that were reinforced by means of nonlinguistic resources, in the English presentations most of the emphasis falls on the adverb (in 6 out of 7 instances), while in the Spanish presentations, the 18 instances are balanced with 9 placed on the adverb and 9 on the adjective. None of them, however, follows a common pattern as might be expected.

With reference to the types of nonlinguistic resources that accompanied the intensifying adverbs, the following features were identified from the video recordings of the presentations included in the dataset:

- paralinguistic features
    a) pitch in the utterance of the adverb and adjective
    b) silence before or after the collocation of adverb and adjective, or even in between
    c) syllable duration in any of the words involved in the adverb-adjective collocation
- kinesic features
    a) hand movement
    b) head movement
    c) body movement, referring to the trunk of the body

This analysis of these features revealed that it was impossible to establish any clear pattern because up to 18 different combinations of the resources appeared just in our limited dataset. Among the nonlinguistic resources that were observed, the most frequent ones co-occurring with the 25 intensifying expressions analyzed are hand movements (18 occurrences) and pitch (15 occurrences), followed by head movements (10 occurrences), syllable prolongation (9 occurrences), silence (6 occurrences) and body movements (2 occurrences).

Within the paralinguistic resources, features related to pitch, silence and syllable prolongation were found. As explained earlier (Table 3.3), high pitch is not always placed on the adverb itself, but also on the adjective modified. Although we may assume that most of the time the speakers purposely stress one word or another, the analysis has shown that this is not always true. We have found one example (6) in which the marking of the expression does not seem to be caused by any preplanned intention of stressing the word/s:

(example 6) diferente, siempre mucho **más** eh **marcada,** pues siempre (Sp1)
different, always much ***more*** *eh* ***marked,*** *as it always*

Here the speaker slightly stops her speech before *siempre (always),* then she lengthens the duration of the adverb *más (more),* which is followed by the discourse filler *eh,* and then she utters the adjective *marcada (marked),* while adding hand movements, as can be seen in the second and third images shown in Figure 3.1.

A tentative interpretation of this example could be that the silent period that occurred before the first image when the speaker utters the word *siempre (always)* and the discourse filler were due to the same reason: the speaker's hesitation when seeking the word needed for her speech, *marcada.*

Figure 3.1 Example 6

As we expected, an intensifier modifying an adjective does not need to always be stressed by means of the pitch, since a number of other resources are available for this purpose. A longer syllable duration, for instance, is found mainly on the modified adjective in speaker Sp1's 6 occurrences (out of a total 7 items in which the syllable is prolonged, ***largas, rimbombante, alto, poquito, pomposa, elevada***). In all occurrences, the stressed syllable is the one being lengthened. The other 2 instances of syllable prolongation take place in the English presentations, 1 occurrence in each presentation (*more* in both cases). In addition, silence [S] seems to be another important resource to emphasize the use of intensifiers. Its distribution among three of the presentations analyzed (Eng1, Sp1 and Sp2) shows that it may be a common option in both languages. However, the use of silence does not seem to be characteristic of all presentations analyzed. Eng1 keeps a short silence to indicate this after the adjective in *because it's* ***so rich*** [S] and between the adverb and the adjective in ***more*** [S] ***tenuous.*** In contrast, Sp1 keeps the short silence before the adverb in both occurrences (example 6 above and in [S] ***muy rimbombante*** *[very ostentatious],* and Sp2 after the adjective, twice in ***más dudosos*** [S] *[more uncertain]* and ***más completa*** [S] *[more complete]*).

Hand movements (including also arm movements) seem to be the most frequent among the kinesic resources analyzed. Most of them occur together with other nonlinguistic resources, except in 3 instances in which hand movements are the only way of reinforcing the utterance. However, Spanish speakers seem to use their hands more often than English speakers (only 2 occurrences out of 18 and only performed by speaker Eng2), resulting in a greater difference which might because of cultural variation (cf. Heino, Tervonen & Tommola, 2002). Between the two Spanish speakers, Sp1 uses her hands in every instance analyzed and Sp2 nearly in all of them. For example, Speaker Eng2 uses her hands to reinforce the expression *very very interesting* and *very very technical.* In the first expression, she raises her pitch in the first *very* and adds an up-and-down movement of her hand like a spiral. In the second, speaker Eng2 accompanies the utterance *very very* raising her left hand, palm up, pointing at the screen and looking directly at the audience, probably to highlight the difficulty implied by the word *technical.* In the case of Spanish speakers, the two main functions of their hand movements seem to be pointing out the relevance or importance of the utterance (example 7) or illustrating, in a metaphorical way, what is being uttered (examples 8 and 9).

In example (7), the speaker moves her hands and arms, which are slightly open; both hands are touching by the fingertips, and when saying the utterance, she exemplifies such "length" *(largas)* by opening the arms and separating the hands.

(example 7) sintaxis es se utilizan frases **muy largas,** así un lenguaje (Sp1)
syntaxis is they are used in ***very long*** *sentences, so a language*

In example (8), the speaker has her palms up, fingers slightly curved, and then she moves her hands up and down reinforcing in this way the idea expressed by *fidedignos (reliable)*

(example 8) amplio para poder tener datos más fidedignos. Y además hemos (Sp2)
wide to have ***more reliable*** *data. Besides, we have*

In the following example (9), the speaker tilts her head to the right as a kind of excuse or meaning "I have done my best," and at the same time, she shrugs her shoulders. Figure 3.2 illustrates this movement by showing the body movement before the utterance, when she utters the expression, and after that, when the shoulders and head have come to a more relaxed position, from left to right.

(example 9) hemos intentado escoger **lo más similar posible.** El campo (Sp2)
we have tried to choose it as similar as possible. The field

The head movements show similar results as the hand movements, as only 1 occurrence happens in English (Sp1) and the rest (9) occur between the Spanish speakers (6 for Sp1, and 3 for Sp2). In these cases, all head movements are accompanying other paralinguistic and kinesic resources, such as pitch, silence, syllable prolongation, hand movements or a combination of some of them. Finally, when we refer to body movement, we mean

Figure 3.2 Example 9

the trunk of the body rather than the head and hands (or arms) as they are explained separately. In this case, there were only 2 occurrences and both were performed by the Spanish speakers (1 each). The following example (10) will be used to illustrate this distinction between trunk and hand or head movements:

(example 10) es gente que es que es así, **muy pomposa, muy elevada,** que no es nada (Sp1)
it is people who is that way, **very overwritten, very profound,** that is nothing

In this case, the speaker utters two consecutive phrases including an intensifying adverb and adjective. Apart from lengthening the syllables in both adjectives (as explained earlier), she accompanies her speech with a movement of the trunk of her body. Before uttering the intensifying expressions, as can be seen in Figure 3.3 she is leaning on the table (image A) and moves her body towards the back of the chair. At the same time, she moves her hand at a middle height, palms towards herself, and in a kind of circular way (image B). She also adds a head movement, tilting it to the left (image C), and moving the head back to the central position after uttering the two expressions (image D). From our point of view, her body language is probably trying to mitigate the implicit criticism she is expressing by means of the spoken language.

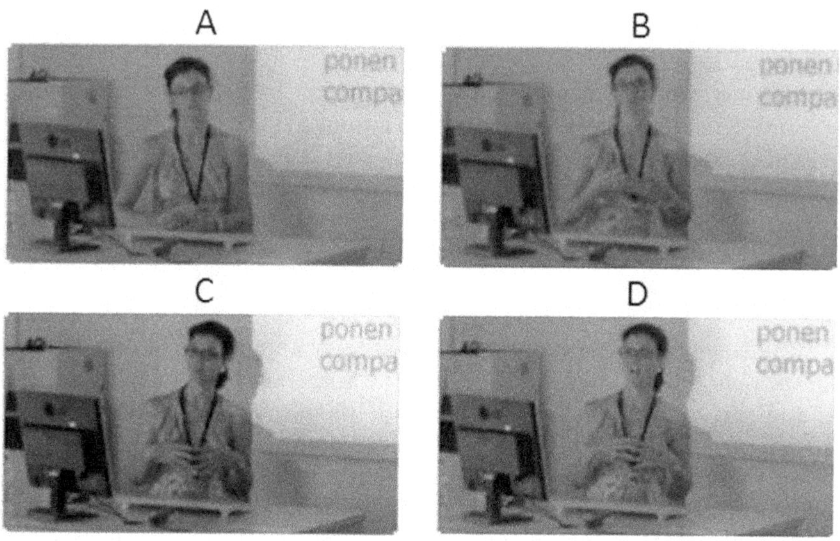

Figure 3.3 Example 10

3.7 CONCLUSIONS AND FURTHER RESEARCH

Needless to say, the limited number of speakers involved in this study, as well as the recognized degree of subjectivity in the interpretation, means that our results must be viewed with caution. As with any study that involves individuals, results may depend on several factors we cannot know or discover. However, we believe this kind of analysis that focuses on the observation of real academic events (even if limited in number) allows us to go deeper into the multimodal dimension of intensification in spoken academic discourse, thus providing an important contribution to applied linguistics.

Our research has shown that the type of adverbs of degree used in academic spoken discourse seems to be quite similar with respect to other studies, even though each person may have a tendency to use some rather than others. This outcome could be expected since, following Recski (2004), even fluent speakers may have problems when planning many thoughts units ahead and tend to rely on the intensifying words that are more accessible in their lexicon, as *very, so, more, muy, más* or *tan*.

According to the research questions posed at the outset of this study, some conclusions can be drawn. Our findings have shown that certain intensifying adverbs are quite frequent in academic spoken English and Spanish, such as *very (muy), more (más)* or *so (tan),* among others, although no significant differences in their frequency of usage were observed. These results support previous studies based on larger corpora. However, according to our study, the Spanish speakers tend to use a higher percentage of adverbs of degree than the English speakers. A more extensive study would be required to confirm or reject this conclusion. Additionally, it seems that a more conversation-like style causes a more frequent use of those common adverbs of degree.

Moreover, we have found that no pattern can be proposed to categorize the nonlinguistic resources used when emphasizing intensifiers in spoken academic discourse. We have observed that paralinguistics and kinesics could play an important role when speaking in public, and in our case, when supporting the intensification expressed by means of words. In our analysis, pitch, silence and syllable prolongation, on the one hand, and head, hand and body movement, on the other, were used to support the spoken language.

Additionally, we agree that intensifiers carry an internal weight as words that try to highlight an expression or an idea, and they can be used to attract the audience's attention or even persuade them. Yet our results show that intensifying adverbs may also be further emphasized so that their intensifying function becomes even clearer (even though this may not always take place). When an intensifier is nonlinguistically reinforced, it cannot be assumed that this happens because the speaker did it on purpose; sometimes it may also be caused by a second thought when speaking, or not finding the right word, for example. However, it is important to be aware of these kinesic and paralinguistic aids in order to determine whether they may be misleading for the audience. We understand, in a more or less conscious way, that speakers tend to use these nonlinguistic resources to reinforce the intended meaning of the expression uttered.

How to use intensifiers, how they collocate with other linguistic items and how to accompany them by means of nonlinguistic resources are issues that need further study, as well as application in the classroom. Some authors (e.g., Pérez-Paredes & Díez-Bedmar, 2012, and Recski, 2004) support the idea that teaching the use of intensifiers in academic writing (especially when it is in a foreign language) can be useful. In the same way, the awareness of how intensifiers are used, their common collocations, but also the possibility of using paralinguistic and kinesic devices to reinforce their meaning should be taken into account when teaching spoken academic discourse.

ACKNOWLEDGMENTS

I am grateful to Dr. María Boquera, Universitat Politècnica de València, and Dr. Paula de Santiago, Universidad de Valladolid, for kindly granting me permission to use their recorded conference presentations and to reproduce their images for this research.

NOTES

1. http://talkbank.org/media/MICASE/.
2. The wordlist returned these adverbs as the most frequent ones. Other adverbs, which, according to the literature, could have been found were also searched across the dataset, but there were none, or they occurred in quantities that were too small to be included, or they did not modify an adjective.
3. The prolongation of the pronunciation of the conjunction *y* in Spanish (*and* in English) was transcribed in the original Spanish text by repeating it. We have tried to maintain that same prolongation in English by repeating the letter *a* in the word *and*.

REFERENCES

Albelda Marco, M. (2005). *La intensificación en el español coloquial* (PhD dissertation). Universitat de València, València, Spain.

Biber, D., Johansson, S., Leech, G., Conrad, S., & Finnegan, E. (1999). *Longman grammar of spoken and written English*. Harlow: Pearson Education Limited.

Björkman, B. (2011). English as a lingua franca in higher education: Implications for EAP. *Ibérica, 22*(Fall), 79–100.

Bolinger, D. (1972). *Degree words*. The Hague: Mouton.

Bondi, M. (2008). Emphatics in academic discourse: Integrating corpus and discourse tools in the study of cross-disciplinary variation. In A. Ädel, & R. Reppen (Eds.), *Corpora and discourse: The challenge of different settings* (pp. 31–55). Amsterdam: John Benjamins.

Boquete Martín, G. (2011). *El uso del juego dramático en la enseñanza de lenguas: Las destrezas orales* (PhD dissertation). Retrieved from http://hdl.handle.net/10017/16981.
Briz Gómez, A. (1997). Los intensificadores en la conversación coloquial. In A. Briz Gómez, J.R. Gómez Molina, M.J. Martínez Alcalde, y Grupo VAL.ES.CO. (Eds.), *Pragmática y gramática del español hablado: El español coloquial* (pp. 13–36). Zaragoza: Pórtico.
Briz Gómez, A. (1998). El español coloquial en la conversación: Esbozo de pragmagramática. Barcelona: Ariel.
Carter-Thomas, S., & Rowley-Jolivet, E. (2003). Analysing the scientific conference presentation (CP): A methodological overview of a multimodal genre. *ASp, 39–40,* 59–72.
Crawford Camiciottoli, B. (2012). "Bigger, a lot bigger, massively much bigger": A comparative study of hyperbole in business and economics lectures. In H. Herrera Soler, & M. White (Eds.), *Metaphors and mills: The use of figurative language in business and economics* (pp. 201–222). Berlin: De Gruyter Mouton.
Diani, G. (2008). Emphasizers in spoken and written academic discourse: The case of *really*. *International Journal of Corpus Linguistics, 13*(3), 296–321.
Drescher, N. (2003, July 19–20). The relationships among gender, power, and register in the American academic community. Paper presented at the international conference of Perception and Realization in Language and Gender Research, Michigan State University. Retrieved from http://www.powershow.com/view1/1fadfa-ZDc1Z/The_Relationships_among_Gender_Power_and_Register_in_the_American_Academic_Community_powerpoint_ppt_presentation.
Dudley-Evans, T., & Johns, T.F. (1981). A team teaching approach to lecture comprehension for overseas students. In T. Dudley-Evans, & T.F. Johns (Eds.), *The teaching of listening comprehension* (pp. 30–46) (ELT Documents Special). London: British Council.
Gilbert, G.N., & Mulkay, M. (1984). *Opening Pandora's box: A sociological analysis of scientists' discourse*. Cambridge: Cambridge University Press.
Heino, A., Tervonen, E., & Tommola, J. (2002). Metadiscourse in academic conference presentations. In E.Ventola, C. Shalom, & S. Thompson (Eds.), *The language of* conferencing (pp. 127–146). Frankfurt: Peter Lang.
Hyland, K. (2000). *Disciplinary discourses: Social interactions in academic writing*. London: Longman.
Hyland, K. (2009). *Academic discourse: English in a global context*. London: Continuum.
Jeon, J., & Choe, J. (2009). A key word analysis of English intensifying adverbs in male and female speech in ICE-GB. In *Proceedings of the 23rd Pacific Asia Conference on Language, Information and Computations (PACLIC)* (pp. 210–219). Retrieved from http://www.aclweb.org/anthology/Y09–1023.
Jespersen, O. (1922). *Language: Its nature, development, and origin*. London: George Allen & Unwin.
Kreuz, R.J., & Roberts, R.M. (1995). Two cues for verbal irony: Hyperbole and the ironic tone of voice. *Metaphor and Symbolic Activity, 10*(1), 21–31.
Lakoff, R. (1973). Language and women's place. *Language in Society, 2*(1), 45–80.
Lakoff, R. (1975). *Language and women's place*. New York: Harper and Row.
Lakoff, R. (1990). *Talking power*. New York: Basic Books.
Lin, C-Y. (2010). '. . . that's actually sort of you know trying to get consultants in . . .': Functions and multifunctionality of modifiers in academic lectures. *Journal of Pragmatics, 42*(5), 1173–1183.
Lorenz, G. (1999). *Adjective intensification—learners versus native speakers: A corpus study of argumentative writing*. Amsterdam: Rodopi.

Mauranen, A., Pérez-Llantada, C., & Swales, J. (2010). Academic Englishes: A standardized knowledge? In A. Kirkpatrick (Ed.), *The Routledge handbook of world Englishes* (pp. 634–653). Oxon: Routledge.

Mustanoja, T. (1960). *A Middle English syntax*. Helsinki: Société Néophilologique.

Partington, A. (1993). Corpus evidence of language change—the case of the intensifier. In M. Baker, G. Francis, & E. Tognini-Bonelli (Eds.), *Text and technology: In honour of John Sinclair* (pp. 177–192). Amsterdam: John Benjamins.

Pérez-Paredes, P., & Díez-Bedmar, B. (2012). The use of intensifying adverbs in learner writing. In Y. Tono, Y. Kawaguchi, & M. Minegishi (Eds.), *Developmental and crosslinguistic perspectives in learner corpus research* (pp. 105–123). Amsterdam: John Benjamins.

Poos, D., & Simpson, R.C. (2000, March). Hedging and disciplinary variation. Paper presented at the American Association of Applied Linguistics, Vancouver.

Portero Muñoz, C. (1997). *Intensificación: Estudio de un clasema* (PhD dissertation). Universidad de Córdoba, Córdoba, Spain.

Querol-Julián, M. (2011). *Evaluation in discussion sessions of conference paper presentations: A multimodal approach*. Saarbrücken, Germany: LAP Lambert Academic Publishing.

Querol Julián, M., & Fortanet-Gómez, I. (2012). Multimodal evaluation in academic discussion sessions: How do presenters act and react? *Journal of English for Specific Purposes, 31*(4), 271–283.

Quirk, R., & Greenbaum, S. (1973). *A university grammar of English*. London: Longman.

Quirk, R., Greenbaum, S., Leech, G.N., & Svartvik, J. (1985). *A comprehensive grammar of the English language*. London: Longman.

Räisänen, C. (1999). *The conference forum as a system of genres: A socio-cultural study of academic conference practices in automotive crash-safety engineering*. Göteborg: Acta Universitatis Gothoburgensis.

Recski, J.L. (2004). ". . . It's really ultimately very cruel . . .": Contrasting English intensifier collocations across EFL writing and academic spoken discourse. *DELTA, 20*(2), 211–234.

Rowley-Jolivet, E. (1999). The pivotal role of conference papers in the network of scientific communication. *ASp, 23–26*, 179–196.

Rowley-Jolivet, E. (2002). Visual discourse in scientific conference papers: A genre-based study. *English for Specific Purposes, 21*(1), 19–40.

Ruiz-Garrido, M.F., & Fortanet-Gómez, I. (2008). El lenguaje de las comunicaciones. In I. Fortanet-Gómez (Coord.), *Hablar inglés en la universidad: Docencia e Investigación* (pp. 125–157). Oviedo: Septem ediciones.

Sanz Álava, I. (2007). *El Español professional y académico en el aula universitaria: El discurso oral y escrito*. Valencia: Tirant Lo Blanch.

Scott, M. (2008). *WordSmith Tools version 5*. Liverpool: Lexical Analysis Software.

Silver, M.S. (2006). *Language across disciplines: Towards a critical reading of contemporary academic discourse*. Boca Raton: Brown Walker Press.

Stenström, A. (1999). He was really gormless—she's bloody crap: Girls, boys and intensifiers. In H. Hasselgård, & S. Okesfjell (Eds.), *Out of corpora: Studies in honour of Stig Johansson* (pp. 69–78). Amsterdam and Atlanta: Rodopi.

Stoffel, C. (1901). *Intensifiers and downtoners*. Heidelberg: Carl Winter.

Swales, J.M., & Burke, A. (2003). "It's really fascinating work": Differences in evaluative adjectives across academic registers. In C. Meyer, & P. Leistyna (Eds.), *Corpus analysis: Language structure and use* (pp. 1–18). Amsterdam and Atlanta: Rodopi.

Swales, J., & Malcewski, B. (2001). Discourse management and new episode flags in MICASE. In R.C. Simpson, & J. Swales (Eds.), *Corpus linguistics in North*

America: Selections from the 1999 symposium (pp. 145–164). Ann Arbor: University of Michigan Press.
Tagliamonte, S., & Roberts, C. (2005). So weird; so cool; so innovative: The use of intensifiers in the television series 'Friends.' *American Speech, 80*(3), 280–300.
Tao, H. (2007). A corpus-based investigation of *absolutely* and related phenomena in spoken American English. *Journal of English Linguistics, 35*(1), 5–29.
Vergara Heidke, A. (2012). El realce: Una propuesta para su conceptualización e identificación. *Filología y Lingüística, 38*(2), 163–181.
Wulff, S., Swales, J., & Keller, K. (2009). "We have about seven minutes for questions": The discussion sessions from a specialized conference. *English for Specific Purposes, 28*(2), 79–92.
Xiao, R., & Tao, H. (2007). A corpus-based sociolinguistic study of amplifiers in British English. *Sociolinguistic Studies, 1*(2), 241–273.

4 Visual Communication in Applied Linguistics Conference Presentations

Giuliana Diani

4.1 INTRODUCTION

Conference presentations are a common means for knowledge dissemination in plenaries or regular sessions (Räisänen, 1999). As Rowley-Jolivet (2002a) points out,

> Conferences play an essential role in the life of research communities, and the conference presentation fulfils distinctive functions in claim-making and in marking out a research territory. [. . .] Conference presentations provide a fast track to information on the latest developments in the field, both in terms of hard data and trends or research areas which are opening up.
>
> (p. 99)

This research genre has received considerable scholarly attention over the years. One of the major contributions to its study is the seminal work by Ventola, Shalom and Thompson (2002), which focuses on the language of conferencing. Further, the conference presentation has been investigated from a variety of perspectives: as a genre (Dubois, 1980a; Räisänen, 2002; Rowley-Jolivet, 2002b; Shalom, 2002; Carter-Thomas & Rowley-Jolivet, 2003; Rowley-Jolivet & Carter-Thomas, 2005; Yates & Orlikowski, 2007); as a narrative discourse (Thompson, 2002); as an information design (Tufte, 2003); and as a speaker-audience interaction (Webber, 2005).

Significant attention has also been paid to the multimodal dimension of conference presentations, where the visual semiotic plays an essential role (e.g., Dubois, 1980b; Rowley-Jolivet, 2004a; Charles & Ventola, 2002; Carter-Thomas & Rowley-Jolivet, 2003). With the advent of digital media technologies, communication tools have increased their degree of multimodality, defined by Kress and van Leeuwen (2001, p. 20) as "the use of several semiotic modes in the design of a semiotic product or event." In the past decade, extensive research has been conducted on linguistic and non-linguistic semiotic resources (Kress & van Leeuwen, 1996; Lemke, 1998;

Kress, 2000), contributing "to an evolving 'inventory' of semiotic modal resources" (Jewitt, 2008, p. 246).

The combination of multiple modes of communication, verbal and visual in particular, has become increasingly common, as "both paper-based and digital texts rely on words and images to create meaning" (Tardy, 2005, p. 320). As Tardy points out, the visual mode carries a heavy functional load in scientific discourse in which visuals (e.g., tables, figures, graphs) may be the only way to communicate certain types of information. This echoes Lemke's (1998) finding that scientific texts typically contain at least one graphic and one numeric visual per written page.

As mentioned above, the visual mode is also particularly evident in academic presentations. The use of multimedia packages has become increasingly common among conference presenters as these tools facilitate combining semiotic resources or modes such as images, writing, layout, sound, gestures, speech and 3D objects (Kress, 2010) with the verbal mode.

During most conferences, visuals are provided to accompany the speaker's discourse, and audiences are expected to listen and read simultaneously. In the complex multimodal semiotics of the conference, substantial work has been devoted to the interaction of extralinguistic aspects, such as the use of slides and the interaction between speech and these visual aids (e.g., Dubois, 1980b, 1982; Rowley-Jolivet, 2000, 2004b, 2012; Charles & Ventola, 2002). Most of this research has concentrated on conference presentations in biomedical, geology, physics and medicine, illustrating the disciplinary nature of the genre. However, analyses in 'soft' domains[1] are still relatively rare (see Tardy, 2005; Campagna, 2009; D'Angelo, 2010; Degano, 2012).

In academia, PowerPoint presentations have become increasingly common not only in the hard sciences, but also in the humanities, showing how the fast-paced, visually attractive data-driven presentations have invaded even the most traditional settings. In this study, I attempt to shed further light on the use of PowerPoint (henceforth PPT) in conference presentations in the field of the humanities, in particular, in applied linguistics, by exploring the visual dimension of the conference presenter's talk, as it is during this phase that slides are shown. More specifically, the research objective is to examine PPT presentations in terms of their visual resources and overall macrostructure. For this purpose, I draw on Bertin's (1973) and Rowley-Jolivet's (2002b) typologies of visuals and Swales's (1990) Introduction-Methods-Results-Discussion (IMRD) model that structures the written genre from which the conference talk originates, i.e., the research article (RA). More specifically, I aim to answer the following research questions:

1. Which types of visuals are used in the PPT conference presentations?
2. What are the similarities and differences in PPT presentation macrostructure with regard to Swales's (1990) IMRD model in written genres?

This chapter is organized as follows: Section 4.2 provides a brief overview of the literature on the conference presentation genre. The corpus and methodology used in the present study are outlined in Section 4.3. Section 4.4 presents the results of the analysis. The chapter concludes with a summary of the findings (Section 4.5).

4.2 THE CONFERENCE PRESENTATION: A REVIEW OF THE LITERATURE

The academic conference presentation has been the center of intense scholarly interest over the past decade, as evidenced by numerous studies analyzing different linguistic aspects of this communicative genre, such as interactive features (e.g., personal deictics and markers, questions and answers) and their role in creating a relationship with the audience (Vassileva, 2002; Webber, 2002, 2005), narrative features (Thompson, 2002), rhetorical features (Rowley-Jolivet & Carter-Thomas, 2005) or pragmatic features (e.g., use of humor, Frobert-Adamo, 2002; Reershemius, 2012).

Although the analysis of conference presentations has focused more on the verbal mode, the visual mode has also received some attention. In her pioneering study of biomedical speeches, Dubois (1980b) emphasizes the pivotal role of slides, which, "in addition to providing visual interest and reinforcement of key points, carry the crucial information of the body of the speech, information which is often not imparted orally by the speaker" (p. 50). Additional research has been done on the use of visuals (e.g., Rowley-Jolivet, 2002b, 2004b) to investigate their potential for structuring discourse and expressing logical relations. As Degano (2012) notes, the synergy between text and talk in PPT-aided conference presentations contributes to creating a scaffolding frame for global coherence, on the one hand, and elaborating on specific points and clarifying meaning relations between notions, ideas and slides, on the other.

Interest has also been shown in the study of paralinguistic aspects of the verbal mode in conference talks. Hood and Forey (2005) explore the combination of body language mode and the verbal mode. Interestingly, they found that, in addition to language, gesture enhances an alignment of the audience with the speaker. Similarly, Querol-Julián and Fortanet-Gómez's (2012) study of the multimodal discourse in conference discussion sessions shows how paralanguage and kinesic features contribute to create the overall meaning of the speech event. Also Morell (2015) explores the contributions of the different semiotics (i.e., spoken and written English, nonverbal material and body language modes) used in conference presentations and observes that they enhance awareness of what and how communication takes place in conferences.

A significant development in this area of research is the view that verbal and visual modes constitute a continuum along which speakers situate their talks. In their inspiring work, Charles and Ventola (2002) discuss the interactivity between the semiotic codes with the staging of the "Slide Show genre" (p. 170). More recently, Wecker (2012) and Rowley-Jolivet (2012) investigated the integration of oral speech with written information on slides in the context of different settings: Wecker (2012) focuses on an educational context, while Rowley-Jolivet (2012) explores an academic context. In an additional contribution to this field, Fernández Polo (2012) analyzes the intertextual relationship between the presenter's topic announcement and the title slide.

Attention has also been paid to the interpersonal aspect of slideware discourse. For example, Campagna (2009) examined patterns of self/otherness focusing on the interplay of referential (endophoric and exophoric) voices involved in the process of constructing visual reasoning. The analysis has also been extended to EAP pedagogy with important implications for teaching oral presentation skills. Tardy (2005) investigated the ways students use various verbal and visual expressions in their Microsoft PowerPoint presentation slides in order to project their own identities. Along the same line, Zareva (2013) explored how TESOL (Teaching English to Speakers of Other Languages) graduate students position themselves through their authorial self-mention choices in their presentations. These studies show the range of possible intersections between verbal and visual modes in the conference presentation genre from a multimodal perspective.

4.3 DATA AND METHODOLOGY

The data used for the study comprise 56 PPT presentations (hereinafter the Slideware Corpus), each 20 minutes in length, given at three international applied linguistics conferences held at the University of Modena and Reggio Emilia (Italy) by native and nonnative speakers between 2009 and 2012. The conferences were organized by the CLAVIER research group (Corpus and Language Variation In English Research), founded in 2009 by the Universities of Bergamo, Florence, Milan, Modena and Reggio Emilia, Pisa, Rome 'Sapienza,' Siena, and Trieste. The conferences covered different themes combining two complementary strands of linguistic investigation, corpus analysis and discourse analysis, to research language variation in English, in both quantitative and qualitative terms. The specific themes of the three conferences were as follows:

- 2009: Corpus Linguistics and Language Variation
- 2011: Tracking Language Change in Specialized and Professional Genres
- 2012: Corpus and Genre in English for Academic Purposes

The 2009 and 2011 three-day conferences included four and three plenary talks, respectively, and 45 full papers each, while the 2012 two-day conference included two plenary talks and 15 full papers. In both conferences, the speakers represented a range of language backgrounds, including native speakers of British and American English, as well as native speakers of other languages, i.e., Italian, French, German, Spanish, Polish, Russian, Chinese, Japanese, Swedish, Albanian, Slovenian and Latvian. The language of all the presentations was exclusively English.

Most speakers used slides to accompany their talk. For the present study, the PPT presentations were kindly provided to me by 56 speakers who had delivered short presentations across the three conferences.[2] Plenaries were excluded from the corpus as it was hypothesized that they may form a different genre (for discussion of plenary addresses, see Chapters 1 and 2, this volume). The presentations were not audio or videotaped. In the 56 presentations, a total of 1,680 slides were projected.

The Slideware Corpus was analyzed in terms of:

1. semiotic resources, i.e., types of visuals
2. structural organization of PPT presentations

As regards the analysis of semiotic resources, I refer to Bertin's (1973) and Rowley-Jolivet's (2002b) typologies of visuals. Bertin (1973) distinguishes *monosemic* images (such as graphs, diagrams and maps), which he calls *graphical* images, and *polysemic* images (such as photographs) which he calls *figurative* images. Rowley-Jolivet (2002b) integrates these two basic categories with two others that were observed in scientific conference papers. She distinguishes *scriptural* visuals (presenting texts), and *numerical* visuals (covering mathematical formulae and numerical tables). To explore how visual communication is projected in conference presentations, the Slideware Corpus was observed in terms of how information was organized on the slides. Thus, the types of visuals contained in the Slideware Corpus were identified.

Attention was also paid to the structural organization of the PPT presentation in order to determine to what extent it may reproduce Swales's (1990) IMRD model, which is common to scientific discourse and research genres. The analysis was carried out using Swales's move structure for research articles. His three-move schema for article introductions, known as the Create a Research Space (CARS) model, is outlined below, showing the preferred sequences of move types and steps, which are largely predictable in research article introductions.

- Move 1: Establishing a territory
  - Step 1: Claiming centrality, and/or
  - Step 2: Making topic generalization(s), and/or
  - Step 3: Reviewing items of previous research
- Move 2: Establishing a niche
  - Step 1A: Counter-claiming, or
  - Step 1B: Indicating a gap, or

- Step 1C: Question-raising, or
- Step 1D: Continuing a tradition

- Move 3: Occupying the niche

    - Step 1A: Outlining purposes, or
    - Step 1B: Announcing present research
    - Step 2: Announcing principal findings
    - Step 3: Indicating the RA structure

As can be seen, Swales's model includes three basic move types in research article introductions. Move 1—'Establishing a territory'—introduces the general topic of research. Move 2—'Establishing a niche'—identifies the more specific areas of research that require further investigation. Move 3—'Occupying the niche'—introduces the current research study in the context of the previous research described in Moves 1 and 2. Each of the three moves is then further articulated in steps (as shown above) that carry out various rhetorical functions and may be combined in a number of different ways, including all or only some of them. More specifically, Move 1 can have a maximum of three steps (Step 1, Step 2, Step 3). In Move 1, Step 1, 'Claiming centrality,' the author can make a centrality claim by claiming interest or importance in referring to research perspectives, or by claiming that there are other researchers working in the area. This step is usually, but not always, at the beginning of the introduction. Here are some examples taken from Swales (1990, p. 144) to illustrate Move 1, Step 1: *In recent years, applied researchers have become increasingly interested in . . .; Many investigators have recently turned to. . . .* Move 1, Step 2, 'Making topic generalizations,' represents a neutral general statement. It typically takes the form of either statements about knowledge or practice, or statements about phenomena. Examples are (p. 146): *There is now much evidence to support the hypothesis that . . .; Education core courses are often criticized for. . . .* The last step of this Move, Step 3, 'Reviewing items of previous research,' presents selected reviews considered relevant to the research study. Here the RA author reports previous findings of the study and situates his/her own work. Examples are (p. 150): *Generative grammarians influenced by Chomsky have recently . . .; Sang et al. (1972) found that X was impaired.* In establishing territory, then, the author tries to persuade the readers of the study by contextualizing its current state of knowledge.

Move 2, 'Establishing a niche' plays a central role in research article introductions as it functions as a link between Move 1 and Move 3 to show the need for the research presented. Move 2 may be realized by the following four steps: Step 1A 'Counter-claiming,' Step 1B 'Indicating a gap,' Step 1C 'Question-raising' and Step 1D 'Continuing a tradition.' Step 1A serves to counter that previous research has given little attention to the study, as shown in the following example: *The research has tended to focus on . . ., rather than . . .* (p. 156). Step 1B signals that previous research "suffers from some limitations" (p. 154), as shown in the following example: *The . . . method (upon which the present study is based) eliminates many of these limitations by . . ., but it can treat only. . . .* Step 1C raises questions like *A question remains whether . . .* (p. 156). Finally, Step 1D gives evidence of the weakness of previous research, implying that the present study is well worth carrying out to continue the tradition, as illustrated in the following example: *The differences need to be analyzed . . .* (p. 156).

The final move type proposed by Swales (1990) is Move 3 'Occupying the niche,' whose function is "to turn the niche established in Move 2 into the research space that justifies the present article" (p. 159). This is realized by either 'Outlining research purpose(s)' (Step 1A), e.g., *The aim of the present paper is . . .* (p. 160), or 'Announcing present research' (Step 1B), e.g., *In this paper we give preliminary results of . . .* (p. 160), then, by 'Announcing the principal findings' (Step 2), e.g., *The paper hopes to show that . . .* (p. 160), and finally by 'Indicating the research article structure' (Step 3), e.g., *We have organized the rest of this paper in the following way . . .* (p. 161).

Swales (1990) extends his analysis to the whole structure of the research article and identifies, in addition to the 'Introduction' section, three further ones: 'Methods,' 'Results' and 'Discussion,' as outlined in the following:

- Methods
- Results
- Discussion
    - Move 1: Background information
    - Move 2: Statement of results
    - Move 3: (Un)expected outcomes
    - Move 4: Reference to previous research
    - Move 5: Explanation
    - Move 6: Exemplification
    - Move 7: Deduction and Hypothesis
    - Move 8: Recommendations

The 'Methods' section describes the data and methodology adopted in the study. The 'Results' section focuses on the findings that emerged from the analysis carried out. The 'Discussion' section is further articulated into eight moves. Move 1—'Background information'—is a "free standing" move that can emerge at any point in the sequence. It is employed to strengthen the author's discussion by "recapitulating main points, highlighting theoretical information and reminding the reader of technical information" (Swales 1990, p. 172). Move 2—'Statement of results'—is labeled "a quasi-obligatory move" of the discussion and is the starting point of a recurrent cycle (p. 172). Move 3—'(Un)expected outcomes'—consists of the researcher's comments on whether the results are unexpected or not. Move 4—'Reference to previous research'—is an obligatory and the most common move, with two principal functions: "references for purposes of comparison and references that provide support for the present research" (p. 173). Move 5—'Explanation'—is common when the writer suggests reasons for unexpected results. Move 6—'Exemplification'—provides examples supporting an explanation (Hopkins & Dudley-Evans, 1988). Move 7—'Deduction and Hypothesis'—allows writers "to make a claim about the generalizability of the results" (p. 173). Move 8—'Recommendations'—is where the writer proposes further research.

With this description in mind, I proceeded to determine whether these moves were also present in the Slideware Corpus.

4.4 RESULTS AND DISCUSSION

4.4.1 Preliminary Overview

The importance of the visual channel in the corpus of conference presentations is manifested in the very large number of slides that were projected. In the 56 papers given, a total of 1,680 slides were projected for an average of 30 per presentation. However, from a preliminary observation, there was actually a considerable variety in the number of the slides used in each presentation, ranging from a minimum of 11 to a maximum of 63 per presentation. This difference in numbers varies according to how the presenter opted to manage his or her space to describe the results. In fact, as we will see later, the presenter may choose to condense the results into a few slides or extend them over many slides.

Following Bertin's (1973) and Rowley-Jolivet's (2002b) typologies of slides used in scientific conference presentations, I attempted to classify the types of visuals characterizing the Slideware Corpus. Table 4.1 presents the overall distribution of the types of visuals detected in the corpus.

As can be seen from the table, of the 1,680 slides used by the conference presenters, the vast majority are *scriptural* (1,274 slides—75.83%). Types of slides under this category were used to accomplish a range of different functions as indicated by their titles, i.e., outline of the talk, aim(s) of the study, research questions, overview of previous research, description of data and methodology, concluding remarks, future work and references. An example is represented in Figure 4.1.

An interesting point to note is that some titles of scriptural slides listed above clearly reflect Swales's (1990) IMRD model for RAs. More specifically,

Table 4.1 Frequency and distribution of visual types in the Slideware Corpus

Type of visual	Raw frequency count	% of total (n = 1,680)
Scriptural	1,274	75.83
Numerical	157	9.34
Figurative	141	8.39
Graphical	108	6.42

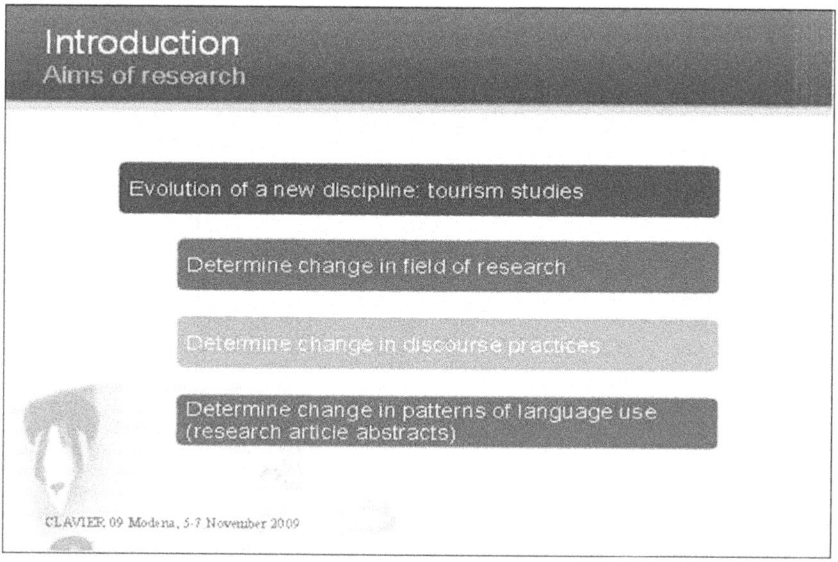

Figure 4.1 Scriptural slide

the 'Aim(s) of research,' 'Research questions' and 'Review of previous research' slides realize the 'Introduction' move; the 'Corpus and Methods' slide reproduces the 'Methods' move; and the 'Conclusion' and 'Future work' slides realize the 'Discussion' move. It is worth pointing out that in the Slideware Corpus this move is always referred to as 'Conclusion' where final remarks on the key results that emerged from the study are provided. Table 4.2 provides an overview of how the scriptural slides conform to Swales's IMRD model.

If we take a closer look at the distribution of the scriptural slides across Swales's (1990) IMRD model as illustrated in the table, undoubtedly the most striking (albeit predictable) feature is the heavy concentration of the 'Aim(s) of research' slide, which was found in 96.42% of the 56 presentations analyzed, as it sets the scene for the audience by indicating the main purpose of the presenter's talk. The 'Corpus and Methods' and 'Conclusion' slides also figure prominently in the corpus, occurring in all the slides analyzed.

With respect to the other scriptural slides found in the corpus, however, the analysis points to variation. A significant difference exists in the frequency of occurrence of the 'Outline of talk' slide, being present in 45.71% of the presentations or the 'Research questions' (12.50%) and the 'Review of previous research' (0.94%). Although rare, it was also found that linguists used the 'Future work' slide with the function of outlining suggestions for future research (present in only four presentations).

A further point which needs underlining is that in the Slideware Corpus, scriptural slides are also used to show extracts of the data analyzed by the

Table 4.2 Distribution of scriptural slides in terms of Swales's (1990) IMRD model

Scriptural slides							
Introduction slide	**%**	**Corpus and Methods slide**	**%**	**Results slide**	**%**	**Conclusion slide**	**%**
• Aim(s) of research	96.42	Description of data and methodology	100	• Extracts of data	27.62	• Concluding remarks	100
• Outline of talk	45.71			• Discussion of results	5.88	• Future work	0.31
• Research questions	12.50						
• Review of previous research	0.94						

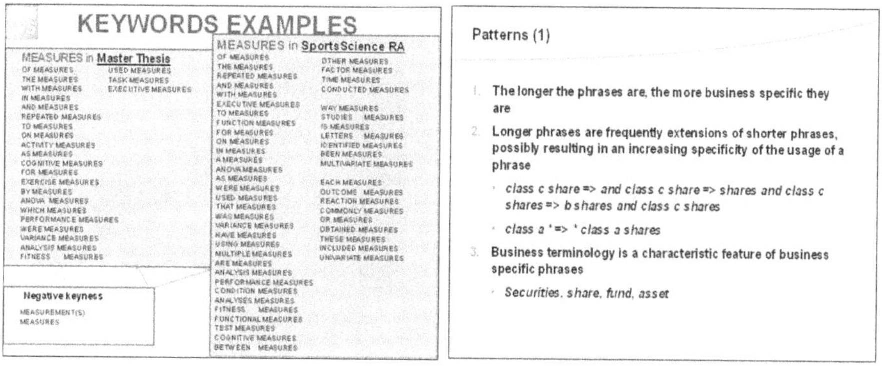

Figure 4.2 Scriptural slides showing extracts of data (left) and discussion of results (right)

presenter (27.62%), or to discuss the results (5.88%), as shown in Figure 4.2, thus corresponding to the 'Results' section of the presentation.

An interesting point to note is that scriptural slides also often incorporate various colors of fonts used to structure verbal content, as well as arrangements of boxed shapes with different colors. In Figure 4.1 the slide reproduces the color scheme automatically selected as initial background when building a PowerPoint presentation (e.g., blue, white and brown in the 'Aims of research' slide). In Figure 4.2, instead, the slide on 'Keywords examples' presents two boxes with different colors (light blue and violet) to draw the audience's attention to two different results. Slides like those exemplified above abound in the Slideware Corpus, thus emphasizing the potential use of colors as important meaning-making resources in visual communication (Kress & van Leeuwen, 2002).

Apart from the scriptural slides, the corpus shows a significant number of slides in which three different types of visual modes are used (406/1,680–24.16%), accounting for the remaining. They consist of (1) *numerical* slides (157/1,680–9.34%), containing numerical tables, or (2) *graphical* (108/1,680–6.42%), containing line charts, histograms or pie charts. Their presence may find an explanation in the type of research methodology used in the field of applied linguistics that often involves quantitative methods. These slides play a central role in the presentation as they summarize the main findings of the study presented. They realize the 'Results' move within the IMRD model. Examples of numerical and graphical slides are represented in Figure 4.3.

Although much less frequent, it was also found that numerical slides are sometimes accompanied by a series of illustrative examples (13 cases) that incorporate verbal language in the form of explanatory notes or illustrative examples. Similarly, there were cases in which graphical slides were accompanied by explanatory notes (4 cases) or illustrative examples (2 cases), as shown in Figure 4.4.[3]

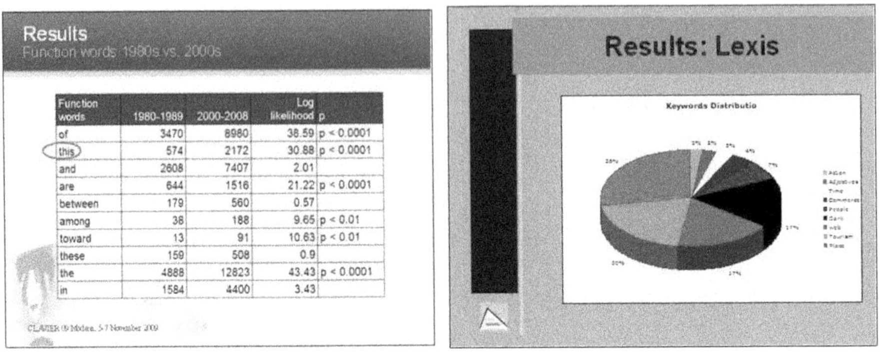

Figure 4.3 Numerical (left) and graphical (right) slides

The third type of visual resource used in the corpus is reflected in *figurative* slides (141/1,680–8.39%), containing images, photos and webpages. They are typically used to introduce the topic of the talk (e.g., the 'About' page of university websites), as illustrated in Figure 4.5.

This initial examination indicates that there is a considerable degree of variety in the types of slides produced for each presentation. Although scriptural slides are the most frequently used in the Slideware Corpus (75.83% of the cases), the frequency of visual slides is also significant (24.16%).

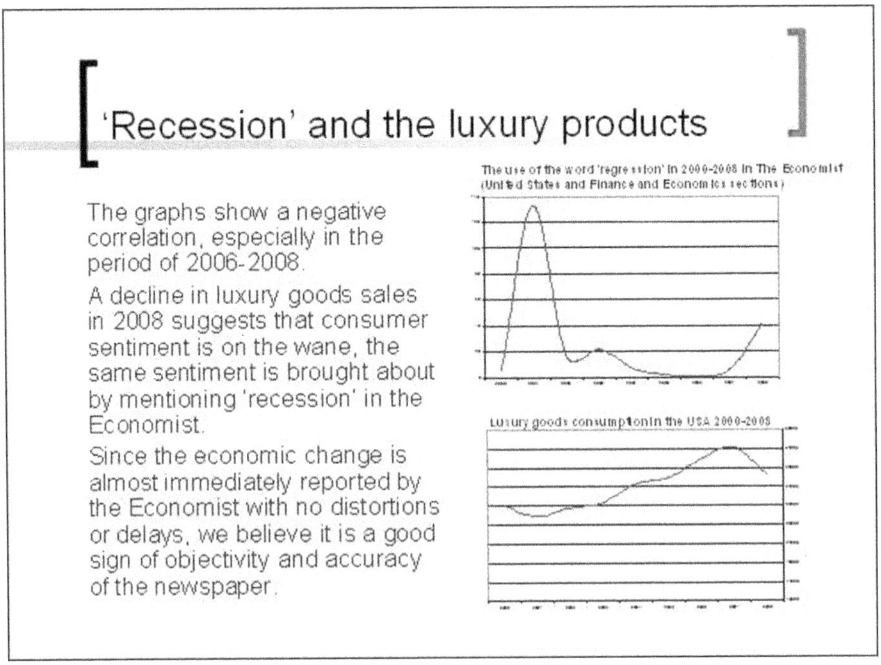

Figure 4.4 Graphical slide with explanatory notes

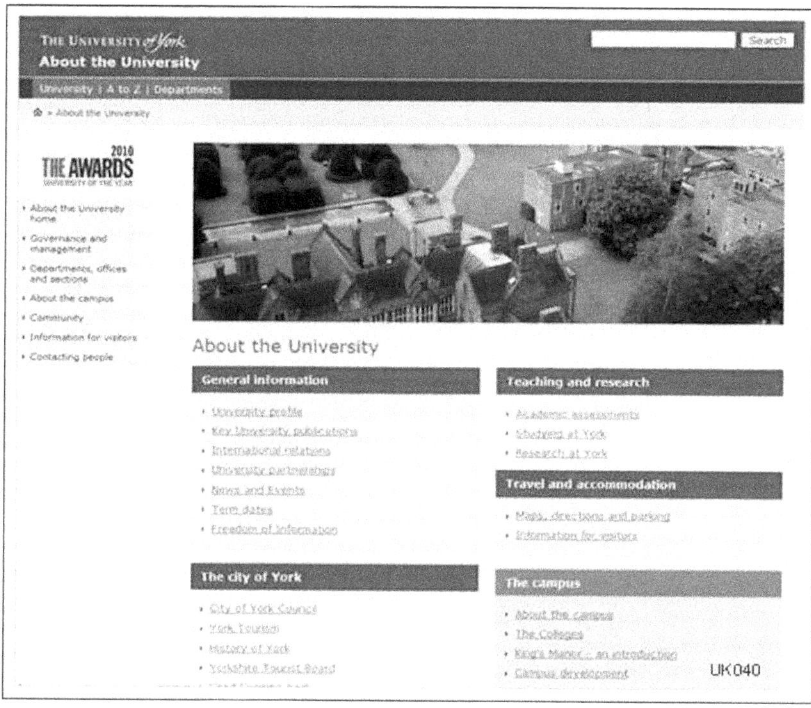

Figure 4.5 Figurative slide introducing the topic of the talk

As regards the distribution of the three visual types found in the corpus, the data show a relatively balanced proportion: numerical slides amount to 9.34%, figurative slides account for 8.39%, followed by graphical slides (6.42%).

Among the variety of visual resources used in the presentations as described above, no audio or video clips incorporated into the slides were found in the Slideware Corpus. This is an unexpected finding as their use has become increasingly common in conference papers, not only in the hard sciences, but also in the humanities (Kousha, Thelwall & Abdoli, 2012). Let us now complete the analysis by examining the overall structural organization of the PPT presentations in the Slideware Corpus.

4.4.2 Structural Organization of PPT Presentations

The structure of slide sequences in each presentation was observed to identify whether it reflects the section and move structure of the written genre from which it originates, i.e., the research article, adopting Swales's (1990) IMRD model. Table 4.3 provides an overview of how the IMRD model is reflected in the Slideware Corpus. Each of the four sections (Introduction-Corpus and Methods-Results-Conclusion) will be discussed in detail in the following subsections.

Table 4.3 The Slideware Corpus macrostructure in terms of Swales's (1990) IMRD model

Introduction slide	%	Corpus and Methods slide	%	Results slide	%	Conclusion slide	%
• Move 1: Establishing a territory	100		100		100	• Move 1: Background information	0
• Move 2: Establishing a niche	12.50					• Move 2: Statement of results	100
• Move 3: Occupying the niche	100					• Move 3: (Un)expected outcomes	31.52
						• Move 4: Reference to previous research	75.14
						• Move 5: Explanation	31.52
						• Move 6: Exemplification	0
						• Move 7: Deduction and Hypothesis	5.35
						• Move 8: Recommendations	7.14

4.4.2.1 The 'Introduction' Slide

As can be seen from the table, the 'Introduction' slide is realized in the PPT presentations predominantly through two moves as described by Swales (1990) in his CARS model for RA introductions: Move 1, 'Establishing a territory,' by means of which the presenter introduces the topic of the talk, and Move 3, 'Occupying the niche,' in which s/he indicates the main purpose of the study and outlines the talk. These two moves occurred in all of the presentations (100%). Move 2, 'Establishing a niche,' is instead rarely used (12.50%), and is often limited to identifying the research questions.

However, differences in the preferences of move sequences as opening strategies of the presentation do seem to exist. The overwhelming majority of the corpus opens with either an outline of the talk (45.71%) or an indication of purposes (20.37%), corresponding to Steps 3 and 1A of Move 3, as shown in examples (1) and (2), which reproduce the content of two slides.

(example 1) Outline

- the 'About' page as a genre
- some examples from UWs (University Websites)
- previous findings
- research hypotheses
- tracking change (2008/2011)
- conclusions

(example 2) Purpose of the study

- Investigating regulative patterns (speech acts) considering their rhetorical functions in the MoU (Memorandum of Understanding)
    - Identification of categories
    - Quantitative presence
    - Rhetorical function
- Exploring differences with regulative patterns in contracts
    - Categories topology
    - Quantitative presence

Only 33.92% of all the PPT presentations open with an indication of the topic (Move 1), as shown in example (3).

(example 3) Elements of Change in Contemporary Institutional Discourse: A Longitudinal and Corpus-based Analysis
The role played by the institutional discourse of the EU in cultural construction and identity representation

In spite of these different opening strategies, all the presenters used the moves connected to the 'Introduction' section, as described by Swales (1990), and no instances of moves outside the parameters of this model were found across the Slideware Corpus. However, an alteration of the linear order of presentation in move sequence was noted. More specifically, a sequential 'disorder' is exemplified by presentations starting with a talk outline (Move 3, Step 3), then moving on to discuss key concepts of the talk (job ads), review previous research (Move 1, Step 2 and Step 3) and indicate the aims of study (goal) (Move 3, Step 1A). Figure 4.6 is an illustration.

These results echo those of Campagna (2009), who found that the 'Introduction' slide identified in her corpus of PPT applied linguistics conference presentations does not always follow the linear order of moves as displayed by Swales's CARS model for RA introductions. As rightly noted by Campagna (2009, p. 382), this may be related to the hybrid nature of the slideware medium in research conference presentations as "a fluid note-taking tool for oral delivery." Another trait that characterizes the 'Introduction' slide in the Slideware Corpus is a considerable degree of variety in the number of slides used to realize Move 1. More specifically, it can be condensed in one or two slides or extended over a sequence of slides. If compared with RA introductions, this analysis indicates that the Slideware

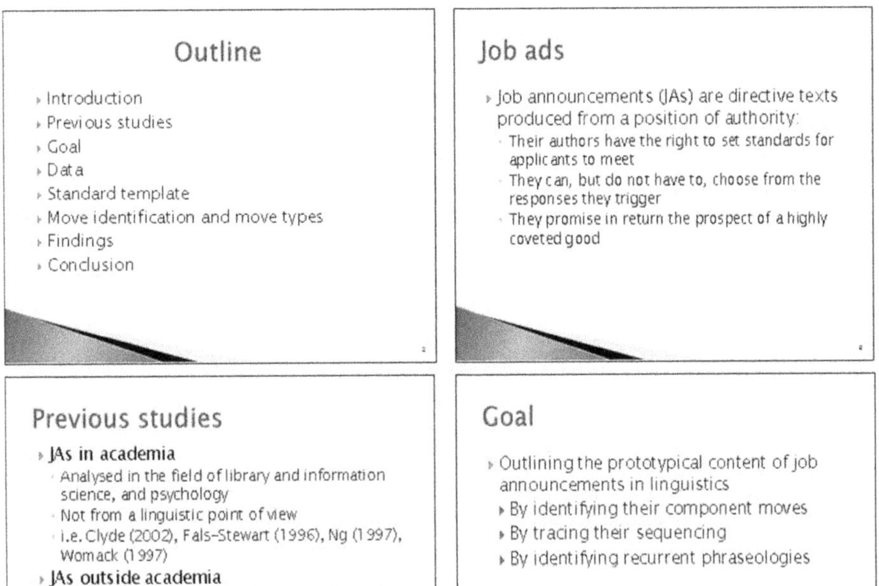

Figure 4.6 Sequential 'disorder' in move sequence in the 'Introduction' slide: Move 3-Move 1-Move 3

Corpus displays longer introductions in which only some of the slide titles fit in the traditional 'Introduction' structure, as is the case for 'Talk outline,' 'Aim(s),' 'Research questions' and 'Review of previous research.'

4.4.2.2 *The 'Corpus and Methods' Slide*

This slide provides information on the design of the study in terms of materials, approaches and procedures. It occurs in all the PPT presentations analyzed and its description can be condensed in one single slide, or two independent slides on data and methodology can be produced, as shown in Figure 4.7.

However, although less frequent (in only 4 cases out of 56), a description of data and methodology may be embedded in the 'Research aims' slide of the 'Introduction' section.

4.4.2.3 *The 'Results' Slide*

This slide summarizes the main findings of the study presented. It occurs in all the Slideware Corpus presentations. Variety was noted in the number of slides used in the realization of this move, ranging from a minimum of 6 to a maximum of 35. A feature that characterizes the 'Results' slide of the Slideware Corpus is its categorization of the results into boxes corresponding to the slide title, i.e., 'Function words 1980s vs. 2000s,' as shown in the slide on the left in Figure 4.3 above. Figure 4.8 reproduces another typical 'Results' slide that shows the audience extractions of data relating to the elaboration of an analysis.

A further trait that characterizes this slide is the combination of scriptural with numerical, graphical or figurative slides, as exemplified in Figure 4.4 above. This multiplicity of use of visual typologies highlights the 'multimodal' character of PowerPoint presentations, encompassing talk, text, graphics and images, which all work together in a synergistic way.

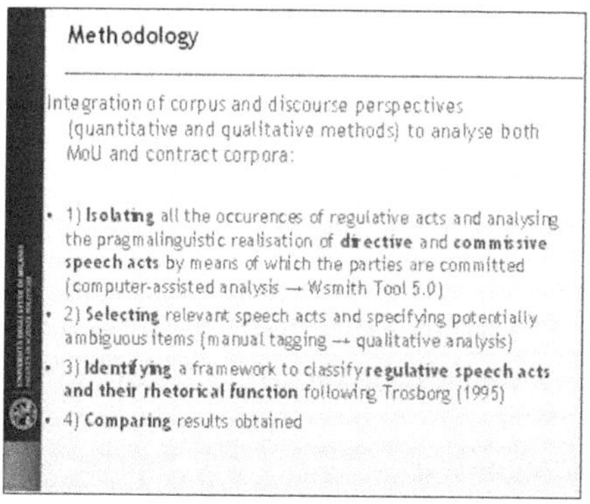

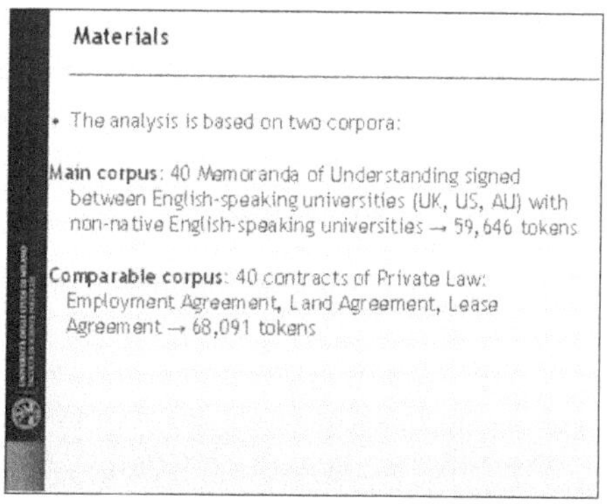

Figure 4.7 Two slides encompassing methods (left) and materials (right)

Top 30 key keywords EU

Member	2900	Treaty	603
shall	2817	are	598
Article	2166	Community	569
be	2152	their	565
State	1513	residence	521
States	1501	Any	514
This	1332	has	496
EUROPEAN	1169	provisions	496
is	1038	such	468
not	852	paragraph	459
application	739	have	450
may	735	referred	432
Council	658	Protection	424
Directive	636	persons	415
national	635	under	413
asylum	630	should	407
accordance	624		
UNION	606		

Figure 4.8 The 'Results' slide

As we have seen in 4.4.1, scriptural slides are often used to show extracts of the data analyzed by the presenter or to describe the results, as exemplified in Figure 4.2 above.

In comparing the use of scriptural slides to other types, however, the Slideware Corpus displays a much higher incidence in the use of numerical, graphical and figurative slides that represent the 'Results' slide. A possible explanation derives from the fact that tables, graphs and images are much more efficient in terms of visualizing certain types of results with respect to the written mode. Although less frequent, it was also found that the presenters integrated their results with explanatory notes in one single slide.

4.4.2.4 *The 'Conclusion' Slide*

This slide draws some concluding remarks on the results discussed during the talk. It occurs in almost all the PPT presentations analyzed (54/56–96.4%). Concluding remarks can be condensed in one single slide or extended over a sequence of slides, as shown in Figure 4.9.

As can be seen in the figure, the concluding remarks are represented in a bullet-point list, summing up the main points discussed during the presentation. This strategy reflects a common pattern of "circularity," as

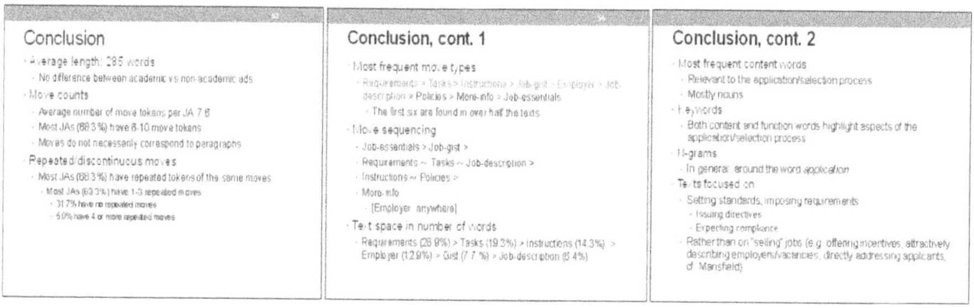

Figure 4.9 A sequence of slides for the 'Conclusion'

Campagna (2009, p. 385) calls it, in slideware discourse as in RAs, which responds to the need of briefly restating the focal points of the presentation.

4.4.2.5 Additional Slides

An interesting point to note is that the 'Conclusion' slide is not always the final slide of the PPT presentations. It was found that in four cases that slide was followed by a slide outlining suggestions for future research, as shown in Figure 4.10.

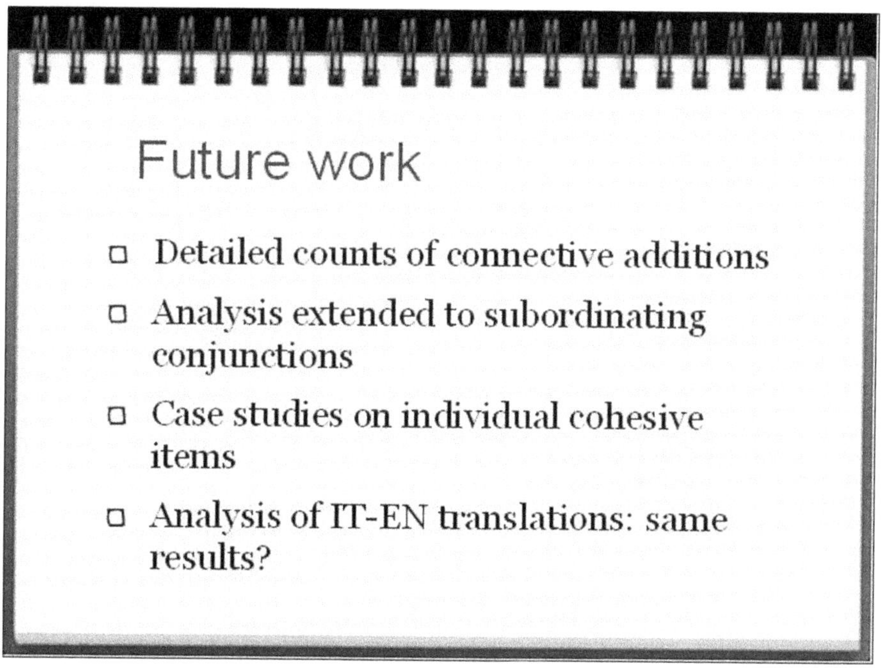

Figure 4.10 The 'Future work' slide

This rhetorical strategy conforms to the conclusion section of RAs, as described in Swales's model, i.e., 'Recommendation: need for further research and/or suggestions about possible lines of further investigation.'

Another trait which is congruent with the canonical bibliographical references included at the end of RAs is the slideware version of the 'References,' taking the shape of a final slide in which the presenter's publications considered relevant to the research presented or mentioned in the talk are reported. The 'References' slide occurs in 25/56 presentations (44.64%) and is illustrated in Figure 4.11.

A further feature which, instead, does not conform to Swales's model for the RA 'Discussion/Conclusion' move is the inclusion of thanking expressions in the very last slide of the Slideware Corpus, as illustrated in Figure 4.12.

This strategy was reported in 25 out of 56 PPT presentations (44.64%) and complies with the kinds of formulaic expressions commonly used by speakers as markers of politeness in the oral delivery of their conference presentations. The 'Thanking expressions' slide may also contain the presenter's contact details. A trait that characterizes the 'Thanking' slide is the presence of attractive images, as shown in Figure 4.12. This strengthens the multimodal nature of the slideware medium with its integration of visual and verbal modes.

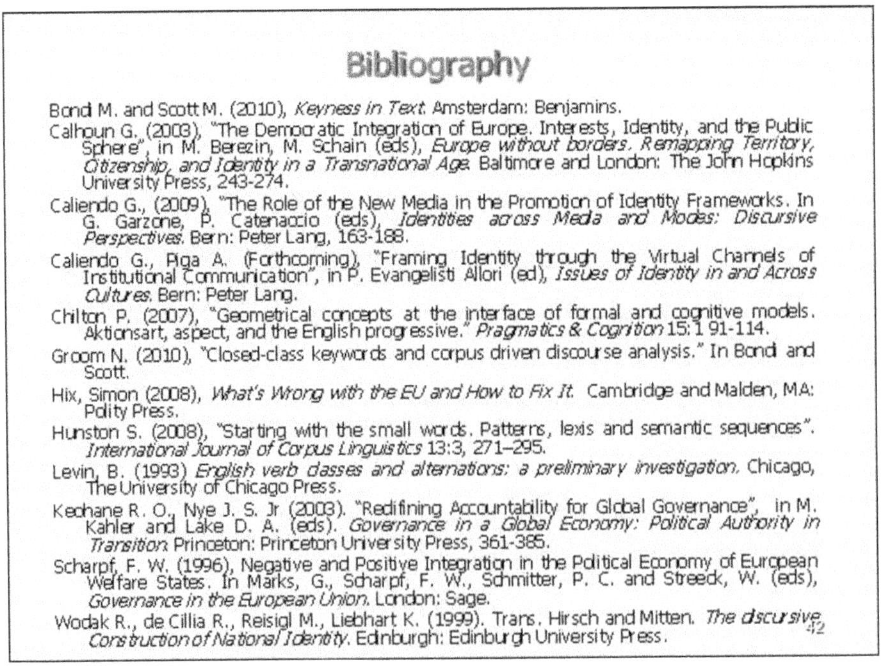

Figure 4.11 The 'References' slide

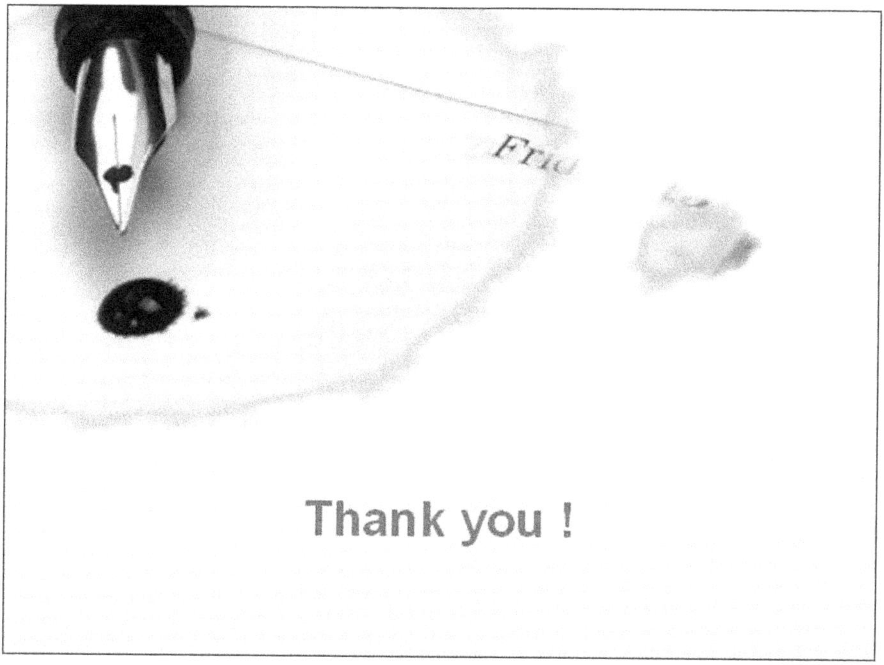

Figure 4.12 The 'Thanking expressions' slide

4.5 CONCLUSION

This study has highlighted how visual communication in applied linguistics conference presentations is manifested through a multiplicity of visual typologies that act together synergetically. Thus, although slides are considered 'visuals,' they are actually multimodal in themselves, also because they may incorporate different semiotic modes within a single slide. Most significantly, the analysis has shown a synchronous combination of scriptural slides, on the one hand, and numerical, figurative and graphical slides, on the other. In this sense, there is bound to be much "semiotic spanning" (Ventola, 2002, p. 43) between both synchronized modes: written (to be spoken) and visual. These two modes are complementary: the scriptural slides serve various functions specific to the delivery of the conference talk, i.e., outlining the talk, presenting aim(s) of the study, posing research questions, giving an overview of previous research, describing data and methodology, providing concluding remarks, suggesting future work, etc.; the visual slides, exemplified by tables, images or graphs, afford the speakers the opportunity of 'showing' their results. This need to visualize, and to see, is an essential part of scientific communication.

As regards the rhetorical structure of the PPT presentation identified in the Slideware Corpus, the analysis shows similarities and differences at the macrostructural level, if compared with written RAs. The main similarity is its conformity to the linear order of presentation in the IMRD sequence, while difference has been noted in the variety of opening strategies used in the first slides realizing the introduction section. More specifically, a sequential 'disorder' was observed in move sequences, exemplified by an altered order of presentation, starting with a talk outline (Move 3, Step 3), moving on to discussing key concepts of the talk and/or reviewing previous research (Move 1, Step 2 and/or Step 3), and then outlining the aims of the study (Move 3, Step 1A). This sequential disorder may be interpreted in relation to the hybrid nature of the slides that may also function as notes that the presenters use to support their oral delivery (Campagna, 2009).

A further difference was also noted in the conclusion section of the Slideware Corpus. This resides in the inclusion of thanking expressions in the very last slide of the PPT presentations. This constitutes a clearly distinctive rhetorical element in the conference presentation genre, which has no counterpart in RAs. Interestingly, in the thanking slides the multimodal aspect is particularly in focus. These slides often contain some kind of attractive or somehow meaningful image, perhaps designed to end the presentation on a lighter interpersonal note, and thus engender the sympathy of the audience.

The analysis carried out here confirms the "scaffolding" function of slides to create coherence across the whole presentation (Degano, 2012, p. 150). In this respect, the slide titles play a crucial cataphoric role, as they anticipate the content of the upcoming slide and also contribute to the macrostructural design of the presentation, thus allowing the audience to form a mental model at the highest level of meaning.

Although macrostructural differences exist between the visually supported conference presentation and the research article, both are essential vehicles for the overall research process of disseminating scientific knowledge. This aspect helps to suggest that the "slideware conferencing product" (Campagna, 2009, p. 387) constitutes a genre of its own as it finds its distinctiveness in a combination of verbal and visual modes to realize a coherent communicative event (Degano, 2012).

On the whole, it appears that the pervasive use of technology leads to discipline-specific academic presentation genres not only in hard sciences (Rowley-Jolivet, 2002b), but also in the soft knowledge domains (Campagna, 2009). This seems to find confirmation in the Slideware Corpus analyzed in the present work. In fact, in the 56 papers given, a total of 1,680 slides were projected. Nevertheless, there is a need to do further research on visual communication in paper presentations held at international conferences in the many different fields of hard and soft sciences to provide more evidence of its role in structuring the discourse. Further research into multimodality may offer new insights into how speakers work with both verbal and visual modes in many diverse fields.

Some implications can be drawn from this study for the teaching of oral presentation skills in EAP settings. For novice speakers at international conferences, who may be unfamiliar with generic norms in the verbal mode, visuals offer them an alternative means of expressing their ideas. This does not mean that visual modes of expression are easier to learn or use than verbal modes, but simply that they allow for "different possibilities" (Tardy, 2005, p. 335) or, in Kress's (2005) words, "new freedoms" for speakers (p. 19).

NOTES

1. The concept of 'hard' and 'soft' knowledge domains refers to the traditional distinction between scientific disciplines such as medicine, engineering and physics classified as hard, and social sciences and humanities disciplines such as economics, sociology, linguistics, history and philosophy classified as soft (Belcher, 1989; Hyland, 2000).
2. I would like to thank the colleagues who kindly sent me their slides and consented to my using them for research purposes.
3. This type of visual echoes Lemke's (2002) 'imagetext,' i.e., an image combined with texts. In this case, the combination enhances the explanatory function of the visual.

REFERENCES

Belcher, T. (1989). *Academic tribes and territories: Intellectual inquiry and the cultures of disciplines*. Milton Keynes: The Society for Research into Higher Education and Open University Press.

Bertin, J. (1973). *Semiologie graphique: Les diagrammes, les résaux, les cartes*. Paris: Gauthier-Villars.

Campagna, S. (2009). Projecting visual reasoning in research conference presentations. In M. Gotti (Ed.), *Commonality and individuality in academic discourse* (pp. 371–392). Bern: Peter Lang.

Carter-Thomas, S., & Rowley-Jolivet, E. (2003). Analysing the scientific conference presentation (CP): A methodological overview of a multimodal genre. *ASp, 39–40*, 59–72.

Charles, C., & Ventola, E. (2002). A multi-semiotic genre: The conference slide show. In E. Ventola, C. Shalom, & S. Thompson (Eds.), *The language of conferencing* (pp. 169–209). Frankfurt am Main: Peter Lang.

D'Angelo, L. (2010). Rethinking the design of presentation slides: The assertion-evidence structure. In G. Garzone, P. Catenaccio, & C. Degano (Eds.), *Diachronic perspectives on genres in specialized communication: Conference proceedings* (pp. 61–63). Milano: CUEM.

Degano, C. (2012). Texture beyond the text: Slides and talk in conference presentations. In S. M. Maci, & M. Sala (Eds.), *Genre variation in academic communication: Emerging disciplinary trends* (pp. 135–152). Bergamo: CELSB.

Dubois, B. L. (1980a). Genre and structure in biomedical speeches. *Forum Linguisticum, 5*(2), 140–169.

Dubois, B. L. (1980b). The use of slides in biomedical speeches. *The ESP Journal, 1*(1), 45–50.

Dubois, B. L. (1982). "And the last slide please": Regulatory function at biomedical meetings. *World Language English, 1*(4), 263–268.

Fernández Polo, F.J. (2012). "The title of my paper is . . .": Introducing the topic in conference presentations. In C. Berkenkotter, V.K. Bhatia, & M. Gotti (Eds.), *Insights into academic genres* (pp. 149–168). Bern: Peter Lang.

Frobert-Adamo, M. (2002). Humour in oral presentations: What's the joke? In E. Ventola, C. Shalom, & S. Thompson (Eds.), *The language of conferencing* (pp. 211–226). Frankfurt am Main: Peter Lang.

Hood, S., & Forey, G. (2005). Introducing a conference paper: Getting interpersonal with your audience. *Journal of English for Academic Purposes, 4*(4), 291–306.

Hopkins, A., & Dudley-Evans, T. (1988). A genre-based investigation of the discussion sections in articles and dissertations. *English for Specific Purposes, 7*(2), 113–121.

Hyland, K. (2000). *Disciplinary discourses: Social interactions in academic writing.* London: Longman.

Jewitt, C. (2008). Multimodality and literacy in school classrooms. *Review of Research in Education, 32*(1), 241–267.

Kousha, K., Thelwall, M., & Abdoli, M. (2012). The role of online videos in research communication: A content analysis of YouTube videos cited in academic publications. *Journal of the American Society for Information Science and Technology, 63*(9), 1710–1727.

Kress, G. (2000). Multimodality: Challenges to thinking about language. *TESOL Quarterly, 34*(2), 337–340.

Kress, G. (2005). Gains and losses: New forms of text, knowledge, and learning. *Computers and Composition, 22*(1), 5–22.

Kress, G. (2010). *Multimodality: A social semiotic approach to contemporary communication.* London: Routledge.

Kress, G., & van Leeuwen, T. (1996). *Reading images: The grammar of visual design.* London: Routledge.

Kress, G., & van Leeuwen, T. (2001). *The modes and media of contemporary communication.* London: Arnold.

Kress, G., & van Leeuwen, T. (2002). Colour as a semiotic mode: Notes for a grammar of colour. *Visual Communication, 1*(3), 343–368.

Lemke, J.L. (1998). Multiplying meaning: Visual and verbal semiotics in scientific text. In J.R. Martin, & R. Veel (Eds.), *Reading science: Critical and functional perspectives on discourses of science* (pp. 87–113). London: Routledge.

Lemke, J. L. (2002). Travels in hypermodality. *Visual Communication, 1*(3), 299–325.

Morell, T. (2015). International conference paper presentations: A multimodal analysis to determine effectiveness. *English for Specific Purposes, 37*(1), 137–150.

Querol-Julián, M., & Fortanet-Gómez, I. (2012). Multimodal evaluation in academic discussion sessions: How do speakers act and react? *English for Specific Purposes, 31*(4), 271–283.

Räisänen, C. (1999). *The conference forum as a system of genres: A sociocultural study of academic conference practices in automotive engineering.* Gothenberg, Sweden: Acta Universitatis Gothoburgensis.

Räisänen, C. (2002). The conference forum: A system of interrelated genres and discursive practices. In E. Ventola, C. Shalom, & S. Thompson (Eds.), *The language of conferencing* (pp. 69–93). Frankfurt am Main: Peter Lang.

Reershemius, G. (2012). Research cultures and the pragmatic functions of humor in academic research presentations: A corpus assisted analysis. *Journal of Pragmatics, 44*(6–7), 863–875.

Rowley-Jolivet, E. (2000). Image as text: Aspects of the shared visual language of scientific conference participants. *ASp, 27–30*, 133–154.

Rowley-Jolivet, E. (2002a). Science in the making: Scientific conference presentations and the construction of facts. In E. Ventola, C. Shalom, & S. Thompson (Eds.), *The language of conferencing* (pp. 95–125). Frankfurt am Main: Peter Lang.

Rowley-Jolivet, E. (2002b). Visual discourse in scientific conference papers: A genre-based study. *English for Specific Purposes, 21*(1), 19–40.
Rowley-Jolivet, E. (2004a). Different visions, different visuals: A social semiotic analysis of field-specific visual composition in scientific conference presentations. *Visual Communication, 3*(2), 145–175.
Rowley-Jolivet, E. (2004b). Visual textual patterns in scientific conference presentations. In D. Banks (Ed.), *Text and texture: Systemic functional viewpoints on the nature and structure of text* (pp. 383–410). Paris: L'Harmattan.
Rowley-Jolivet, E. (2012). Oralising text slides in scientific conference presentations: A multimodal corpus analysis. In A. Boulton, S. Carter-Thomas, & E. Rowley-Jolivet (Eds.), *Corpus-informed research and learning in ESP: Issues and applications* (pp. 137–165). Amsterdam: John Benjamins.
Rowley-Jolivet, E., & Carter-Thomas, S. (2005). The rhetoric of conference presentation introductions: Context, argument and interaction. *International Journal of Applied Linguistics, 15*(1), 45–70.
Shalom, C. (2002). The academic conference: A forum for enacting genre knowledge. In E. Ventola, C. Shalom, & S. Thompson (Eds.), *The language of conferencing* (pp. 51–68). Frankfurt am Main: Peter Lang.
Swales, J.M. (1990). *Genre analysis. English in academic and research settings.* Cambridge: Cambridge University Press.
Tardy, C.M. (2005). Expressions of disciplinarity and individuality in a multimodal genre. *Computers and Composition, 22*(3), 319–336.
Thompson, S. (2002). "As the story unfolds": The uses of narrative in research presentations. In E. Ventola, C. Shalom, & S. Thompson (Eds.), *The language of conferencing* (pp. 147–167). Frankfurt am Main: Peter Lang.
Tufte, E.R. (2003). *The cognitive style of PowerPoint.* Cheshire, CT: Graphics Press LIC.
Vassileva, I. (2002). Speaker-audience interaction: The case of Bulgarians presenting in English. In E. Ventola, C. Shalom, & S. Thompson (Eds.), *The language of conferencing* (pp. 255–276). Frankfurt am Main: Peter Lang.
Ventola, E. (2002). Why and what kind of focus on conference presentations? In E. Ventola, C. Shalom, & S. Thompson (Eds.), *The language of conferencing* (pp. 15–50). Frankfurt am Main: Peter Lang.
Ventola, E., Shalom, C., & Thompson, S. (Eds.). (2002). *The language of conferencing.* Frankfurt am Main: Peter Lang.
Webber, P. (2002). The paper is now open for discussion. In E. Ventola, C. Shalom, & S. Thompson (Eds.), *The language of conferencing* (pp. 227–254). Frankfurt am Main: Peter Lang.
Webber, P. (2005). Interactive features in medical conference monologue. *English for Specific Purposes, 24*(2), 157–181.
Wecker, C. (2012). Slide presentations as speech suppressors: When and why learners miss oral information. *Computers and Education, 59*(2), 260–273.
Yates, J.A., & Orlikowski, W. (2007). The PowerPoint presentation and its corollaries: How genres shape communicative action in organizations. In M. Zachry, & C. Thralls (Eds.), *The cultural turn: Communicative practices in workplaces and the professions* (pp. 67–92). Amityville, NY: Baywood.
Zareva, A. (2013). Self-mention and the projection of multiple identity roles in TESOL graduate students' presentations: The influence of the written academic genres. *English for Specific Purposes, 32*(2), 72–83.

5 A Multimodal Approach to Persuasion in Conference Presentations

Julia Valeiras Jurado

5.1 INTRODUCTION

The mastery of a genre such as conference presentations is a key to success in many academic contexts. However, mastery of any genre implies not only a deep understanding of its communicative situation and its communicative purpose, but also an awareness of the variety of semiotic resources available, which go far beyond speech. Especially in the case of oral genres such as conference presentations, research has frequently overlooked the fact that speakers can resort to much more than words to convey their meaning (Kress & van Leeuwen, 2001; van Leeuwen, 2004; Kress, 2010). This is precisely the gap that a multimodal approach to genre analysis tries to fill.

Multimodality intersects with discourse by focusing on the variety of available semiotic modes from which users of genres can select to better suit their needs in particular communicative situations. The more acquainted users are with these modes, the more likely they are to convey their meaning successfully and use genres effectively. Among these modes, three of them are particularly salient in oral genres: gestures and head movements (both kinesic features) and intonation (paralinguistic feature). They are virtually unavoidable in any instance of oral discourse and they deeply affect the way the message is perceived.

In the case of conference presentations, these modes can also contribute to the communicative purpose of the genre: presenting a scientific novelty to the scientific community and persuading this community that the research described is valuable. In this sense, conference presentations play a crucial role in the dissemination of scientific knowledge, as argued by Rowley-Jolivet (1999).

By means of a case study, I aim to demonstrate that academics resort to a variety of semiotic modes to make their conference presentations more persuasive. In particular, I attempt to address the following research questions:

1. How do intonation, head movements and gestures contribute to create a persuasive conference presentation?
2. To what extent is persuasion in conference presentations genre-specific?

In the next section, I provide a brief literature review of different approaches to academic discourse and genres that highlights the suitability of a multimodal approach to the study of an oral persuasive genre such as conference presentations. I then examine the conference presentation itself, focusing on its multimodal nature and its persuasive character. The remaining sections of the chapter are dedicated to a case study of an analysis of a conference presentation, which aims to highlight the contribution of the multimodal approach towards understanding how a persuasive message is designed in this genre.

5.2 APPROACHES TO ACADEMIC DISCOURSE ANALYSIS

Discourse analysis (often abbreviated as DA) is an approach to the study of discourse that focuses on how language is actually used (Fasold, 1990). There are different trends within DA, but they all agree that we need to avoid looking at language as an abstract system independent from its users. Instead, DA focuses on how people use language to show their attitude, to express feelings, to exchange information and to socialize, among other aims (Brown & Yule, 1983; Schiffrin, 1994). DA also emphasizes the need to take into account the *purpose* of using certain linguistic forms, instead of studying them in isolation. According to Swales (1990), this purpose is usually determined by the *discourse community* and its social practice, and this communicative purpose allows us to differentiate between different types of discourse. We can often associate a discourse community with a professional community, which makes it possible to speak of professional discourses such as business discourse, legal discourse, academic discourse, etc. Each type of discourse is, in turn, manifested in different genres.

Regarding academic discourse in particular, Hyland (2009) identifies the following main trends in the study of academic discourse:

1. A textual trend, which focuses on language choices, meanings and patterns in texts. Within this trend, we could include corpus analysis and genre analysis.
2. A contextual trend, which takes the wider situational aspects as a point of departure and looks at how language is socially enacted in specific situations.
3. A critical trend, which tries to bring to the fore the ideologies and relations of power revealed through texts.

I consider the present study to be included in the field of genre analysis, and therefore devote the next section to a discussion of the relevant literature.

5.3 APPROACHES TO GENRE ANALYSIS

In his seminal study on genres in academic settings, Swales (1990) describes genres as communicative events with a recognizable communicative purpose within a discourse community. Over the years, Swales's conception of genres has proved very influential and, as pointed out by Valeiras and Ruiz (in press), many authors have developed and expanded on the original concepts introduced by him (Paré & Smart, 1994; Berkenkotter & Huckin, 1995; Yates & Orlikowski, 2002; Virtanen & Halmari, 2005).

Two crucial aspects that recur in the literature on genres are *recursiveness* and *regularity*. A genre is recognizable by its recurrent use in particular situations, as well as by regularities in form, content and purpose (Paré & Smart, 1994; Yates & Orlikowski, 2002). Likewise, *acceptance by a community* is a requirement for a genre to be considered as such. Through this acceptance, a genre raises expectations in its community (Paré & Smart, 1994; Berkenkotter & Huckin, 1995; Yates & Orlikowski, 2002). This connection with a *community of use* also highlights a genre as a social and professional tool that allows users to become competent members of a community (Berkenkotter & Huckin, 1995). Furthermore, the genre–society relationship entails a reciprocal influence, which Paré and Smart (1994) call *duality of structure*. On the other hand, genres are *dynamic* entities that change according to users' needs and also respond to social changes (Berkenkotter & Huckin, 1995).

As society and the way people communicate evolve, new texts that do not seem to fit into existing genre typologies emerge and a revision of the concept of genre is needed. Along this line, Kress (2003, p. 36) emphasizes the need to move from a theory that accounts for language alone to "a theory that can account equally well for gesture, speech, image, writing, 3D objects, colour, music and no doubt others." Kress describes genres as dynamic entities that are the result of a creative process. This is particularly salient in the case of persuasive genres, as pointed out by Halmari and Virtanen (2005). Since persuasion is more effective when it is unexpected (O'Keefe, 2002; Perloff, 2003), it also prompts genre dynamism and the integration of new elements (i.e., new semiotic modes) that consequently add to the description of the genre.

A multimodal approach to genre analysis is based on the assumption that the genre-creation process is multimodal because users select among different modes to express meaning (Kress & van Leeuwen, 2001; Kress, 2003; Norris, 2004; Kress & van Leeuwen, 2006). The concepts of *mode* and *media,* which are central to multimodal analysis, can help to shed light on the production and interpretation processes involved in genres. Jewitt (2004) clarifies the difference between these concepts, stating that modes enable *representation* of meaning, while media allow for the *dissemination* of meaning. Kress (2003) further claims that the production process of a text is closely related to design. Users design the most appropriate way of communicating their meaning in a given situation. This implies choosing the most suitable combination of modes, bearing in mind that each mode has different affordances and epistemological commitments. At the same time, the practices of the community in which the genre is used also impose certain restrictions and rule out certain things as unacceptable. These issues will be discussed further in relation to conference presentations in the following section.

5.4 THE CONFERENCE PRESENTATION AS A GENRE

The conference presentation can be classified as an academic genre since it is mainly used by discourse communities within academia. In order to better understand the nature of this genre and the way it is related to other genres within academic discourse, I draw on Fortanet's (2005) classification of spoken academic genres, which uses the purpose of the genre as the main criterion and distinguishes three main categories:

1. *Classroom genres,* within which we can include lectures, seminars, students' presentations and oral exams, among others.
2. *Institutional genres,* which include academic year opening lectures, honoris causa speeches and rectors' addresses to the faculty, among others.
3. *Research genres,* which can be further subdivided into a) *conference genres* that include plenary lectures, poster presentations, workshops and conference presentations, which are central to this study, and b) *other research genres* such as PhD thesis defenses, master's thesis presentations, etc.

Classroom genres seem to have been privileged in research on spoken academic discourse, but conference presentations have recently attracted the attention of many scholars who have tackled its study from different angles. Among these, we can mention Dubois (1982), who presents a detailed account of biomedical conferences. Later Rowley-Jolivet (1999, p. 179) claimed what she termed the "pivotal role" of conference presentations in academic research, and identified three main functions of this genre: to present a scientific novelty, to give visibility to research and to reinforce social cohesion within the discourse community. This work was expanded by Rowley-Jolivet and Carter-Thomas (2003, 2005), who studied presentations from three different approaches (see the discussion in the next section). They also compared the rhetorical structure of conference introductions with research article introductions. In these studies, they highlight an important feature of conference presentations that is of particular relevance for this chapter: They are not only novelty-oriented and informative, but they are also inherently persuasive. This idea is shared by Räisänen (1999, 2002), who suggests that the function of conference presentations is to publicize, critically discuss and ratify research. Another issue of particular relevance raised in the literature on conference presentations is the immediacy in time and place in relation to an expert audience with whom a great amount of shared knowledge can be expected. This is discussed by Hood and Forey (2005) and Rowley-Jolivet & Carter-Thomas (2005), who maintain that the immediacy of an audience and the consequent need for real-time processing strongly influence the way a presentation is designed.

The relationship of conference presentations with other genres has also been the focus of several studies that see this genre as part of a macrogeneric event embedded in the wider conference experience. With the term *semiotic spanning,* Ventola (2002) tries to explain the connection between the presentation itself and the discursive practices of the participants during the whole conference event. This implies that every presentation an academic delivers is necessarily influenced by the previous presentations in the conference event and the future presentations that will come after it, as well as by related genres such as the abstract or the research article. This relationship has also been explained through the concept of *genre chain,* which identifies a chronological sequence of academic genres that are produced during the unfolding of a communicative event, e.g., Call for papers–Abstract–Presentation–Research article (Räisänen, 2002; Shalom, 2002).

The idea that a conference presentation is associated with (and influenced by) a written paper is also discussed by Rowley-Jolivet (1999), Rowley-Jolivet and Carter-Thomas (2005) and Hood and Forey (2005). Presentations are a way of testing research before a definitive paper is published. They may also present research that is still ongoing. This dynamic process is usually diluted and idealized in the written paper (Hyland, 2009). For this reason, we can argue that a conference presentation is a process genre (Swales, 1990; Rowley-Jolivet & Carter-Thomas, 2005), since it often takes place while research is still in progress.

There are also some interesting studies that deal with specific sections of conference presentations. The discussion session or Q&A has been dealt with by Shalom (1993), Wulff, Swales & Keller (2009) and Querol-Julián (2011). I follow Wulff et al. (2009) in considering the Q&A session as part of the conference presentation and not as a separate genre, because I consider the communicative situation and purpose still to remain much the same, despite the more active role of the audience during this session. For the same reason, I also consider the chair's introduction as part of the conference presentation genre.

Rather than concentrating specifically on genre, other studies have dealt with the narrative discourse of presentations (Thompson, 2002), or the language used within them (Ruiz-Garrido & Fortanet-Gómez, 2008). Finally, Hood & Forey (2005) and Hyland (2009) identified several challenges when studying conference presentations as a genre. On the one hand, we need to consider their inherent *variety*. Presentations can range from a one-hour plenary to a short parallel session, they can present research at various levels of completion, and their audience can differ in size and homogeneity. On the other hand, we cannot ignore the difficulties of collecting and coding *multimodal data*. The multimodal nature of conference presentations is the focus of the next section of this chapter.

5.4.1 Multimodality in Conference Presentations

Dubois (1982) was among the first to draw attention to the multimodal nature of presentations, pointing out the increasing importance and abundance of visuals, as well as their role in helping to structure the presentation.

Later, Carter-Thomas and Rowley-Jolivet (2003) suggested that the study of conference presentations must be approached from three different perspectives:

1. A microscopic bottom-up analysis to identify recurrent linguistic features and relate these choices to the communicative context (but which fails to account for the rhetorical macrostructure of the text)
2. A macroscopic top-down analysis (analysis of moves) to explore the rhetorical structure (but which fails to account for the variety of modes employed)
3. A multimodal approach to account for the essential role of visuals in presentations, and how the affordances of this mode make it particularly suitable for easy processing during real-time delivery

The role of visuals is also dealt with in Rowley-Jolivet's work (2002, 2005), in which she claimed that visuals constitute a major resource for meaning-making in presentations. Moreover, because they provide immediate access to data discussed, visuals serve to reinforce newness and immediacy of the presentation. Hyland (2009) further claimed that visuals fulfill the three metafunctions postulated in systemic functional linguistics, and thus can provide information, help to structure the talk and appeal to the imagination of the audience. Finally, with a slightly different focus, Bellés and Fortanet (2004) discussed the characteristics of the handouts used in academic presentations in the field of linguistics, identifying references, schematic outlines and short summaries as common traits in their corpus.

From this brief and selective review, we see that visuals have enjoyed a privileged treatment in multimodal analyses of conference presentations. However, some studies have also looked at the role of kinesic or paralinguistic features in academic discourse. With reference to classroom settings, English (1985) discussed the role of kinesics in academic lectures to facilitate understanding. Pozzer-Ardenghi and Roth (2005) pointed out how gestures in lectures can reduce the ambiguity of visuals, while Crawford Camiciottoli (2007) included nonverbal behavior in her description of business lectures. Regarding academic research genres, Rendle-Short (2006) found that presenters in seminars announce silent periods through paralanguage and kinesics. Hood and Forey (2005), in their multimodal study of introductions of plenary presentations, showed how gestures express attitudinal meaning and encourage alignment between audience and presenter. Räisänen and Fortanet (2006) tackled the use of nonverbal communication in conference presentations, looking at gestures, gaze, facial expression and posture.

They concluded that discussion sessions display a greater variety of kinesic features than the monologic presentation. Finally, Querol-Julián (2011) provided a detailed study of the multimodal expression of evaluation in discussion sessions of specialized conference paper presentations.

In this chapter, I focus on paralinguistic and kinesic features (i.e., intonation, head movements and gestures) as crucial meaning-making resources in oral discourse in general, and conference presentations in particular. I draw on the above-cited research to analyze the multimodal expression of persuasion in this genre, arguing that conference speakers use a variety of modes to deliver a persuasive presentation.

5.4.2 Persuasion in Conference Presentations

Because their primary aim is to convince an audience of the validity, originality and usefulness of a piece of research (Rowley-Jolivet, 1999; Räisänen, 1999, 2002; Rowley-Jolivet & Carter-Thomas, 2003, 2005), conference presentations can be considered to be a persuasive genre. According to authors such as O'Keefe (2002), Perloff (2003) and Halmari and Virtanen (2005), persuasive messages tend to be more effective when a) speakers have credibility and the audience can identify with them, b) the message is made memorable, c) the message is innovative and surprising and d) the message is perceived as not imposed, but inferred.

In this chapter, I attempt to demonstrate that paralinguistic and kinesic features play a key role in providing a conference presentation with the above-mentioned characteristics to make it more persuasive, i.e., speakers communicate a persuasive message through the use of different modes. Towards this aim, I have focused on four persuasive strategies that can be hypothesized to be enacted through intonation, head movements and gestures, as well as with words (Brazil, 1997; Kendon, 2004; Hood & Forey, 2005; Querol-Julián, 2011). These strategies, as discussed in Valeiras and Ruiz (in press), are the following:

1. *Emphasis:* This refers to highlighting parts of the message so that they receive more attention. Intonation can contribute through the use of prominent syllables. It can also be used in combination with rhetorical devices that make the text more memorable, such as lexical creativity (Lakoff, 1982; Bamford, 2007, 2008).
2. *Evaluation:* This occurs when speakers evaluate something and are thus implicitly inviting the listener to accept their point of view (Bamford, 2007; Querol-Julián, 2011). Hood and Forey (2005) point out how speakers can include multimodal expressions of attitude in their introductions that subtly evaluate their presentations in positive terms and seek alignment with their audience. Also along this line, Pomerantz (1986) notes how extreme case formulations are frequently used to legitimize claims when speakers expect possible counterclaims. Interestingly,

these claims are commonly accompanied by head shakes, which seem to deny in advance a potential counter-argument (Kendon, 2002).

3. *Projection of understanding of the situation:* This allows speakers to present some parts of the message as shared with the audience and agreed upon, as opposed to new and open to discussion. Intonation, for example, plays an important role in this. It can be used in combination with inclusive pronouns that can help establish rapport with the audience and enhance the sense of shared knowledge (Fortanet, 2002; Bamford, 2007, 2008; Rowley-Jolivet & Carter-Thomas, 2005). Gestures can also help create this sense of inclusivity, bringing the audience into the discussion and establishing common ground (Hood and Forey, 2005; Holler, 2010).
4. *Anticipation and direction of responses:* This happens when speakers tend to predict reactions and adapt their discourse accordingly in order to obtain a desirable response. Very frequently, we do this with gestures and head movements (e.g., gestures or head shakes to prevent potential counterclaims) and also with intonation (e.g., a final high pitch shows that the speaker expects the listener to be surprised) (Brazil, 1997).

However, some modern research on persuasion (O'Keefe, 2002; Perloff, 2003) suggests that a persuasive message cannot be created as a template, but needs to be adapted to particular circumstances. In the specific case of conference presentations, this means that it is necessary to take into account how persuasion adapts to the communicative situation and especially to the community addressed. Hyland (2006, 2009) points out that belonging to a community means engaging with their discourses and practices. Thus, when speakers produce meaning in interaction with a community, their rhetorical choices are determined by their purpose, the setting and the audience. In Hyland's own words, "Persuasion in the academy [. . .] involves using language to relate independent beliefs to shared experience" (2009, p.13). Here I go a step further and argue that persuasion in academic contexts involves using not only *language,* but a *combination of semiotic modes.*

According to Thompson (2002) and Hyland (2006), humanities lack the highly formalized reporting system of hard sciences and, for this reason, researchers cannot minimize their presence that easily. Instead, they require more personal projection in their texts to prompt solidarity, acceptance and credibility and create a convincing discourse. Rowley-Jolivet and Carter-Thomas (2005), however, maintain that the greater presence of the researcher may also be due to the requirements of the communicative situation of the oral presentation, which calls for more interactive efforts to engage with the audience as opposed to written genres. Engaging with the audience, according to Hyland (2006), is a twofold process. On the one hand, it means addressing the audience as participants in an argument, and on the other, it means anticipating potential responses and directing the audience towards intended interpretations.

Persuasion in conference presentations, therefore, is discipline-dependent and contextually dependent, and also requires the speaker to meet the following conditions: a) prove the originality and value of the piece of research described, b) prove that it has been done according to disciplinary rules, c) share practices and admit responsibility for decisions and d) be part of the whole communicative event in which research is being disseminated.

As Hyland (2006, p. 21) puts it, "We are more likely to persuade readers of our ideas if we shape our message so as to appeal to appropriate community recognized relationships." In the case study presented in the remainder of this chapter, I show how speakers make an effort to fulfill these conditions in order to communicate their research persuasively.

5.5 DATA AND METHODOLOGY

5.5.1 The Conference Event[1]

ABC (Association for Business Communication) is an international organization devoted to business communication. The organization holds an annual general conference, as well as other events organized by its four regional branches. These events are announced through a call for abstracts, which is also the basis for the selection of the presentations that will form the event. In the specific case of the symposium that concerns this study, there are plans to publish a volume compiling the different contributions. The event was devoted to exploring the two 'ends' of professional discourse research: a) obtaining data for analysis on the one hand (the "ins") and b) translating these data into useful recommendations for practitioners on the other (the "outs"). The conference presentation selected for analysis was scheduled on the second day of the event (devoted to the "outs" of professional discourse). It presents a case study of business English students doing an internship at a company. The presentation will be followed up by a written paper that will be part of the above-mentioned volume.

In this presentation, I have identified the following semiotic modes:

1. Verbal linguistic elements, i.e., the text delivered by the speakers
2. Paralanguage: intonation, pauses, nonverbal vocalizations, among others
3. Kinesics: gestures, body posture, head movements, gaze, among others
4. Image (visuals): projected on screen as the presentation proceeds
5. Writing: written text projected in the same way as images

All of these modes, and potentially more that could be identified and added, help express meaning and play an important role in communicating a persuasive message.

5.5.2 The Methodology

The methodology employed for the study combined a multimodal analysis of four modes (i.e., speech, intonation, head movements and gestures), which was integrated with ethnographic interviews with speakers to enable a triangulation of results.

First, a video recording of one conference presentation in the field of business discourse was taken using one stative camera focused on two speakers who co-presented. The presentation included a Q&A session at the end. The video was later transcribed orthographically. Shortly after the presentation, interviews were held with both speakers individually to gain insight into their views about the presentations and the communicative event. Towards this aim, the interviews included questions about their purpose and the preparation of their presentation. In addition, speakers were also asked about other presentations that they had seen that day in order to include their point of view as part of the audience. These interviews allowed me to probe into key aspects such as:

- What speakers assumed is a good presentation
- What speakers assumed was expected of them and how they prepared accordingly
- What speakers were trying to achieve with their presentation
- Their self-evaluation of the effectiveness of their presentation
- The relationship of the presentation with the corresponding written paper

The next step was an analysis of the macrostructure of the presentation. From this analysis, integrated with the information obtained from the interviews with speakers, a series of potentially persuasive points were identified. These are moments in the presentation which are particularly rich in terms of persuasive efforts from the speakers, and are also especially rich in modal density (Norris, 2004). This approach was adopted to avoid prioritizing any semiotic mode in particular, which has proved useful to keep the focus on the multimodal ensemble as a whole and the way different modes interact to encode a persuasive message. If each mode had been studied in isolation, this comprehensive view would not have been possible, and it would have been difficult to avoid the tendency to focus on the verbal element as the primary semiotic source.

A multimodal analysis of the expression of persuasion in these rich points constituted the next step of the process. Despite an effort to focus on the multimodal ensemble, for the sake of feasibility this study only focuses on a limited number of modes, i.e., speech, intonation, head movements and gestures, while leaving out others such as proxemics, gaze or visuals, which can equally contribute to the message. The reason why the modes specified above have been selected is that they have received less attention in academic discourse (compared, for example, to visuals), and yet they are quite conspicuous whenever we speak. Indeed, it is possible to give a presentation without visuals, even if it would probably be more difficult. However, it would be virtually impossible to deliver a presentation using a flat intonation throughout or without moving at all.

The speakers' gestures were analyzed following the work of Kendon (2004) and McNeill (1992). Where possible, their terminology has been applied for easier identification and description of the gesture. Particular attention was paid to the interaction of the gestures with the other modes studied, and how they work together in the expression of meaning. In the case of head movements, my analysis drew mainly on the research of McClave (2000) and Kendon (2002), focusing especially on amplitude and repetition, as well as interplay with other modes. The approach adopted for the analysis of intonation is Discourse Intonation (DI) (Brazil, 1997). DI looks at the communicative value of intonation by analyzing four systems in which speakers can make a range of meaningful choices. Through these choices speakers project a particular understanding of the communicative situation, direct the interpretation of the message or favor certain responses, all of which can function as highly persuasive tools. Table 5.1 offers a summary of these.

Finally, the results obtained from the analysis described above were discussed with the speakers themselves, who confirmed some of them but, more interestingly, also provided alternative interpretations that highly enriched the analysis.

Table 5.1 Discourse Intonation (Adapted from Brazil, 1997)

System	Definition	Options
Prominence	Prominent syllables are louder and longer	Prominent vs. non-prominent
Tone	Pitch movement	Rise-fall Fall Level Rise Fall-rise
Key	Relative pitch of onset syllables in relation to the onset syllable of the previous tone unit. (onset = first prominent syllable in a tone unit) (tone unit = basic intonation unit consisting of at least one prominent syllable)	High Mid Low
Termination	Relative pitch of tonic syllables in relation to the onset syllable in the same tone unit (tonic = prominent syllable in a tone unit that carries pitch movement)	High Mid Low

Before proceeding to the results of the analysis, I would like to make a further comment about the modes selected. I have differentiated intonation as a separate mode rather than including it within speech because I consider it capable of fulfilling Halliday's metafunctions (Halliday & Greaves, 2008). In addition, I argue that people in general exploit it communicatively to a great extent, even if not so consciously or systematically as words. We are all familiar with the expression "it's not what you say, it's the way you say it." Therefore, it meets the two requirements suggested by Kress (2010) to be considered a mode.

5.6 RESULTS AND DISCUSSION

In this section, I provide an overview of my results regarding the macrostructure and the multimodal analysis of persuasive rich points. I close this section by contrasting my results with the views of the speakers.

5.6.1 Macrostructure of the Presentation

The presentation macrostructure is illustrated in Table 5.2. As usual in academic conferences, there is an introduction by the chair before the presentation itself. In this case, the presentation is co-presented, and four turns are established for the two speakers, who alternate. The presentation is followed by a Q&A session with four questions/comments and a closing remark from the chair.

Table 5.2 Macrostructure of the presentation

(1) Chair introduction		
(2) Monologue section	Self-introductions of both speakers	
	1st turn of speaker 1	
	1st turn of speaker 2	
	2nd turn of speaker 1	
	2nd turn of speaker 2	
(3) Q&A section	Question 1	Answer of speaker 1
	Question 2	Answer of speaker 2
	Comment 3	Answer of speaker 2
		Answer of speaker 1
	Question 4	Answer of speaker 2
		Answer of speaker 1
(4) Closing remarks of chair		

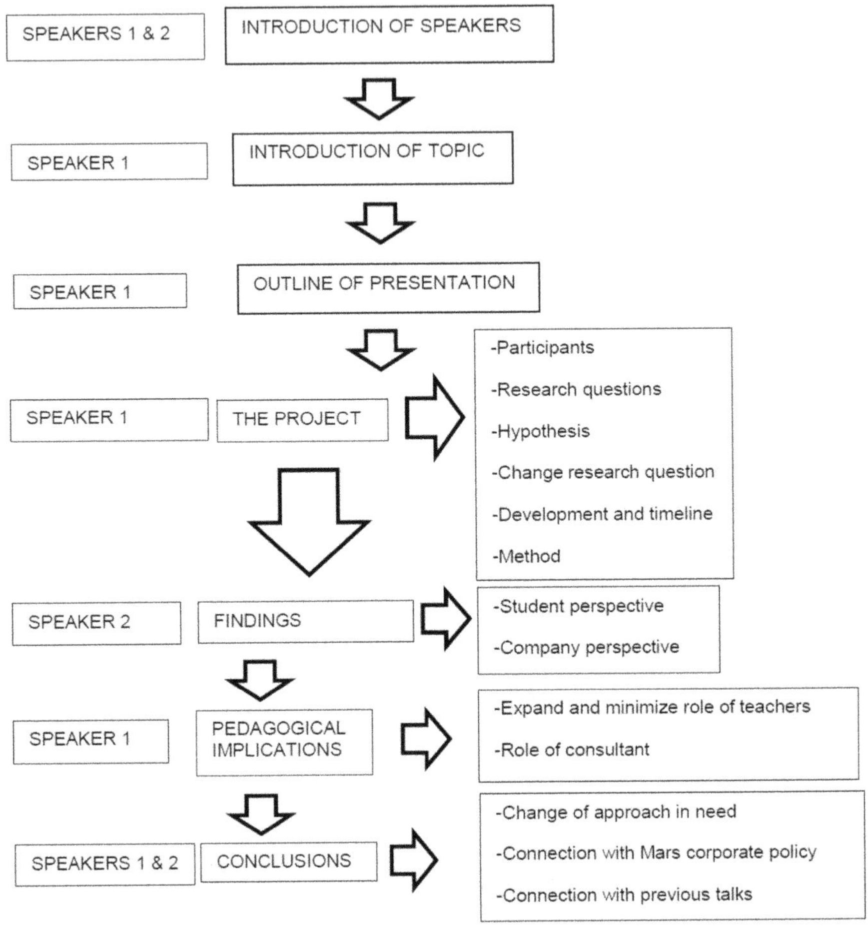

Figure 5.1 Macrostructure of the monologue section

The macrostructure of the monologue section can be represented schematically as shown in Figure 5.1.

5.6.2 Multimodal Analysis of Persuasion

The main point of this presentation (as confirmed by the interviews) is the tension between academic and professional profiles, and the complex interplay between key players in an internship project. Therefore, it could be expected that a) references to this tension will be particularly persuasive, b) this persuasion will be expressed multimodally and c) intonation, gestures and head movements are likely to play an important role in the multimodal ensemble.

These hypotheses were confirmed by the analysis. Many of the points that were identified as particularly persuasive correspond to the discussion of the results and the implications that can be derived from them. In addition, they are also related to the tension identified as the main point of the presentation. On the other hand, it should also be noted that these points also constitute the original contribution of this research, which further explains the need to highlight them and make them particularly persuasive. This is connected to an attempt to conform to the discursive rules of the community (i.e., prove originality and relevance of research) that is present throughout the presentation. In the following paragraphs, I zoom in on two relevant extracts to illustrate these points.

In Figure 5.2 below, Speaker 1 is discussing one of the main findings of their study, i.e., during an internship project, the role of the teacher must be diminished so that students can evolve to become professionals. As the speaker is pronouncing the utterance "we should stop at a certain point" he makes an open hand prone gesture (Kendon, 2004) that implies the idea of 'stop' or 'halt,' and interestingly coincides with the word "stop." This word is also made prominent because it is the tonic syllable of the tone unit (Brazil 1997). The speaker is thus emphasizing the idea of stopping, which is a main finding, through intonation and gesture.

Figure 5.3 is another example of highlighting a main finding multimodally. Speaker 2 is commenting that students need to be encouraged to become "truly consultants." As the word "truly" is pronounced it receives prominence and, at the same time, a finger bunch gesture (Kendon 2004) is made that ends in a closed fist, signifying the idea of 'seizing' something,

Figure 5.2 "We should stop"

of 'grasping' the exact meaning of something. This meaning complements what is expressed by the word "truly."

Hyland's (2006) claim that the presence of the researcher is rather prominent and serves to give credibility to research in humanities is confirmed by both speakers' emphasis on the honest sharing of the research experience and the process. In addition, references to the researchers themselves are relevant here, as expressed by the pronouns "our" and "we," also reinforced through gestures, as Figure 5.4 exemplifies:

Note how Speaker 2 points to herself as she mentions "our everyday practice," directing attention to the figure of the researcher and the progress of the research process. Interestingly, the word "our" also receives prominence.

Both speakers mention several times that they changed their research questions as they progressed in their research, and they seem to emphasize this point throughout the presentation. My interpretation of this is as follows: This change is something that could be objected to, given the assumptions among the scientific community on how research should be done. Because of this, the decision is carefully justified, and particularly persuasive efforts can be expected whenever there is a reference to this change. There is a special need to persuade the audience that the study presented

Figure 5.3 "Become truly consultants"

Figure 5.4 "Our everyday practice"

has been done according to accepted conventions in the discourse community that forms the audience. This was, however, refuted by later discussion with speakers. Both emphasized that the reason for the emphasis on the change of research question was to build an interesting narrative about the research process, and mainly stemmed from an interest in sharing research experiences with the audience. This is, in turn, very revealing about generic practices and expectations: Oral presentations allow for this sharing of research experiences, while written papers do not. Both speakers referred to this difference in their interviews, as I expand on in the next section. Some examples clarifying this point are:

(example 1) WE //CHANGED //our RESEARCH question
(example 2) *WE* felt // it was time for *US* // to *CHANGE* our *APPROACH*[2]

Both ideas are conveyed in utterances made up of shorter tone units than usual and with prominence on key words such as "change," "we," "us," "research" or "approach."

Speaker 1 repeats several times during his first turn that they were scheduled in the "outs"-themed section for the sake of consistency. I interpret this as a way of proving the relevance of their presentation in the whole communicative event, and of showing that the presentation coheres with it. This is further supported by the references to other presentations. The following example illustrates this point:

(example 3) WE were *SCHEDULED*// to *DAY* // in the *OUT* sessions

Note how the word "today" is singled out as a tone unit in itself, and "out" is the tonic syllable of the next tone unit, both becoming prominent.

During the Q&A session, for both speakers the nodding of the head during the posing of a question serves as a backchannel, but it sometimes becomes particularly emphatic and assumes an interpersonal and modal meaning (i.e., showing alignment). A good example of this is the third question in the discussion session, which takes the form of a comment:

(example 4) I feel also as a student, they don't feel that's legitimate to step into the company or be very aggressive or very authoritative.

During this comment (which was actually longer than the extract shown above), both speakers nod subtly as they start listening. As the discussant makes her point, both nod more frequently and emphatically. My interpretation is that this is a way of anticipating a positive response or, in other words, a way of showing agreement with the views expressed in the comment. This is in line with Querol-Julián's (2011) findings in her multimodal study of Q&A sessions in conference presentations. It is also supported by the fact that Speaker 2 uses a high key (involving a higher pitch) as she answers, which according to Brazil (1997) is adjudicating, and can be paraphrased as "you are right" as shown in example (5):

(example 5) Yes, thank you so much. I'm glad you brought that out.

5.6.3 Insights from Speaker Interviews

Ethnographic interviews with both speakers shed additional light on the results presented in the previous section. They also allowed me to compare the results with the speakers' views. In some cases, the speakers confirmed these results. In others, however, they gave alternative views that differed from my interpretations. In both cases, their insights provided the case study with more objectivity and made the analysis considerably richer.

5.6.3.1 Views on the Presentation and the Event

For both speakers, it was their second experience at the ABC conference, but Speaker 1 seemed to make a closer connection and draw more from his experience at the first conference. In fact, he mentioned that his motivation to attend this second conference was derived from his successful experience the first time.

Speaker 2 admitted during the interview that, although it was not the first time she participated in an ABC conference, she felt "like an outsider." This leads me to think that she was making a greater effort to create rapport and build common ground with the audience. In my opinion, this explains her more frequent hedging, which gives her presentation an overall humble tone. In example (6), we see this during her discussion of the students' perception of the communication flow between themselves and the company, which she admits was not positive.

(example 6) So we looked at the interviews on the complex interactions between the company and the students and we noticed a couple of things. I'll guide you through some of the quotes here. The students were basically not that happy, that's a way of summarizing it.

In example (7), the attempt to sound noncategorical materializes through paralanguage and kinesics instead of lexically: a pause immediately before and a longer syllable duration in "difficulty," accompanied by a minimizing hand gesture signifying something small.

(example 7) So when we, as researchers, confronted the company with this—well, difficulty in working together, the trust, the giving access, they were totally surprised.

The frequent open hand supine gestures through which she offers and shares ideas with her audience with palms facing up, suggesting honesty and willingness to draw on shared knowledge, seem to serve the same purpose (Holler 2010). This is further supported by her acknowledgement during the interview that she tried to find a common ground with the audience by appealing to shared teaching experiences, whereas in more familiar contexts she tends to be more direct. Interestingly, she mentioned that she particularly liked another presentation in the conference because the speaker was 'humble but confident,' which is very much in line with the relationship she seems to be trying to establish with her audience.

Concerning the emphasis on being scheduled on the "outs"-themed section of the conference, both speakers agreed that it was an effort to make their contribution cohere with the whole communicative event. This is in line with Speaker 2's efforts to make references to other contributions at the end of the presentation.

Finally, concerning the difference between the oral presentation and the paper that will be based on it, Speaker 1 claimed that the paper will be more result-oriented, while the oral presentation is more apt for methodological discussion. A reason for this is that he considers a presentation to be more flexible and interactive than a written paper. Speaker 2 believes the main difference between them is that the presentation needs to "sell something quickly," while the paper will focus on the importance of the contribution.

In the written paper, there is no room for honest sharing of research experiences. Speaker 1 also gave a lot of importance to visuals in this presentation because he thinks they help make the presentation more to the point and therefore more effective, which is in line with Speaker 2's idea of "selling something quickly."

5.6.3.2 *Other Issues*

Regarding the change of the research question, Speaker 1 claimed that there was no need to justify it in his opinion. Rather, it is a metareflection that he considered would be more interesting for the audience (and in this he agreed with Speaker 2). He added that sharing the process is more interesting in the case of group work rather than in the case of an individual researcher. Speaker 1 also mentioned that he particularly liked a specific presentation because the speaker was "honest," which connects with this idea of sharing research experiences in a transparent way.

Speaker 2 explained that this change was somehow prompted by the initial results obtained, and rather than feeling the need to justify this decision, she thought it was a good hook for the audience, who she assumed would be more interested in an honest and transparent narrative of the research process.

In relation to the head nods during the Q&A session, both speakers found the possibility of anticipating a positive response plausible, but Speaker 2 added that in her case she uses these nods to help her maintain concentration after the draining experience of presenting.

5.7 CONCLUSIONS

A multimodal approach to conference presentations allows for a more comprehensive perspective on how a persuasive message is communicated. Throughout this chapter, I have shown how it is actually a complex interplay of different modes that makes a presentation persuasive. Towards this aim, I have combined a multimodal analysis of a video-recorded presentation with interviews that provided insight into the speakers' views and allowed contrasting interpretations.

The number and complexity of modes that contribute to the genre of conference presentations is a challenge for any comprehensive study. There are other modes not dealt with in this chapter, such as posture or gaze, which equally contribute to creating a persuasive message. The study of these modes can constitute an interesting and enlightening line for further research. In addition, a wider corpus of conference presentations should be collected and analyzed for the sake of representativeness.

In this chapter, I have illustrated through a case study how speakers present their research in a persuasive way by resorting to intonation, gestures and head movements. A mode such as intonation serves as a signposting tool, highlighting important aspects, directing interpretation and monitoring responses. Through intonation, a speaker marks what is assumed as shared knowledge and what is expected to be accepted as an innovative and valuable contribution to the field. It is no coincidence that in the conference presentation analyzed, many of the richest points in terms of persuasion correspond to the discussion of results and their relevance or applicability. Rather than explicitly evaluating these results verbally (which would probably not fit into discourse practices), speakers direct attention to them and highlight them as new and potentially interesting through intonation, i.e., giving them prominence in their tone units.

Gestures and head movements, on the other hand, frequently reinforce and complement meaning expressed with words, or even substitute for them. Interestingly, many of the rich points referred to in the previous paragraph are also supported by hand gestures that either complete or reinforce the meaning expressed through other modes. Gestures and head movements also make it possible to express in a subtle way aspects of meaning that would be problematic to express with words in the communicative situation of a conference (e.g., strong agreement or disagreement). This was particularly evident during the Q&A session, where discourse is highly controlled by academic hedging. We have seen in the example analyzed that head nods can be used to anticipate strong agreement with the views expressed by a member of the audience who poses a question or makes a comment.

Persuasion in conference presentations is also highly dependent on the communicative event. This implies proving that the presentation fits into the broader conference and coheres with other presentations. The high number of references to other presentations and the way these are made prominent through intonation indicates that both speakers are aware of this in the example analyzed.

Finally, persuasion in conference presentation also implies respect for disciplinary practices. In the case analyzed in this study, this entailed a number of aspects such as focusing on honest and transparent sharing of research methods, taking responsibility of research decisions, as well as highlighting the novelty, value and applicability or usefulness of the results obtained. It is also interesting to note that these practices may change from one discipline to another, and probably in a conference in a different field we could expect a different stance from the speaker.

These are all important aspects that novel researchers should be made aware of as they go through a process of enculturation into a discipline to become competent members of the community. However, they are largely neglected in academic English courses, which tend to play a stronger emphasis on language accuracy. Novel researchers are typically left on their own to infer this knowledge about the genres and communicative practices of their disciplines. This turns science communication into a stressful business, something that could be avoided if researchers were directed towards the right communicative tools and resources to effectively disseminate their work. Using Hyland's words (2009, p. 2), "Ultimately a theory prevails because it is presented in a way which academics recognize as persuasive: knowledge, in other words, is what people can be persuaded to accept."

ACKNOWLEDGMENTS

I would like to express my sincere thanks to Astrid Vandendaele and Tom Bruyer for granting me permission to record their presentations and reproduce their speech and images, and for their patience in dealing with my interviews.

NOTES

1. I would like to thank Geert Jacobs, president of ABC Europe, for the useful account of the organization and its communicative practices, and for facilitating access to the conference that is the object of this study.
2. I use the following DI notation conventions: uppercase letters for prominent syllables, lowercase letters for non-prominent syllables, and // to delimit tone units.

REFERENCES

Bamford, J. (2007). Accentuating the positive: Evaluation and persuasive discourse in business presentations. In J. Bamford, & R. Salvi (Eds.), *Business discourse: Language at work* (pp. 135–155). Rome: Aracne Editrice.

Bamford, J. (2008). Telling a convincing story: A corpus assisted analysis of business presentations. In A. Martelli, & V. Pulcini (Eds.), *Investigating English with corpora. Studies in honour of Maria Teresa Prat* (pp. 277–291). Monza: Polimetrica International Scientific Publisher.

Bellés, B., & Fortanet, I. (2004). Handouts in conference presentations. In I. Fortanet, J. Palmer, & S. Posteguillo (Eds.), *Linguistic studies in academic and professional English* (pp. 211–235). Castellón: Publicacions de la Universitat Jaume I.

Berkenkotter, C., & Huckin, T. (1995). *Genre knowledge in disciplinary communication*. Hillsdale, NJ: Erlbaum.

Brazil, D. (1997). *The communicative value of intonation in English*. Cambridge: Cambridge University Press.

Brown, G., & Yule, G. (1983). *Discourse analysis*. Cambridge: Cambridge University Press.

Carter-Thomas, S., & Rowley-Jolivet, E. (2003). Analysing the scientific conference presentation (CP): A methodological overview of a multimodal genre. *ASp 39–40*, 59–72.

Crawford Camiciottoli, B. (2007). *The language of business studies lectures: A corpus assisted analysis*. Amsterdam: John Benjamins.

Dubois, B. L. (1982). And the last slide please: Regulatory function at biomedical meetings. *World Language English, 1*(2), 263–268.

English, S. (1985). Kinesics in academic lectures. *The ESP Journal, 4*(2), 161–170.

Fasold, R. (1990). *The sociolinguistics of language*. Oxford: Blackwell.

Fortanet, I. (2002, April). Enhancing the speaker–audience relationship in academic lectures. Paper presented at the *International Symposium on Social and Cognitive Pragmatics*. Seville, Spain.

Fortanet, I. (2005). Honoris Causa speeches: An approach to structure. *Discourse Studies, 7*(1), 35–51.

Halliday, M., & Greaves, W. (2008). *Intonation in the grammar of English*. London: Equinox.

Halmari, H., & Virtanen, T. (2005). Towards understanding modern persuasion. In H. Halmari, & T. Virtanen (Eds.), *Persuasion across genres* (pp. 229–244). Amsterdam: John Benjamins.

Holler, J. (2010). Speakers' use of interactive gestures as markers of common ground. In S. Kopp, & I. Wachsmuth (Eds.), *Gesture in embodied communication and human-computer interaction* (pp. 11–22). Berlin: Springer Berlin Heidelberg.

Hood, S., & Forey, G. (2005). Introducing a conference paper. Getting interpersonal with your audience. *Journal of English for Academic Purposes, 4*(4), 291–306.

Hyland, K.B. (2006). *Academic discourse across disciplines*. Bern: Peter Lang.

Hyland, K.B. (2009). *Academic discourse*. London: Continuum.

Jewitt, C. (2004). Multimodality and new communication technology. In P. Levin, & R. Scollon (Eds.), *Discourse and technology: Multimodal discourse analysis* (pp. 184–195). Washington DC: Georgetown University Press.

Kendon, A. (2002). Some uses of the head shake. *Gesture, 2*(2), 147–183.

Kendon, A. (2004). *Gesture: Visible action as utterance*. Cambridge: Cambridge University Press.

Kress, G. (2003). *Literacy in the new media age*. London: Routledge.

Kress, G. (2010). *Multimodality: A social semiotic approach to contemporary communication*. London: Routledge.

Kress, G., & van Leeuwen, T. (2001). *Multimodal discourse: The modes and media of contemporary communication*. London: Arnold.

Kress, G., & van Leeuwen, T. (2006). *Reading images: A grammar of visual design*. London: Routledge.

Lakoff, R. (1982). Persuasive discourse and ordinary conversation, with examples from advertising. In D. Tannen (Ed.), *Analysing discourse: Text and talk* (pp. 25–42). Washington, DC: Georgetown University Press.

McClave, E. (2000). Linguistic functions of head movements in the context of speech. *Journal of Pragmatics, 32*(7), 855–878.

McNeill, D. (1992). *Hand and mind: What gestures reveal about thought*. Chicago: The University of Chicago Press.

Norris, S. (2004). Multimodal discourse analysis: A conceptual framework. In P. Levine, & R. Scollon (Eds.), *Discourse and technology: Multimodal discourse analysis* (pp. 101–115). Washington, DC: Georgetown University Press.

O'Keefe, D. (2002). *Persuasion: Theory and research*. London: Sage Publications.

Paré, A., & Smart, G. (1994). Observing genres in action: Towards a research methodology. In A. Freedman, & P. Medway (Eds.), *Genre and the new rhetoric* (pp. 146–54). London: Taylor & Francis.

Perloff, R. (2003). *The dynamics of persuasion*. Mahwah, NJ: Lawrence Erlbaum Associates, Inc.

Pomerantz, A. (1986). Extreme case formulations: A way of legitimizing claims. *Human Studies, 9*(2–3), 219–229.

Pozzer-Ardenghi, L., & Roth, W. (2005). Photographs in lectures: Gestures as meaning-making resources. *Linguistics and Education, 15*(3), 275–293.

Querol-Julián, M. (2011). *Evaluation in discussion sessions of conference paper presentations: A multimodal approach*. Saarbrücken: LAP Lambert Academic Publishing.

Räisänen, C. (1999). *The conference forum as a system of genres. A socio-cultural study of academic conference practices in automotive crash-safety engineering.* Gothenberg, Sweden: Acta Universitatis Gothoburgensis.
Räisänen, C. (2002). The conference forum: A system of interrelated genres and discursive practices. In E. Ventola, C. Shalom, & S. Thompson (Eds.), *The language of conferencing* (pp. 69–93). Frankfurt: Peter Lang.
Räisänen, C. & Fortanet, I. (2006, June). Do genres have body language? Nonverbal communication in conference paper presentations. Paper presented at the *Conference in honour of John Swales*, Ann Arbor, Michigan.
Rendle-Short, J. (2006). *The academic presentation: Situated talk in action.* Hampshire: Ashgate.
Rowley-Jolivet, E. (1999). The pivotal role of conference papers in the network of scientific communication. *ASp, 23–26,* 179–196.
Rowley-Jolivet, E. (2002). Visual discourse in scientific conference paper: A genre-based study. *English for Specific Purposes, 21*(1), 19–40.
Rowley-Jolivet, E., & Carter-Thomas, S. (2005). The rhetoric of conference presentation introductions: Context, argument and interaction. *International Journal of Applied Linguistics, 15*(1), 45–70.
Ruiz-Garrido, M. F., & Fortanet-Gómez, I. (2008). El lenguaje de las comunicaciones. In I. Fortanet-Gómez (Ed.), *Hablar inglés en la universidad: Docencia e Investigación* (pp. 125–157). Oviedo: Septem ediciones.
Schiffrin, D. (1994). *Approaches to discourse.* Oxford: Blackwell.
Shalom, C. (1993). Established and evolving spoken research process genres: Plenary lecture and poster session discussions at academic conferences. *English for Specific Purposes*, *12*(1), 37–50.
Shalom, C. (2002). The academic conference: A forum for enacting genre knowledge. In E. Ventola, C. Shalom, & S. Thompson (Eds.), *The language of conferencing* (pp. 51–68). Frankfurt: Peter Lang.
Swales, J. (1990). *Genre analysis: English in academic and research settings.* Cambridge: Cambridge University Press.
Thompson, S. (2002). As the story unfolds: The uses of narratives in research presentations. In E. Ventola, C. Shalom, & S. Thompson (Eds.), *The language of conferencing* (pp. 147–168). Frankfurt: Peter Lang.
Valeiras, J., & Ruiz, N. (in press). A multimodal approach to product presentations. *Procedia Social and Behavioral Sciences.* http://www.sciencedirect.com/science/journal/18770428
van Leeuwen, T. (2004). Ten reasons why linguists should pay attention to visual communication. In P. Levine, & R. Scollon, *Discourse and technology: Multimodal discourse analysis* (pp. 7–19). Washington, DC: Georgetown University Press.
Ventola, E. (2002). What and what kind of focus on conference presentations. In E. Ventola, C. Shalom, & S. Thompson (Eds.), *The language of conferencing* (pp. 15–50). Frankfurt: Peter Lang.
Ventola, E., Shalom, C., & Thompson, S. (Eds.). (2002). *The language of conferencing.* Frankfurt: Peter Lang.
Virtanen, T., & Halmari, H. (2005). Persuasion across genres: Emerging perspectives. In H. Halmari, & T. Virtanen (Eds.), *Persuasion across genres* (pp. 2–24). Amsterdam: John Benjamins.
Wulff, S., Swales, J., & Keller, K. (Eds.). (2009). "We have seven minutes for questions": The discussion sessions from a specialized conference. *English for Specific Purposes*, *28*(2), 79–92.
Yates, J., & Orlikowski, W. (2002). Genre systems: Structuring interaction through communicative norms. *Journal of Business Communication, 39*(1), 13–35.

Part II

Classroom Applications

6 There Is More to Multimodality Than Discourse Features and Nonverbal Behaviors!

Christine Räisänen

> Language matters. Discourse matters. Culture matters. There is an important sense in which the only thing that does not seem to matter anymore is matter.
>
> —(Barad, 2003, p. 801)

6.1 WHY DOES 'MATTER' MATTER?

Discourse and genre studies tend to focus on structure, on discrete activities, genres and/or particular textual instantiations. From this perspective, performance resides in the cognitive achievement of one or several individuals. Learning, teaching and knowing how to perform discursively, at least in higher education, most often assumes that discursive practices are predicated on human agency. Knowing and learning is assumed as taking place from "standing at a distance and representing" (Barad, 2007, p. 49). The contextual, material, nonhuman entities that configure particular discursive practices tend to be "relegated to the status of brute tools subordinated to human intention and design" (Fenwick, 2014, p. 45).

However, for a message (text) to be appropriated by a receiver, engagement has to take place, manifested through some form of enactment. Scollon (1998) refers to the real-time, unique social space in which engagement occurs as a 'site of engagement' and defines it as a moment when a text leading to action is in actual use, not just passively present in the situation. Scollon described a 'site of engagement' as "the window opened through the intersection of social practices in which participants may appropriate a message for mediated action" (1998, p. 11). To transform a conference presentation into a site of engagement is not an easy feat. Presenters need to be attuned and in concert with several very different modalities, many of which they cannot control. Sociocultural theories of action, such as mediated-action theory (e.g., Wertsch, 1993), situated action (e.g., Lave & Wenger, 1991) and mediated discourse (Scollon, 1998) assume that talk and action are inherently interwoven and that both construct and maintain structure, social practices and contractual arrangements. It is in these interactions that information may be appropriated, and subsequently enacted. To facilitate appropriation of information and knowledge requires competent mediators and an understanding of the affordances and constraints of the different available modalities. The implication of these perspectives for studies of discursive practices is that the unit of analysis cannot be reduced to only actors, social contexts or mediating tools. Rather, practice or activity needs to be viewed as social practice, involving the interaction of interlocutors, contexts, semiotic systems, artifacts, technologies, spatial arrangements and time. In such interactions, there often exist inherent tensions between human and nonhuman entities and spatial arrangements in particular contexts of use (Carlile et al., 2013; Dale & Burrell, 2008; van Marrewijk & Yanow, 2010; Orlikowski, 2007; Orlikowski & Scott, 2008; Yanow, 2010).

The reason for the tensions is that matter and materials also have agency, which we need to take into account when we prepare for participation in discourse practices, such as conference presentations. We need to think *multimodally,* not only in terms of the modalities we can control and use as mediating tools, such as discourse, paralanguage, kinesic features, as well as the available technology (I will call these *internal* modalities), but also those modalities that may wield power and control over our performance, which are *external* to the performer, for example, spatial arrangements, traditional conference props and time of day, to name a few. These modalities may have unanticipated effects on the performance of a presenter, and consequently on the interpretations of the audience. Material modalities may facilitate a presenter's attempt to create a site of engagement, which would enable the audience to appropriate the text. Scollon (1998) describes a site of engagement as a real-time, social space and moment in which mediated action occurs when a text leading to action is in actual use, not just passively present in the situation.

Seeing, hearing, talking and sense-making, all of which occur simultaneously during a conference presentation are as much discursive practices as material practices. They "involve the intra-twining, or the entanglement, of certain of our material bodily processes with those of the material world" (Shotter, 2013, p. 36). In other words, human and nonhuman bodies are not independent and self-contained entities located in a space that serves as a static repository for the deployed activity; rather they exist as "dynamic stabilities" in temporary relations to each other and to the space they momentarily share (p. 36). Materials available in particular contexts and practices are not inert, innocent objects; they are imbued with agential authority and shape the practice over time. A multimodal approach to research and learning of conference-presentation genres needs to attend to these external modalities since they intra-act[1] (Barad, 2003) with internal modalities as the practice is being deployed, i.e., in the doing of the practice.

The social and the material are therefore not separable entities; they are entangled, and are interdependently in perpetual becoming (Tsoukas & Chia, 2002). What this means for the learning, teaching and knowing of conference-presentation genres and discursive practices is that we need to move from a structural, performer-centric position to a process-oriented position, where perform*ing* or present*ing* are viewed as enactments in a sociomaterial assemblage (e.g., Carlile et al., 2013; Orlikowski & Scott 2008). We need to encompass the interplay between the social and the material and, more importantly, learn to adapt acquired cognitive multimodal strategies to ongoing, situated contingency modalities. In the interplay of the social and the material, neither human *nor* nonhuman agencies are predefined; rather they emerge temporally in a relational process of resistance and accommodation. This dialectic process is deployed in a certain place, with its particular spatial organization, and at a certain time, both of which also have agency.

In this conceptual chapter, I suggest a broadening of a multimodal approach to include matter/material (e.g., artifacts, spatial layout, bodies as well as less obvious 'things' as weather and time), as proposed in social semiotics (e.g., Ravelli & Stenglin, 2008; O'Halloran & Smith, 2011; Jewitt, 2014). I suggest a move from merely representing structure to focusing on agential processes in interactions between human and nonhuman entities in social practices. Rather than treating mental activities such as cognition, learning and knowing as ideational endeavors that reside in the minds of individuals and are learnt cognitively, we need to reflect on the ways in which materials deeply implicate not only practices and identities (Crawford Camiciottoli, 2009), but also our enactment of a practice in a specific situation, regardless of what role we perform in the practice. We need to build experience of the inherent constraints of matter as well as its affordances, its possibilities of action, both of which may not emerge until individuals act. Learning and knowing a practice involves both the mind and the body; it involves preparing for the unexpected, the chaotic—sometimes even for catastrophic consequences that arise when the materials meant to serve us do not perform in the ways we anticipated. My reflections stem from several decades of research and teaching of discursive practices in a wide variety of academic and professional contexts, and draw on the literature of several fields. In the following section, I briefly review some of this literature.

6.2 THEORETICAL FRAMING

Although successful performance at conferences is critical for knowledge dissemination and sharing in academic disciplinary fields (e.g., Räisänen, 1999, 2002; Rowley-Jolivet, 1999; Carter-Thomas & Rowley-Jolivet, 2003; Rowley-Jolivet & Carter-Thomas, 2005; Ventola et al., 2002), conference-presentation genres (paper presentations, plenary lectures and panel discussions) have tended to be eclipsed by research-paper genres (experimental, theoretical and review articles and conference papers) both as research topic and as classroom genre. One important reason for neglecting conference-presentation genres is the historically status-laden position of peer-reviewed research-paper genres in academia. Indeed, in the 1960s the influential physicist and humanist John Ziman (1968, p. 108) referred to conferences as "new vulgarities," sites for informal meetings and coffee-table conversations concerning unpublished work-in-progress. Conferences were not sites in which knowledge could become public and consensual, i.e., considered as fact, since this transformation from information to consensual knowledge could only be achieved through peer review and publication in internationally recognized research journals (Ziman, 1968, pp. 9–12).

This privileged status of the research article has driven research and the teaching of academic genres in higher education since the 1980s. Most of this work has been influenced by the seminal research of John Swales (1981, 1990) on the structure and textual realization of research article introductions, of Caroline Miller's (1984) definition of genre-as-social action and of Charles Bazerman's (1988) historical study of the origin of the scientific research article genre.

Another reason for the neglect of conference-presentation genres as an object of study is the ephemerality of speech as opposed to the durability as well as the ability of written text to travel across time and space. Written texts have been easy to access and amenable to research, aided by fast-developing corpus analytical tools. In this respect, oral research genres have lagged behind since, as this book highlights, oral genres are deployed in a situated dynamic context in which meaning-making is made "on the hoof" and is co-constructed by presenter and audience (e.g., Hood & Forey, 2005; Räisänen, 1999; Rowley-Jolivet & Carter-Thomas, 2005; see also Querol-Julián & Fortanet-Gómez, 2012). Analyzing oral research genres and practices entails paying attention not only to textual and contextual characteristics, but also to the interactional features of speaker/audience, speech/visuals, the verbal/nonverbal, and, as this chapter argues, the entanglement of the social and the material.

During the 1980s, the only comprehensive research on conference presentations was that of Dubois (e.g., 1980, 1982, 1987). Grounded in genre theory, she examined a variety of characteristics of biomedical conference presentations, comparing their structure with those of the biomedical research article genres. Dubois's work on conference presentations, in the context of this book, needs to be acknowledged since she was the first scholar to comprehensively highlight the multimodal and persuasive dimensions of conference presentations, even though she did not examine paralinguistic and kinesic features.

To date, research on conference-presentation genres from a wide variety of perspectives is growing (Hood & Forey, 2005; Carter-Thomas & Rowley-Jolivet, 2003; Rowley-Jolivet & Carter-Thomas, 2005; Shalom, 1993, 2002; Thompson, 2002; Ventola et al., 2002; Wulff, Swales & Keller, 2009; see Valeiras Jurado, this volume, for a brief review of some of this literature). Thanks to the development of sophisticated software programs such as ELAN,[2] which allows for annotations synchronized with streaming videos, researchers are now able to attend to speakers' uses of paralanguage and kinesic features (e.g., Querol-Julián, 2011; Querol-Julián & Fortanet, 2012, as well as Crawford Camiciottoli and Zhang, this volume). These studies contribute to a richer understanding of the ways in which speakers' verbal and nonverbal texts align, or misalign, and how audience behavior may influence speakers positively or negatively and vice versa. This latter dimension is addressed by Campoy-Cubillo and Querol-Julián (this volume), and hopefully will encourage more studies.

Although the analysis of the multimodal interplay between linguistic/discursive features, nonverbal behaviors and use of visual illustrations have enriched the teaching and learning of oral presentation genres in academic and professional contexts (for a comprehensive overview of previous research, see fellow chapters in this volume), these studies tend to focus solely on the cognitive processes of individual agents; they pay far less attention to the contexts in which the presentations play out, and how different contexts implicate individual and collective enactments.

6.3 THE SHIFTING COMMUNICATION FUNCTION OF CONFERENCE PRESENTATIONS

Although previous literature on conference presentations highlights their important function in the production, sharing and dissemination of knowledge, it also most often defines these presentations as a process genre (Swales, 1990) since the work presented is seen as ongoing. From this perspective, conference presentations may be compared to Goffman's (1990) back-stage performance as a rehearsal for a final front-stage publication in a research journal, a view that is reminiscent of Ziman's claim in the 1960s. However, in a growing number of disciplines in applied science, engineering and social science, conference associations now function as peer-reviewed publication forums; information disseminated at conferences can therefore no longer be characterized as "in progress," but rather as consensual knowledge (Räisänen, 1999, 2002). This development has implications for the teaching and learning of conference presentations in higher education since the stakes for presenters, especially novices, are higher. The purpose and role of the conference presentations in the applied sciences and engineering, as described by Räisänen (2002), differ from those in the social science and medical fields, which Swales and others have ascribed to process genres. In the former fields, presenters are no longer 'back-stage'; rather they are both metaphorically and literally 'front-stage.' In Sweden we call such front-stage enactment 'skarpt läge' or in my translation 'sharp positioning'; in such a positioning there are always stakes involved, and with stakes come risks. Presenting research at a conference in e.g., engineering, especially for the first time, is daunting for novices. Not only are they novice presenters (chances are they have scant experience of public speaking), they are also in a process of becoming, i.e., they are what Lave and Wenger (1991) refer to as 'legitimate peripheral participants'. They are still not part of the community of practice, but they are not outsiders either.

For these PhD students, presenting their research at academic or trade conferences is an important 'rite of passage' into the professional world (Swales, 1990; Räisänen, 1999). Indeed, publishing and presenting conference papers have become an obligatory passage point in PhD curricula, driven by the 'publish or perish' rationale prevalent in academia. Attending conferences affords them visibility and direct contact with academics and practitioners beyond the purview of their own universities, enabling them to widen their knowledge horizon (Räisänen, 1999, 2002). In engineering for example, conference forums have established their own reviewing processes, and the papers are published in proceedings prior to the conference event (Räisänen, 1999). The conference presentation is therefore no longer a tentative description of ongoing research, but a presentation of published findings. One critical aspect of this kind of conference presentation is that its function is not only to present findings, but, and maybe more importantly from the presenter's perspective (in terms of academic career prospects), to sell the paper. What this means is that the presentation has to persuade the audience that the results and argument are reasonable, reliable and accountable, and he/she must also make the audience want to read the paper, and by extension also cite the paper.

From a multimodal perspective, this conference-presentation process introduces yet another modality (or actor if you will), in the form of an artifact that wields agential power during the process of the presentation. I am here referring to the published conference paper, which members of the audience often have in front of them and are actively annotating during the presentation (Räisänen, 1999). Practices in these after-print conferences are not comparable to those in the before-print events (cf. p. 101), yet by far most of the current research on conference presentations are predicated on the before-print type of conference. I would encourage colleagues to fill this gap by applying a multimodal approach to after-print conference-presentation genres. This research would inform the learning and teaching of conference presentations in a growing number of new and hybrid fields of academic research. One example is nursing, which is an academic field that is currently in the process of establishing its scholarship. It is interesting to note that the number of articles highlighting the critical importance of conference presentations has been growing over the last decade (Cumble et al., 2005; Happell, 2009; Hardicre, Coade & Dewitt, 2007). Most of these articles, however, are normative and prescriptive, providing novices with acontextual (genre) templates. Such hybrid, new academic fields would be a rich soil for a broader multimodal approach, which would not only contribute to enhancing conference-presentation genres in the fields, but would also contribute to growing the theoretical and methodological scholarship presented in this volume.

What follows is a vignette drawn from observations of over 100 conference presentations in a variety of academic and professional fields during the past 15 years. The situation described in the vignette is authentic and has recurred more or less as narrated several times and in different fields. I close the chapter with a brief analysis of the vignette and some suggestions for the teaching and learning of conference-presentation genres.

6.4 IMAGINE! (VIGNETTE)

A large, modern auditorium, curving around a vast raised stage. Projected slides on a white screen compose the full backdrop. Spotlights are directed on the stage; the audience space is in darkness. Front-stage and to the very far left, a rather imposing fixed pulpit. Frida, a second-year engineering PhD student is about to occupy the stage to present her conference paper. Before her, a renowned researcher in the field has presented the opening keynote lecture. Professor Mark Potter is an impressive performer, and a large man. Frida is struck by how comfortable he looks in the situation. The pulpit seems to have diminished; lost authority. Professor Potter avails himself of all the possibilities it affords: For him it is a support and a facilitator. It seems to reinforce his authority and credibility.

Frida, however, is petite; she measures 155 cm. She knows that she tends to speak too softly. This is her second conference presentation, and the experience she brings with her from the first one won't help in this setting. She realizes that she would need to re-think, but does not know where to start. As her turn looms closer, her anxiety grows. The chairperson introduces her, and she takes her ascribed place behind the pulpit. Her anxiety and discomfort increases as she realizes that she almost disappears behind the pulpit. To make matters worse, the fixed microphone is too high. She has to appeal to the chairperson to help her adjust it. Her allotted time is ticking; she feels momentarily paralyzed; her mind is blank. She has to stand on her toes to achieve at least some contact with her audience. If she cannot see them out there in the dark, at least the ones sitting in the first few rows may see her face. For Frida, this presentation was an ordeal that lived with her for a long time. It eroded her self-confidence and she avoided conferences for the next year and a half even though she knew that the consequences would be detrimental to her career as a researcher. She wished she had been better prepared for different situational contingencies and material arrangement. She would have been better equipped to adapt; she might even have had the self-confidence to ignore the pulpit, request a mobile microphone, and place herself front-stage as one speaker did.

The vignette is an aggregated narrative that draws on several similar events at a number of conferences. In my conversations with the speakers after such performances, I became increasingly aware that the talk centered on the feelings of the presenters; on how their bodies felt out-of-place in the space; how their stomachs cramped and they felt sick; and how this bodily discomfort affected their talk and their actions. At one conference, a nonnative speaker of English, in spite of painstaking rehearsals, was so nervous already that the unexpected spatial and material arrangements disconcerted him to the extent that he completely froze, and after a very hesitant start could no longer continue. Many novice nonnative speakers of English already feel at a disadvantage when presenting at international conferences (Räisänen, 1999), and having to face the unexpected settings depicted here can be overwhelming. These factors need to be verbalized and problematized back-stage in a classroom setting. For example, mock conference events could be set up, where students practice in as natural a setting as possible—an auditorium rather than a classroom. Using the technology described and further developed by several authors in this volume, students could collectively view and compare professional conference presentations and compare them with their own, attending to the external modalities of the setting. They could discuss these in terms of inherent as well as unexpected constraints, and also reflect on ways in which they could use possible affordances to resist or overcome constraints. In the medical and healthcare literature, there are some very relevant articles, which could inform both students and teachers of communication for special purposes, e.g., Nordquist et al. (2011) and Poland et al. (2005). Another interesting area of literature to explore is that of activity theory and expansive learning (e.g., Engeström, Miettinen & Punamäki, 1999 and Sannino, Daniels & Gutiérrez, 2009). A broader multimodal approach would raise students' critical awareness and sensitize them to think about contingencies. For me, the most important effect of such training is that it fosters an important skill, namely the ability to improvise on the fly. This in turn builds self-confidence and flexibility.

To improve communication, therefore, would first and foremost require an understanding of the social practices in which the communication is located, how space is organized, what place speakers are ascribed within that space, what media may be available and are used and, more importantly, what agential powers the human as well as nonhuman entities may wield. Moreover, the media available are imbued with inscribed historical, cultural and situational uses from previous uses and practices, which means that time as well plays an important role.

So to end this chapter where I began, I would like once again to echo Barad:

> "We" are not outside observers of the world. Nor are we simply located at particular places in the world; rather, we are part of the world in its ongoing intra-activity. . . . Humans are part of the world-body space in its dynamic structuration.
>
> (Barad, 2003, p. 828)

NOTES

1. Intra-action, in contrast to interaction, is used by Barad (2003) to underscore that agencies are only distinct in a relational sense; they emerge and become distinct through their intra-action with and within their surroundings.
2. ELAN was developed by the Max Planck Institute for Psycholinguistics and has been extensively used by linguists to annotate multimodal data (Wittenburg et al., 2006). ELAN can be downloaded from http://tla.mpi.nl/tools/tla-tools/elan/.

REFERENCES

Barad, K. (2003). Posthumanist performativity: Toward an understanding of how matter comes to matter. *Signs: Journal of Women in Culture and Society, 28*(3), 801–831.

Barad, K. (2007). *Meeting the universe halfway: Quantum physics and the entanglement of matter and meaning.* Durham, NC: Duke University Press.

Bazerman, C. (1988). *Shaping written knowledge.* Madison, WI: University of Wisconsin Press.

Carlile, P., Nicolini, D., Langley, A., & Tsoukas, H. (Eds.). (2013). *How matter matters: Objects, artifacts, and materiality in organization studies.* Oxford: Oxford University Press.

Carter-Thomas, S., & Rowley-Jolivet, E. (2003). Analysing the scientific conference presentation (CP): A methodological overview of a multimodal genre. *ASp, 39–40,* 59–72.

Crawford Camiciottoli, B. (2009). Collective and individual identities in business studies lectures. In M. Gotti (Ed.), *Commonality and individuality in academic discourse* (pp. 141–160). Bern: Peter Lang.

Cumble, S., Weinert, C., Luparell, S., Conley, V., & Smith, J. (2005). Developing a scholarship community. *Journal of Nursing Scholarship, 37*(3), 289–293.

Dale, K., & Burrell, G. (2008). *The spaces of organisation and the organisation of space: Power, identity and materiality at work.* Basingstoke: Palgrave Macmillan.

Dubois, B. L. (1980). Genre and structure of biomedical speeches. *Forum Linguisticum, 5*(2), 140–169.

Dubois, B. L. (1982). "And the last slide please:" Regulatory function at biomedical meetings. *World Language English, 1*(2), 263–8.

Dubois, B. L. (1987). "Something in the order of around 40 to 44": Imprecise numerical expressions in biomedical slide talks. *Language in Society, 16*(4), 527–541.

Engeström, Y., Miettinen, R., & Punamäki, R-L. (1999). *Perspectives on activity theory.* Cambridge: Cambridge University Press.

Fenwick, T. (2014). Sociomateriality in medical practice and learning: Attuning to what matters. *Medical Education, 48*(1), 44–52.

Goffman, E. (1990). *The presentation of self in everyday life.* London: Penguin.

Happell, B. (2009). Presenting with precision: Preparing and delivering a polished conference presentation. *Nurse Researcher, 16*(3), 45–56.

Hardicre, J., Coad, J., & Dewitt, P. (2007). Ten steps to successful conference presentations. *British Journal of Nursing, 16*(7), 402–404.

Hood, S., & Forey, G. (2005). Introducing a conference presentation: Getting interpersonal with your audience. *Journal of English for Academic Purposes, 4*(4), 291–306.

Jewitt, C. (Ed.). (2014). *The Routledge handbook of multimodal analysis*. London: Routledge.
Lave, J., & Wenger, E. (1991). *Situated learning: Legitimate peripheral participation*. Cambridge: Cambridge University Press.
Miller, C. (1984). Genre as social action. *Quarterly Journal of Speech, 70*(2), 151–167.
Nordquist, J., Kitto, S., Peller, J., Ygge, J., & Reeves, S. (2011). Focusing on future learning environments: Exploring the roles of space and place for interprofessional education. *Journal of Professional Care, 25*(6), 391–393.
O'Halloran, K., & Smith, B.A. (2011). Multimodal studies. In K. O'Halloran, & B.A. Smith (Eds.), *Multimodal studies: Exploring issues and domains* (pp. 1–13). London: Routledge.
Orlikowski, W. (2007). Sociomaterial practices: Exploring technology at work. *Organization Studies, 28*(9), 1435–1448.
Orlikowski, W., & Scott, S.V. (2008). Sociomateriality: Challenging the separation of technology, work and organization. *Academy of Management Annals, 2*(1), 433–474.
Poland, B., Lehoux, P., Holmes, D., & Andrew, G. (2005). How place matters: Unpacking technology and power in health and social care. *Health & Social Care in the Community, 13*(2), 170–180.
Querol-Julián, M. (2011). *Evaluation in discussion sessions of conference paper presentations: A multimodal approach*. Saarbrücken: LAP Lambert Academic Publishing.
Querol-Julián, M., & Fortanet, I. (2012). Multimodal evaluation in academic discussion sessions: How do presenters act and react? *English for Specific Purposes, 31*(4), 271–283.
Räisänen, C. (1999). *The conference forum as a system of genres: A sociocultural study of academic conference practices in automotive crash-safety engineering*. Gothenburg: Acta Universitatis Gothoburgensis.
Räisänen, C. (2002). The conference forum: A system of interrelated genres and discursive practices. In E. Ventola, C. Shalom, & S. Thompson (Eds.), *The language of conferencing* (pp. 69–93). Frankfurt: Peter Lang.
Ravelli, L., & Stenglin, M. (2008). Feeling space: Interpersonal communication and spatial semiotics. In G. Antos, & E. Ventola (Eds.), *Handbook of interpersonal communication* (pp. 355–394). Berlin: Mouton de Gruyter.
Rowley-Jolivet, E. (1999). The pivotal role of conference papers in the network of scientific communication. *ASp, 23–26*, 179–196.
Rowley-Jolivet, E., & Carter-Thomas, S. (2005). The rhetoric of conference presentation introductions: Context, argument and interaction. *International Journal of Applied Linguistics, 15*(1), 45–70.
Sannino, A., Daniels, H., & Gutiérrez, K. (2009). *Learning and expanding with activity theory*. Cambridge: Cambridge University Press.
Scollon, R. (1998). *Mediated discourse as social interaction*. Harlow: Longman.
Shalom, C. (1993). Established and evolving spoken research process genres: Plenary lecture and poster session discussions at academic conferences. *English for Specific Purposes, 12*(1), 37–50.
Shalom, C. (2002). The academic conference: A forum for enacting genre knowledge. In E. Ventola, C. Shalom, & S. Thompson (Eds.), *The language of conferencing* (pp. 51–68). Frankfurt: Peter Lang.
Shotter, J. (2013). Reflection on sociomateriality and dialogicality in organization studies: From 'inter-' to 'intra-thinking' in performing practices. In P. Carlile, D. Nicolini, A. Langley, & H. Tsoukas (Eds.), *How matter matters: Objects, artifacts, and materiality in organization studies* (pp. 32–57). Oxford: Oxford University Press.

Swales, J. (1981). *Aspects of article introductions.* Birmingham, UK: Aston University Language Studies.

Swales, J. (1990). *Genre analysis: English in academic and research settings.* Cambridge: Cambridge University Press.

Thompson, S. (2002). "As the story unfolds": The uses of narratives in research presentations. In E. Ventola, C. Shalom, & S. Thompson (Eds.), *The language of conferencing* (pp. 147–168). Frankfurt: Peter Lang.

Tsoukas, H., & Chia, R. (2002). On organizational becoming: Rethinking organizational change. *Organization Science, 13*(5), 567–582.

van Marrewijk, A., & Yanow, D. (Eds.). (2010). *Organizational spaces: Rematerializing the workaday world.* Cheltenham: Edward Elgar.

Ventola, E., Shalom, C., & Thompson, S. (Eds.). (2002). *The language of conferencing* Frankfurt: Peter Lang.

Wertsch, J. (1993). *Voices of the mind: Sociocultural approach to mediated action.* Harvard: Harvard University Press.

Wittenburg, P., Brugman, H., Russel, A., Klassmann, A., & Sloetjes, H. (2006). ELAN: A professional framework for multimodality research. Proceedings of LREC 2006, Fifth International Conference on Language Resources and Evaluation. Retrieved from http://www.lrec-conf.org/proceedings/lrec2006/pdf/153_pdf.pdf.

Wulff, S., Swales, J., & Keller, K. (Eds.). (2009). "We have about seven minutes for questions": The discussion sessions from a specialized conference. *English for Specific Purposes, 28*(2), 79–92.

Yanow, D. (2010). Giving voice to space: Academic practices and the material world. In *Organizational spaces: Rematerializing the workaday world* (pp. 139–158). Cheltenham: Edward Elgar.

Ziman, J.M. (1968). *Public knowledge: An essay concerning the social dimension of science.* Cambridge: Cambridge University Press.

7 Elaborating Explanations During OpenCourseWare Humanities Lectures

The Interplay of Verbal and Nonverbal Strategies

Belinda Crawford Camiciottoli

7.1 INTRODUCTION

In instructional contexts, academics are called upon to explain theories and concepts, as well as their own thoughts and opinions as experts in their particular field. Explanation is therefore a crucial component of the learning process where language is used to transmit information in a way that enables novices to comprehend. According to the Merriam-Webster online concise encyclopedia, explanations are a "set of statements that makes intelligible the existence or occurrence of an object, event, or state of affairs."[1] From a linguistic perspective, explanations are complex phenomena that may take the form of definition, exemplification, reformulation, and argumentation (e.g., discursive patterns based on a claim followed by a justification, or cause and effect sequences). These discourse functions may also be combined to produce elaborate explanatory passages. With particular reference to the argumentative dimension of explanations, Weimer (1977, p. 5) affirms that "explanation is inherently a matter of argument." A typical argumentative pattern is seen in what von Wright (1971) characterizes as *causal explanation*. Here the relationship between two events is explained in terms of the second event being a consequence, result or effect of the first.[2] Causal explanations are encoded on a linguistic level by lexical items such as *because, so, in order to, as a result* and *the reason why*. Sbisá (1987) mentions other types of linguistic markers associated with explanation, including items such as *namely, that is* and *for example,* which are used to elaborate and exemplify propositional content. The explanatory role of such items, also called *code glosses* by Hyland (2005), is evident in their metadiscursive function through which writers and speakers interact with readers or listeners in order to clarify intended meanings and guide comprehension. Explanations have also been studied in terms of speech act theory (Sbisá, 1987, p. 11), where the verb *explain* could be interpreted as a performative verb used to "metacommunicatively present a speech act" that will then be uttered by the speaker, e.g., *now I will explain it.* Thus, we see that explanation is a multifaceted feature of discourse that may manifest itself in numerous ways and can be investigated from diverse theoretical and analytical perspectives.

Some studies in the area of academic discourse have provided insights into how explanations emerge in both written and spoken texts used for teaching purposes. In a corpus based on extracts from introductory level textbooks from different academic disciplines, Hyland (1999) found that code glosses were the second most frequent explanatory device after logical connectives. Furthermore, Bondi's (1999) study of economics textbooks showed that writers in this discipline make frequent use of discursive patterns based on general statements supported by exemplification in explanatory passages. In addition, argumentative patterns of the type claim → justification-of-claim and claim → counterclaim were also prominent. For spoken academic discourse, and with particular reference to the lecture genre as the focus of this chapter, some small-scale studies have shown that repetition and reformulation are important features of university lectures found in the context of explanation (Bamford, 2002; Giménez-Moreno, 2012). Similarly, exemplification that helps learners understand by providing a concrete 'connection' to the real world has been shown to be characteristic of academic lectures (see Young, 1990; Crawford Camiciottoli, 2007). A study on discourse functions in lectures by Deroey and Taverniers (2011) revealed that exemplification could be encoded explicitly through lexical items that incorporated *example* or *instance,* but could also be signaled in a more ambiguous way using discourse markers such as *so* and *you know.* Nesi and Basturkmen's (2006) large-scale study of lexical bundles in a corpus of 160 university lectures across a range of disciplines found that *if you look at* used to signal an upcoming exemplification was among the most frequent.

From the above discussion, it is clear that the process of explanation is a vital component of the learning experience in university classrooms. However, a lecture is obviously much more than just a verbal message delivered to students by the speaker. In fact, today's lectures typically include images or audiovisual input that can be easily incorporated by means of presentation software such as PowerPoint. Brabazon (2006) goes so far as to describe lectures as "multi-modal formations, using sound, vision, gestures, and often scent and touch." In the following section, I shift my focus to the multimodal dimension of academic lectures, with particular reference to its role in the context of explanation.

7.2 MULTIMODALITY AND LECTURES

The important contribution of other communicative modes beyond the verbal message in human interactions has long been recognized, dating as far back as Darwin's (1890/1989) studies of facial expressions and gestures. In more recent times, some systematic accounts of communication from a multimodal perspective have been offered. For example, Poyatos (2002, p. 103) defines communication in terms of a "Basic Triple Structure" that comprises verbal and nonverbal modes, i.e., "language-paralanguage-kinesics." There has also been some pioneering work by linguists who have focused on how semiotic resources beyond language contribute to meaning in social practices. Kress and van Leeuwen (2006) describe a 'grammar' of visual images that analyzes their unique features such as compositional arrangement of elements and colors in a way that is inspired by Hallidayan systemic functional grammar. Similarly, Baldry and Thibault (2006) propose an innovative approach for the analysis of multimodal discourse, i.e., discourse that integrates different semiotic systems that may comprise linguistic, visual, audio and gestural resources, also in this case from a systemic functional perspective. They describe the multimodal transcription of discourse as "a way of revealing both the codeployment of semiotic resources and their dynamic unfolding in time along textually constrained and enabled pathways of trajectories" (Baldry & Thibault, 2006, p. xvi). For instance, a multimodal transcription of a television commercial may be structured into a series of frames from the video recording, which are described in terms of the corresponding image, action and sound, and then interpreted in terms of their metafunctions within the communicative context (Thibault, 2000). In the same way, a video-recorded academic lecture may be transcribed using a multimodal format where visual images extracted from the streaming video are accompanied by the corresponding verbal text, as well as functional descriptions of the co-occurring nonverbal behaviors (Crawford Camiciottoli, 2007). Thus, multimodal analysis and transcription enable discourse analysts to capture a multiplicity of communicative modes that are simultaneously woven together to create meaning in a particular context (Norris, 2004).

Especially in the last few years, there has been growing interest in multimodal discourse analysis (see Jewitt, 2009; O'Halloran, 2011; O'Halloran & Smith, 2013). This trend has likely been impacted by the rapid acceleration in digital technology that has led to the development of software designed specifically for the multimodal annotation of texts (e.g., O'Halloran, E & Tan 2014). However, advances in technology have also greatly expanded possibilities to gain access to multimodal texts. Indeed, forms of multimodal discourse in digital formats that were previously beyond the reach of many analysts are now increasingly available on Internet platforms. Thus, we can expect to find an increasing amount of language research with a multimodal focus, as aptly expressed by O'Halloran and Smith (2013, p. 3): "The ongoing development of interactive digital techniques, along with the increasingly collaborative nature of research in the 21st century, points to a period of further growth in coming years within this field."

Moving closer to the focus of the present study, the multimodal dimension of communication that takes place in instructional settings has been the topic of a number of pedagogically oriented discourse studies, highlighting "the complex ways in which image, gesture, gaze, interaction with objects, body posture, writing, and speech interact in the classroom production of school subject knowledge" (Jewitt, 2008, p. 249). Much of this research has been carried out in mathematics or science education at the level of secondary education, providing insights into how nonverbal communicative modes may be integrated with speech during explanations (see O'Halloran, 1998; Kress et al., 2001; Weinberg, Fukawa-Connelly & Wiesner, 2013). With particular reference to the role of gesturing during explanation, Pozzer-Ardenghi and Roth (2005) analyzed the gestures that accompanied explanations of the scientific content represented in visual images during both secondary school and university-level ecology lectures. Their analysis was based on McNeill's (1992) descriptive and functional classification of hand and arm gestures which includes beats (vague rhythmic hand movements used to accent words), iconic gestures (spatial descriptions of content or specific lexical items), metaphoric gestures (representations of ideas or abstract concepts) and deictic gestures (indication of some referent that may be present or removed from the context). The authors concluded that gestures are an important meaning-making resource in science discourse that can enhance understanding. In instructional settings, gestures may also co-occur not only with speech, but also with gaze directed outward towards the student audience as a way to nonverbally focus students' attention (Coleman, 2006; Crawford Camiciottoli, 2007).[3]

Because research on the nonverbal aspects of explanations of concepts in classroom discourse has been limited mainly to scientific fields (e.g., see O'Halloran, Podlasov, Chua, Tisse, Lim & Smith, 2014, for analysis of MIT online mathematics lecture), it seems important to expand the focus to include other disciplinary areas. In the humanities, for example, knowledge is often derived from philosophical, historical or critical reflections rather than empirical evidence. This could result in different approaches to explanation that are based on diverse verbal patterns and nonverbal cues. In an effort to address this gap in the literature, this study aims to acquire a better understanding of the interplay between the linguistic expression of explanation and the nonverbal signals that may co-occur with it during humanities lectures. More specifically, I seek to answer the following research questions:

1. Which linguistic markers of explanation are used by the lecturers?
2. Which nonverbal features are used to accompany the linguistic markers and what are their functions?
3. How do nonverbal features interact with verbal expressions of explanation to construct meaning and reinforce understanding?

7.3 METHODOLOGY

7.3.1 The Dataset

The lectures utilized for this study were digital recordings collected from Yale University's Open Courses website.[4] Among the many institutions of higher education that now provide OpenCourseWare (OCW) resources,

Yale University offers a particularly rich and well-articulated selection of lectures, in addition to related learning materials from complete introductory courses across a range of academic disciplines that broadly represent natural sciences, social sciences and the humanities. The materials include video and audio recordings, the corresponding transcripts, syllabi, reading materials and lesson handouts. All the lectures were video/audio-recorded on the Yale University campus and were transcribed by people, rather than by machine transcription software.[5] They are offered as free and accessible to the general public. Indeed, their website states that "the aim of the project is to expand access to educational materials for all who wish to learn."

Five lectures dedicated to topics in the field of humanities were selected to comprise the dataset of the study. In particular, the lectures represent the disciplines of philosophy, history, English, religious studies and African American studies. The decision to focus the analysis within this particular disciplinary area was based on two considerations. First, as previously noted, because most research has looked at multimodal features of classroom discourse in the sciences, a shift to a disciplinary area with a different epistemological tradition and pedagogical aims has the potential to offer fresh insights. Second, among the various courses and lectures available on the Open Yale Courses website, with respect to other disciplinary areas, those dealing with the humanities offered greater choice and variety to compile a dataset that would be more representative of the field. At the same time, the fact that all the lectures dealt with humanities topics assured that what emerged from the analysis would not be impacted by radically different types of content, and could thus be more accurately linked to the features of interest to this study.

To identify the specific lectures to be included in the dataset, I carried out preliminary viewings in order to select those recordings that had high-quality images of lecturers who were kept in the focus of the video camera for most of the time. In other words, lectures in which the video camera panned away from the speaker to accompanying visuals for extended periods of time were excluded since they would not permit systematic observation of the speakers' nonverbal signals. Table 7.1 provides an overview of the five lectures that conformed to these criteria.

As can be seen, the five lectures had roughly the same duration, and the speakers included three males and two females. All of the lecturers are described on the Open Yale Courses website as distinguished professors and scholars with extensive teaching experience, as was also evident from the biographical information presented on their course homepages.

The five lecture videos were downloaded in .mp4 format, along with their corresponding transcripts files that are also available on the course homepages. From the digital recordings, it was possible to clearly hear the vocal production of all the lecturers and thus determine that they were all native speakers of US English. To verify the accuracy of the transcripts,

Table 7.1 The Yale lecture dataset

Lecture	Course	Lecture Title	Lecturer	Duration
1	Philosophy 176: Death	The Nature of Persons: Dualism vs. Physicalism (Spring 2007)	Male	41 min
2	English 310: Modern Poetry	Robert Frost (Spring 2007)	Male	46 min
3	African American Studies 162: African American History: From Emancipation to the Present	Public Policy and Presidential Politics (Spring 2010)	Male	46 min
4	Religious Studies 145: Introduction to the Old Testament (Hebrew Bible)	Critical Approaches to the Bible: Introduction to Genesis 12–50 (Fall 2006)	Female	48 min
5	History 116: The American Revolution	Outraged Colonials: The Stamp Act Crisis (Spring 2010)	Female	41 min

I listened to each lecture while following along with the transcripts. The lectures were delivered using a "conversational style" (Dudley-Evans, 1994, p. 148), with lecturers appearing to speak spontaneously, while only occasionally referring to notes. In this type of lecture, the content has been planned, but not the actual sequences of words used to discuss it, resulting in a natural-sounding delivery. On the whole, the transcripts were highly accurate representations of the verbal content of the lectures, even if normal speech dysfluencies such as filled pauses, false starts and repetitions had not been transcribed in most cases. However, this lack of transcription detail is not problematic since the focus of the present study is on other features.

All five lectures can be described as frontal and essentially monologic with very little input from students, thus reflecting a noninteractive style (Morell, 2004). Only the philosophy lecture contained two questions posed by students to which the lecturer responded. The noninteractive format implemented here seems to be at odds with current trends in higher education that encourage greater instructor-student interaction (see Ernst & Colthorpe, 2007; White, 2011). However, noninteractive lectures may have been deliberately selected for the OpenCourseWare platform as likely the most viable format for a remote Internet audience.

All the lecturers were positioned at the front of what appeared to be a large lecture hall that was equipped with a podium, a blackboard and a screen for projecting visuals. Some supporting images were projected during the English lecture, while a short video clip was shown to the audience during the African American studies lecture. The philosophy and religious studies lecturers made use only of the blackboard using the "talk and chalk" format (Mason, 1994, p. 203), while the history lecturer did not integrate any type of visual modalities during the delivery of her lecture.

7.3.2 The Analysis

The first step was to determine which verbal features could be interpreted as manifestations of explanatory processes within the lecture dataset. Given the complexities of explanation as a discursive phenomenon and the variety of forms through which it may be encoded, methods of corpus linguistics were implemented to both identify and extract potentially corresponding linguistic features. The transcripts of the five lectures were compiled into a single file and then processed with text-mining software program WMatrix (Rayson, 2008), a powerful corpus analysis tool, which is capable of performing automatic semantic tagging. More specifically, each word is annotated or tagged according to pre-established semantic categories based on 21 over-arching domains (e.g., *General & Abstract Terms, The Body & the Individual, Education, Money & Commerce, Emotional Actions, States & Processes*), which are further articulated into over 200 specific tags. In corpus linguistics, this approach can be described as inductive or *corpus-driven* as linguistic features of interest emerge from the data itself, rather than deductive or *corpus-based,* which starts from a list of predefined list of features to be analyzed in the data (Tognini-Bonelli, 2001, p. 2). This procedure led to the identification of three key types of verbal explanation across the five lectures, i.e., the linguistic elements that encode (a) the speech act *explain,* (b) exemplification and (c) argumentation (von Wright, 1971; Sbisá, 1987; Weimer, 1997). This semantic tagging process will be illustrated in further detail in the next section. All instances of the three types of explanation were then marked in the five lecture transcripts.

Once the instances of explanation had been identified, it was necessary to identify potentially meaningful nonverbal signals of the lectures that might accompany the verbal explanations. For this purpose, I used the software program ELAN, which allows for complex multimodal annotations in digital audio and video resources.[6] The software permits users to create and insert annotations that are synchronized with streaming videos. Annotations may include the transcript of the speech production, as well as any number of user-defined annotations that code and mark particular verbal and/or nonverbal features of interest. The annotations are organized and displayed in multiple layers or tiers under the streaming digital resource (Wittenburg et al., 2006), which allows for complete visualization of the resources that contribute to the multimodal dimension of the speech event.

Annotation in ELAN of each of the five lecture videos was undertaken in various phases. First, a *Transcript* tier was created directly under the sound wave viewer of the corresponding .wav file that had been extracted from the .mp4 video files and uploaded separately into ELAN. This tier served to display the lexical items that corresponded to the three types of explanation coded in the transcripts, which were inserted in alignment with the corresponding speech production of the streaming videos. A second tier labeled *Explanation* was created to annotate each instance of verbal explanation according to one of the three previously identified types: the speech act *explain,* exemplification, or argumentation. Thanks to the audio waveform viewer, it was also possible to identify prosodic stress used by the lecturers during stretches of discourse in explanatory passages, thus calling attention to them and prioritizing information for listeners.[7] Therefore, an additional tier labeled *Prosody* was inserted to annotate any paralinguistic stress that occurred during verbal explanations.

In a second phase, each video was viewed again in ELAN to pinpoint non-verbal features that accompanied the previously annotated verbal expressions of explanations. From the preliminary overview of the lecture videos, I found that I was able to observe most clearly hand/arm gestures and the direction of the speaker's gaze. However, because the lecturers had not been filmed to show facial close-ups, the analysis of gaze was limited to whether the speaker was gazing downwards (e.g., towards the podium or notes) or outwards towards the student audience. As a result, the analysis of the non-verbal dimension of the lectures will focus mainly on these two features, which were then annotated in three separate tiers: *Gaze, Gesture-description* and *Gesture-function.* The *Gaze* tier was associated with two possible annotations, i.e., 'Down' or 'Out.' For gestures, it seemed important not only to provide a physical description, but also an interpretation of its function in the context of explanation. Thus, a parent tier *Gesture* was created to annotate, first of all, the presence of a gesture, to which two referring tiers were then associated. First, the *Gesture-description* tier provided for a wide range of different descriptions that emerged during the analysis of the lecture videos. Following Querol-Julián (2011), annotations were created based on abbreviated descriptions of the gesture in terms of hand and arm movements. PalmUMUp (palm up and moving upwards), HandsRotOut (hands rotating outward) and FingRing (fingers forming a ring and moving outward) are examples of descriptive annotations inserted into this tier (see Appendix A for the complete list). Then, for the *Gesture-function* tier, I created a series of annotations that were inspired by two previous studies. Kendon (2004) identified three pragmatic functions of gestures in conversational data, namely *modal* (to express certainty/uncertainty), *performative* (to illustrate the type of speech act that the speaker is doing) and *parsing* (to demarcate different units within a stretch of speech). Weinberg,

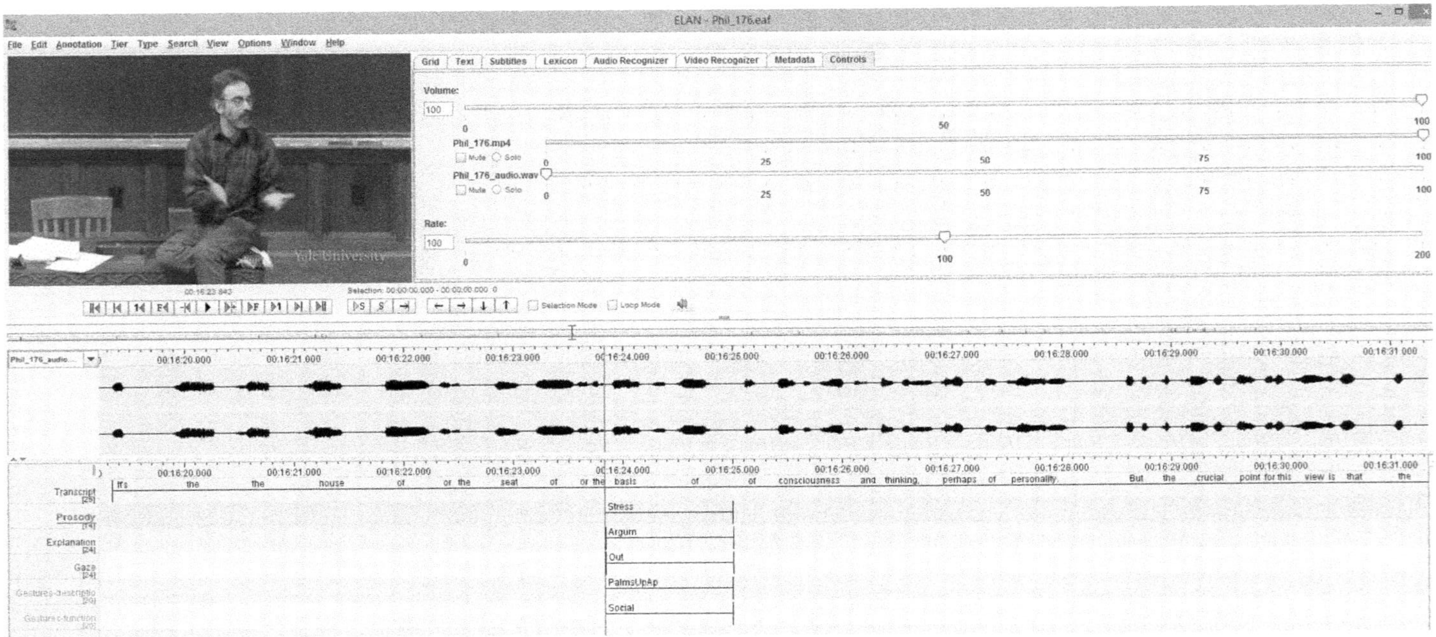

Figure 7.1 Screenshot of multimodal annotation (Source: ELAN software)[8]

Fukawa-Connelly and Wiesner (2013) classified the function of gestures in classroom discourse as *indexical* (to indicate a position), *representational* (to represent an object or idea) and *social* (to emphasize the message or increase the speaker's immediacy with the audience). In an effort to interpret the functions of gestures in the lecture videos as accurately and exhaustively as possible, I opted to utilize both classifications and thus created annotations corresponding to all six functions. For illustrative purposes, a screenshot of Lecture 1 (Philosophy) as elaborated in ELAN is provided in Figure 7.1.

The figure above shows the point in the streaming video where a series of annotations have been inserted to classify the verbal expression of explanation and the accompanying nonverbal features. In particular, the argumentative explanation *on the basis of* (Argum) is accompanied by prosodic stress as shown by the audio wave above the words, which was annotated in the *Prosody* tier (Stress). In addition, the lecturer gazes outwards towards the audience (*Gaze* tier—Out). At the same time, the presence of a gesture was identified. It was then further described as palms up and moving apart (*Gesture-description* tier—PalmsUpAp), which was interpreted as having a social function (*Gesture-function* tier—Social) to give greater emphasis to the explanation and highlight its importance for the audience.

7.4 RESULTS AND DISCUSSION

7.4.1 Linguistic Features of Explanation

As previously mentioned, the dataset compiled from the five lecture transcripts was processed with the software WMatrix (Rayson, 2008). This procedure generated a key semantic domain cloud, i.e. a visual representation of which semantic domains are significantly frequent in the dataset.[9] The key semantic domain cloud is reproduced in Figure 7.2.

Although all the semantic domains displayed in cloud are frequent across the five lectures, those in larger fonts have particularly high frequencies. By clicking on each semantic domain in the cloud, it is possible to see all the various lexical items that have been assigned to it by the software. These items can then be displayed in lists or concordances to facilitate further scrutiny. Through this procedure, I determined that there were three semantic domains whose lexical items could be conceptually mapped onto the previously identified types of explanation. The specific tags of these domains are as follows:

1. *Speech_acts,* which contained items based on the lemma *explain* → the speech act *explain*
2. *Generally_kinds_examples,* which contained items based on the lemmas *example* and *instance,* as well as *such as* → exemplification
3. *Cause&Effect/Connection,* which contained a range of lexical items linked to reasoning processes → argumentation

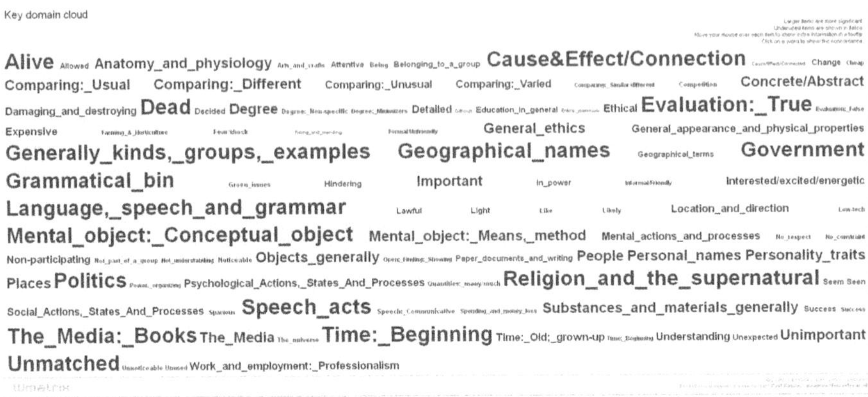

Figure 7.2 Screenshot of key semantic domains (Source: WMatrix, Rayson, 2008)

Not surprisingly, all three of the above-described tags appear in the largest font size, suggesting that the lexical items contained within them are highly characteristic of the lecture genre. This was the basis for my decision to focus the analysis on these three types of explanation.

While the items associated with the speech act *explain* and exemplification could be easily attributed to explanatory discourse on the part of the lecturers, the wide range of items contained in the *Cause&Effect/Connection* tag linked to argumentation were not as straightforward. More specifically, it was necessary to examine each of these items in its context of usage to distinguish those that reflected explanations of concepts, events, situations or entities from those that did not, and therefore needed to be removed from the data. This process is illustrated in examples (1) and (2) in which the lecturers used the item *reason*. In example (1), *reasons* is clearly being used to explain a particular situation. In contrast, in example (2), *reason* is used as a verb in a descriptive capacity and not in an explicitly explanatory sense. Items of this type were eliminated from the dataset.

(example 1) So for all of these *reasons*, these acts are problematic, threatening, frightening and get people thinking. (Lecture 5/History)

(example 2) We are bodies that can think. We are bodies that can plan. We are bodies that can *reason*. We are bodies that can feel. (Lecture 1/Philosophy)

Following this procedure to filter out *Cause&Effect/Connection* items that were not used in an explanatory context, a total of 34 different items remained that could be classified as explanation in the form of argumentation. The complete list is shown in the Appendix B, with items ranked according to their frequencies indicated in parentheses. It is interesting to note that the most frequent item that encoded argumentation (*why*, N = 12) was sometimes used in the interrogative form as a sort of interactional rhetorical question that the lecturer then proceeded to answer in the context of the explanation, as shown in example (3).

(example 3) The construction of Marduk's ziggurat is represented as displeasing to God. *Why?* There are very many possible interpretations . . . (Lecture 4/Religious Studies)

Table 7.2 shows the distribution of the three types of verbal explanation across the dataset. As can be seen, overall the speech act *explain* was used rarely by the lecturers and verbal expressions of *exemplification* were also rather infrequent with the exception of Lecture 3 where they accounted for 40% of the speaker's explanations.

Because exemplification has been found to be a relatively prominent feature of lectures in other disciplines (see Young, 1990; Nesi & Basturkmen, 2006; Crawford Camiciottoli, 2007), the low frequencies here could be impacted by the humanistic content of the lectures that appears to require more elaborate and complex types of explanation. In fact, the majority of the explanations in this dataset were encoded through various lexical items associated with argumentation, accounting for 60% in Lecture 3, 80% in Lecture 2 and Lecture 4, 92% in Lecture 1 and 95% in Lecture 5. Examples (4–6) below illustrate some of the interesting ways the lecturers used such features to formulate their explanations.

(example 4) He actually was protesting against the *implications* of the Stamp Act. (Lecture 5/History)

(example 5) Today literary criticism has a slightly different *connotation* from what it was in the 19th century, so people prefer the term source criticism. (Lecture 4/Religious Studies)

(example 6) There's this always lingering *connection* between African Americans and the "Jewish question" in the Middle East and Palestine. (Lecture 3/African American Studies)

Table 7.2 Types of verbal explanation in the Yale lecture dataset

	Lecture 1		Lecture 2		Lecture 3		Lecture 4		Lecture 5	
	N	%	N	%	N	%	N	%	N	%
Speech act *explain*	1	4	1	10	–	–	–	–	–	–
Exemplification	1	4	1	10	4	40	7	20	1	5
Argumentation	22	92	8	80	6	60	28	80	18	95
Total	24	100	10	100	10	100	35	100	19	100

7.4.2 Nonverbal Features in Explanations

Table 7.3 illustrates the co-occurrence of prosodic stress, gaze towards the audience and gesturing with the verbal expressions of explanation, reflecting Poyatos's (2002, p. 103) model of communication based on "language-paralanguage-kinesics." The figures report the frequency counts of the nonverbal features that occurred in each lecture (N), and the percentage of (N) that was used simultaneously with verbal explanations. In addition, the table shows the percentage breakdown for the functions of the gestures produced by each lecturer according to categories illustrated in the methodology section.

As is evident from the figures reported in the table, hand and arm gestures co-occurred very frequently during verbal explanations, accounting for roughly 80–90% of all the explanatory episodes across the dataset. Gaze directed out towards the audience also co-occurred in relatively high percentages, with the exception of Lecture 2, which registered only 50% co-occurrence. The general tendency of these lecturers to accompany their verbal explanations with gesturing and outward gaze suggests that these nonverbal signals play a key interactional role in explanations (Hyland, 2005). More specifically, they could reflect an attempt to engage with the

Table 7.3 Co-occurrence of nonverbal features with verbal explanations

	Prosodic stress		Gaze outwards		Gesturing		
	N	%	N	%	N	%	Gesture function
Lecture 1	14	58	22	92	20	83	• social (75%) • representational (20%) • indexical (5%)
Lecture 2	4	40	5	50	9	90	• social (67%) • unclassifiable (22%) • representational (11%)
Lecture 3	4	40	8	80	9	90	• social (78%) • parsing (11%) • unclassifiable (11%)
Lecture 4	22	63	27	77	32	91	• social (63%) • unclassifiable (16%) • representational (9%) • parsing (9%) • indexical (3%)
Lecture 5	10	53	17	89	17	89	• social (82%) • indexical (12%) • parsing (6%)

audiences as much as possible, and also to offset to some extent the distance imposed by the physical setting in which the lecturers are positioned remotely from the audience. The following examples illustrate patterns of co-occurrence that emerged from the multimodal analysis. In example (7), the lecturer incorporates two types of verbal explanation into this passage, i.e., exemplification *(example)* and argumentation *(cause),* and reinforces his explanation by gazing outwards towards the audience while gesturing with one hand chopping into the other (HandChop) to depict the action of 'pricking.' In example (8), the lecturer emphasizes her explanation of why the text's focus changes by gazing directly at the audience and gesturing with palms up and moving outwards (PalmsUMOut) when posing the question *why?* before she proceeds to provide the answer.

(example 7) I gave the *example* pricking my body. That's a physical process that *causes* some sorts of changes in the mental processes occurring in my soul. (Lecture 1/Philosophy)

(example 8) So God's focus has shifted dramatically, the text's focus has shifted dramatically. *Why?* When you get to the end of Genesis 11 . . . (Lecture 4/Religious Studies)

Thus, when gaze and gesturing are combined with verbal explanation, they reflect a multiplicity of semiotic resources that are used to create meaning in the instructional setting.

Prosodic stress instead did not accompany verbal explanations at such high percentages, ranging from a minimum of 40% to a maximum of 60% co-occurrence. Further analysis revealed that prosodic stress did not accompany either of the two instances of verbal explanation encoded by the speech act *explain* and only 4 out of the 14 instances of exemplification (see Table 7.2). Thus, prosodic stress tends to be a strategy favored by the lecturers when using more complex argumentative forms of explanation, as shown in the examples below where the lecturers prosodically stress the words *entails* (example 9), and *reasons* and *painfully* (example 10) within these explanatory passages.

(example 9) Now, this guile of his, because that's what it *entails,* this guile is something temperamental, I think. (Lecture 2/English)

(example 10) Civil rights activists are horrified, for *reasons* I hope are *painfully* obvious to you at this point. (Lecture 3/African American Studies)

As can be seen from Appendix A, a wide range of annotations was necessary to kinesically describe the gestures that co-occurred with explanations. The gestures also varied considerably in terms of how they were used by the five individual lecturers. For example, some had what could be described as an understated style of gesturing, i.e., mostly smallish hand gestures with palms in different positions and a restricted range of motion. Others were more 'exuberant' with an extended repertoire of hand and arm movements and a wider range of movement. However, for reasons of space, I will not discuss all the various gestures that emerged on a purely descriptive level, but will instead focus mainly on their functional dimension, which will be illustrated by some of the most interesting cases.

Referring again to Table 7.3, we see that four of the six lecture functions outlined in the methodology section emerged from the analysis. While *social, representational, indexical* and *parsing* functions could be interpreted from the lecturers' gestures, *performative* and *modal* were instead absent. A possible explanation for this absence could be linked to the nature of the communicative event itself. During lectures, expert academics aim to transmit factual knowledge to novices, and would therefore seem to have little use for modal gestures that communicate personal assessments of certainty/uncertainty during explanations. In addition, the lack of performative gestures to illustrate the speech act that is being performed could be linked to the fact that only two explanations in the entire dataset took the form of the speech act *explain*. Moreover, in an instructional setting that is routine for participants, there would seem to be little reason to use gestures to reinforce the act of explaining. Finally, in three of the five lectures there were some gestures that did not have a clearly interpretable function in the communicative context and were thus categorized as *unclassifiable*. Weinberg, Fukawa-Connelly and Wiesner (2013) noted similar issues of ambiguity in gestures that may prove difficult even for expert observers to interpret.

Table 7.3 also shows that gestures classified as *social* accounted for a large majority across all five lectures, ranging from a minimum of 63% to a maximum of 82%. This type of gesture is used to reinforce the message by accompanying speech with vague movements of the hands in various positions, e.g., palm(s)/up/down/sideways and moving up/down/out/apart. These gestures are essentially those described as beats or underliners by McNeill (1992).

An example of gesturing with the *social* function is visible in Figure 7.3. Here the English lecturer gestures with hands rotating at the center of the body to call attention to the argumentative item *results from* when explaining the reason for a particular feature of a poem by Robert Frost: *The special sound of Frost's poems results from the tension between these pairs of opposing forces.*

Although less frequent, gestures performing a *representational* function appeared in four out of the five lectures. In these cases, the lecturer produced a gesture that in some way represents an object or an idea, corresponding to McNeill's (1992) *iconic* or *metaphoric* gestures that may be either *pictographic* to depict the shape of the referent, or *kinetographic* to describe a movement or action. Figure 7.4 provides an illustration of a representational gesture. Here the lecturer is using the argumentative term *link*. Her hands form a square space that oscillates right and left (HandsSqSpM) to represent the kinetic action of linking two entities together in the following explanation: *All of those sections very often that link stories are attributed to the P source.*

Figure 7.3 A social gesture (Lecture 2/English)[10]

Indexical and *parsing* gestures were rather infrequent, each occurring during verbal explanations in only three out of five lectures. Figure 7.5 shows how an indexical gesture, corresponding to McNeill's (1992) *deictic* category, was used by a lecturer to indicate the discourse deictic 'this' in the explanatory passage based on the argumentative element *reasons: For all of these reasons, this would not be a popular thing.*

Figure 7.4 A representational gesture (Lecture 4/Religious Studies)[11]

Figure 7.5 An indexical gesture (Lecture 5/History)[12]

Parsing gestures are instead used to separate a stretch of discourse into separate units. An example is shown in Figure 7.6, where the lecturer gestures with hands sweeping outwards away from the body (HandsSwOut) to visually distinguish 'African Americans' from 'the Jewish question' when using the argumentative device *connection* in the following explanation: *There's this always lingering connection between African Americans and the Jewish question in the Middle East and Palestine.*

The above analysis suggests that the use of gestures to enrich the verbal message is often linked to explanations of the argumentative type, rather than the speech act *explain* or exemplification. Because the former tend to be more complex, they may be perceived by speakers as requiring additional semiotic resources to clarify meaning.

To conclude this section, I would like to briefly comment on the proxemic dimension of the five lectures. Proxemics refers to how people use body posturing and spatial positioning in a physical setting to communicate nonverbally (Hall, 1966). Although this aspect of nonverbal communication was not the focus of the present study, it nonetheless contributed to some interesting differences that are worth mentioning. As illustrated by the figures above, most of the lecturers positioned themselves at the lecture podium and remained there for the duration of the lecture, at most moving a few feet away to the right or to the left, or to the blackboard behind them. However, one lecturer positioned himself closer to the audience, at times sitting on the desk (see Figure 7.1), or often walking back and forth at the front of the lecture hall with a wide range of movement. Thus, even among the limited number of participants in this study, there was considerable variation

Figure 7.6 A parsing gesture (Lecture 3/African American Studies)[13]

in their nonverbal behaviors at various levels. It is important to recognize that all types of nonverbal communication depend very much on individual style and proclivity. As Galloway (1972, p. 11) notes, "A nonverbal cue may manifest itself because of a personal characteristic, perceived role and situation."

7.5 CONCLUDING REMARKS

The multimodal analysis implemented in this study has shed some light on the characteristics of verbal expressions of explanation and their accompanying nonverbal signals in humanities lectures. The first finding of interest emerged from the analysis of linguistic markers of explanation. These humanities lecturers seemed to prefer more complex argumentative forms over simpler explanatory strategies, e.g., exemplification that is common in other disciplinary areas (see Young, 1990; Crawford Camiciottoli, 2007). This could be linked to the epistemological tradition of humanities disciplines in which the construction of knowledge often involves philosophical, historical, cultural or critical reflections that require more elaborate patterns of verbalization. In addition, the fact that all five lecturers often accompanied their explanations with gaze directed towards the audience and with various types of gestures, and sometimes also with prosodic stress, suggests that nonverbal communication is an important component of explanatory passages in humanities lectures. Most of the gesturing corresponded to the social function with the aim to better engage the audience while highlighting particularly salient aspects of the explanation. However, there were also gestures that elaborated explanations in a more explicit way, performing also representational, indexical and parsing functions. Thus, the linguistic expressions of explanation and the co-occurring nonverbal signals seemed to work synergistically on an interpersonal level to reinforce meaning in order to enhance comprehension, but also to promote a classroom atmosphere that facilitates learning.

From a methodological perspective, this study has shown how multimodal annotation software can be used to achieve highly articulated descriptions of verbal and nonverbal interplay during lectures. Although I have offered some interpretation of the multimodal dimension of the explanatory episodes, this should be viewed as tentative since it is based on my perceptions as an observer of the recorded phenomena. More interpretive insights could perhaps be gained by eliciting feedback from the participants in an effort to understand more about the explanatory role of nonverbal cues during lectures. Yet, according to McNeill (1992, p. 72), speakers may be "largely unaware" of the gestures they use to accompany their speech, so input from the lecturers themselves may actually have limited interpretive value.

Perhaps a more useful way to further develop this research would be to extend the sample in quantitative terms to include more speakers, as well as other disciplinary areas. As Adolph (2013) points out, research on the interaction between verbal and nonverbal communicative modes has traditionally been done on a very small scale and often in experimental contexts. However, new technologies that facilitate both the collection and analysis of multimodal corpora have the potential to upgrade this type of research to a larger scale that would result in more generalizable findings.

To conclude this chapter, I would like to point out some pedagogical applications that can be inspired by this study, with particular reference to the medium of instruction that was analyzed. In fact, the widespread availability of OCW digital lectures can be exploited at different levels. On one hand, they could be utilized in educational training programs to help aspiring lecturers become more cognizant of the important contribution of nonverbal signals to reinforce explanations in lecture discourse. On the other hand, OCW lectures could be integrated into academic listening skills courses designed for nonnative speakers of English who must cope with the challenges of comprehending lectures in a language that is not their own. Because there is evidence to suggest that the presence of nonverbal signals is linked to improved listening comprehension in ESL learners (see Wagner, 2010), OCW lectures are a valuable multimodal resource to help learners become more aware of the nonverbal features of lectures and how they can enhance learners' understanding. Moreover, OCW digital lectures provide a strong connection to the increasingly multimodal world of today's learners that requires multiliteracy competence beyond verbal language.

ACKNOWLEDGMENTS

I wish to thank Lucas Swineford, executive director of Digital Dissemination and Online Education at Yale University for granting permission to reproduce all the screenshots from the Yale Open Courses website. I also thank Prof. Diana E.E. Kleiner, founding director of Yale Open Courses, and I am grateful to the five Yale professors whose lectures and kind collaboration made this study possible.

Appendix A
Gesture-Description Annotations

FingBunUD	fingers bunched moving up and down
FingClose	fingers closed into a ball
FingForehd	finger to forehead
FingPtUD	finger pointing moving up and down
FingPtUpMOut	finger pointing up moving out
FingRing	fingers forming a ring moving forward
FingSmSp	fingers forming a small space
ForefingHand	forefinger on fingers of opposite hand
HandChop	one hand chopping into the other
HandGlss	hand touches glasses
HandLftVert	hand lifted in vertical position
HandsApFace	hands apart moving up to face
HandsClsp	hands clasped in front of body
HandsOpSp	hands forming a round open space
HandsRotCtr	hands rotating at the center of the body
HandsRotHd	hands rotating at the sides of the head
HandsRotOut	hands rotating outward
HandsSqSpM	hands forming a square space moving right and left
HandsSwIn	hands sweep inwards towards body
HandsSwOut	hands sweep outwards away from body
PalmDMDn	palm down moving down
PalmDMSd	palm down moving sideways
PalmFwUD	palm forward moving up and down
PalmInw	palm moving inward towards body
PalmSMOut	palm sideways moving out
PalmSMUp	palm sideways moving up
PalmUMDn	palm up moving down
PalmUMOut	palm up moving out
PalmUMSd	palm up moving sideways
PalmUMUp	palm up moving up
PalmUpThUp	palm up with thumb up
PalmsFwdMFwd	palms forward moving forward

PalmsSdAp	palms sideways moving apart
PalmsUMOut	palms up moving out
PalmsUpAp	palms up moving apart
PalmsUpApUD	palms up and apart moving up and down
PalmsUpFing	palms up with fingers touching

Appendix B
Cause&Effect/Connection Items Used in Explanations

(1) why (12)
(2) because of (10)
(3) reasons (7)
(4) based on (4)
(5) connection (4)
(6) basis (3)
(7) depend on (3)
(8) implication (3)
(9) implications (3)
(10) prompted (3)
(11) causes (2)
(12) depending on (2)
(13) in light of (2)
(14) link (2)
(15) reason (2)
(16) results (2)
(17) causal (1)
(18) cause (1)
(19) caused (1)
(20) combine (1)
(21) combined (1)
(22) connotation (1)
(23) connote (1)
(24) depended on (1)
(25) derive (1)
(26) entails (1)
(27) evoke (1)
(28) gave rise to (1)
(29) influence (1)
(30) lead to (1)
(31) linking (1)
(32) result (1)
(33) resultant (1)
(34) resulting in (1)

NOTES

1. http://www.merriam-webster.com/dictionary/explanation.
2. The complex philosophical issues of causality and its role in argumentation are beyond the purview of this study. For more on this topic, see von Wright (1971) and van Eemeren, Grootendorst & Snoeck Henkemans (1996).
3. Gaze has been studied extensively in the context of conversational analysis, by means of detailed microanalysis of eye movements during interactions between interlocutors. It plays a key role in the management of turn-taking and occurs in relation to other communicative aspects, including speech and nonverbal actions of the participants. For more on gaze, see Goodwin (1981) and Heath (1984).
4. http://oyc.yale.edu/.
5. This information was gleaned from a summary of an online interview concerning the Open Yale Courses initiative available at http://christytucker.wordpress.com/2007/12/11/open-yale-courses-good-media-traditional-pedagogy/.
6. ELAN was developed at the Max Planck Institute for Psycholinguistics, the Language Archive, Nijmegen, the Netherlands. It is freely available at http://tla.mpi.nl/tools/tla-tools/elan/.
7. According to Silipo and Greenburg (2000), prosodic stress is an integral part of speech that derives from a complex combination of factors linked to duration, amplitude and fundamental frequency of syllabic sequences. Together with other features (e.g., intonation, rhythm, pitch), stress reflects the paralinguistic dimension of speaking. Because an in-depth analysis of the prosodic patterns of the lecturers' speech is clearly beyond the scope of this study, the analysis will be limited to the presence or absence of stress as illustrated by the ELAN audio waveform viewer.
8. Shelly Kagan, Death (Yale University: Open Yale Courses), http://oyc.yale.edu (accessed December 14, 2013). License: Creative Commons BY-NC-SA.
9. The software automatically compares the dataset with a normative corpus (in this case, the sampler of spoken English of the British National Corpus). This enables the identification of which semantic domains appear in statistically higher frequencies in the dataset as compared to the normative corpus. Statistical significance is calculated at the .01 level of confidence using the log-likelihood measure.
10. Langdon Hammer, Modern Poetry (Yale University: Open Yale Courses), http://oyc.yale.edu (accessed December 14, 2013). License: Creative Commons BY-NC-SA.
11. Christine Hayes, Introduction to the Old Testament (Hebrew Bible) (Yale University: Open Yale Courses), http://oyc.yale.edu (accessed December 14, 2013). License: Creative Commons BY-NC-SA.
12. Joanne Freeman, The American Revolution (Yale University: Open Yale Courses), http://oyc.yale.edu (accessed December 14, 2013). License: Creative Commons BY-NC-SA.
13. Jonathan Holloway, African American History: From Emancipation to the Present (Yale University: Open Yale Courses), http://oyc.yale.edu (accessed December 14, 2013). License: Creative Commons BY-NC-SA.

REFERENCES

Adolph, S. (2013). Corpora: Multimodal. In C. A. Chapelle (Ed.), *The encyclopedia of applied linguistics* (pp. 1–4). Oxford, UK: Wiley-Blackwell. Retrieved from http://onlinelibrary.wiley.com/doi/10.1002/9781405198431.wbeal0233/full.

Baldry, A., & Thibault, P.J. (2006). *Multimodal transcription and text analysis.* London: Equinox.

Bamford, J. (2002). Are economists guilty of anti-economic linguistic behaviour? Repetition and reformulation in economics lectures. In M.L. Bisgnami, G. Iamartino, & C. Pagetti (Eds.), *The economy principle in English linguistic, literary and cultural perspectives* (pp. 63–76). Milano: Edizioni Unicopli.

Bondi, M. (1999). *English across genres: Language variation in the discourse of economics.* Modena: Il Fiorino.

Brabazon, T. (2006). Socrates in earpods? The ipodification of education. *Fast Capitalism, 2*(1). Retrieved from http://www.uta.edu/huma/agger/fastcapitalism/2_1/brabazon.html.

Coleman, D. (2006). A formal integrated view of speech, gesture, gaze and its implications for learning. *LACUS Forum, 32,* 163–172.

Crawford Camiciottoli, B. (2007). *The language of business studies lectures: A corpus-assisted analysis.* Amsterdam: John Benjamins.

Darwin, C. (1890/1989). *The expression of emotions in man and animals.* London: Pickering. (Originally published, London: J. Murray).

Deroey, K.L.B., & Taverniers, M. (2011). A corpus-based study of lecture functions. *Moderna Språk, 105*(2), 1–22. Retrieved from http://ojs.ub.gu.se/ojs/index.php/modernasprak/issue/view/134.

Dudley-Evans, T. (1994). Variations in the discourse patterns favoured by different disciplines and their pedagogical implications. In J. Flowerdew (Ed.), *Academic listening: Research perspectives* (pp. 146–158). Cambridge: Cambridge University Press.

Ernst, H., & Colthorpe, K. (2007). The efficacy of interactive lecturing for students with diverse science backgrounds. *Advances in Physiology Education, 31*(1), 41–44.

Galloway, C.M. (1972). An analysis of theories and research in nonverbal communication. Retrieved from http://files.eric.ed.gov/fulltext/ED059988.pdf.

Giménez-Moreno, R. (2012). The interdependence of repetition and relevance in university lectures. *Journal of Pragmatics, 44*(6–7), 744–755.

Goodwin, C. (1981). *Conversational organization: Interaction between speakers and hearers.* New York: Academic Press.

Hall, E.T. (1966). *The hidden dimension.* Garden City, NY: Anchor Books.

Heath, C. (1984). Talk and recipiency: Sequential organization of speech and body movement. In J.M. Atkinson, & J. Heritage (Eds.), *Structures of social action: Studies in conversation analysis* (pp. 247–265). Cambridge: Cambridge University Press.

Hyland, K. (1999). Talking to students: Metadiscourse in introductory coursebooks. *English for Specific Purposes, 18*(1), 3–26.

Hyland, K. (2005). *Metadiscourse: Exploring interaction in writing.* London: Continuum.

Jewitt, C. (2008). Multimodality and literacy in school classrooms. *Review of Research in Education, 32*(1), 241–267.

Jewitt, C. (Ed.). (2009). *Handbook of multimodal analysis.* London: Routledge.

Kendon, A. (2004). *Gesture: Visible action as utterance.* Cambridge: Cambridge University Press.

Kress, G., & van Leeuwen, T. (2006). *Reading images: The grammar of visual design* (2nd edition). London: Routledge.

Kress, G., Jewitt, C., Ogborn, J., & Tsatsarelis, C. (2001). *Multimodal teaching and learning: The rhetorics of the science classroom.* London: Continuum.

Mason, A. (1994). By dint of: Student and lecturer perceptions of lecture comprehension strategies in first-term graduate study. In J. Flowerdew (Ed.), *Academic listening: Research perspectives* (pp. 199–218). Cambridge: Cambridge University Press.

McNeill, D. (1992). *Hand and mind: What the hands reveal about thought*. Chicago: The University of Chicago Press.

Morell, T. (2004). Interactive lecture discourse for university EFL students. *English for Specific Purposes, 23*(3), 325–338.

Nesi, H., & Basturkmen, H. (2006). Lexical bundles and discourse signaling in academic lectures. *International Journal of Corpus Linguistics, 11*(3), 283–304.

Norris, S. (2004). Multimodal discourse analysis: A conceptual framework. In P. Levine, & R. Scollon (Eds.), *Discourse and technology: Multimodal discourse analysis* (pp. 101–115). Washington, DC: Georgetown University Press.

O'Halloran, K.L. (1998). Classroom discourse in mathematics: A multisemiotic analysis. *Linguistics and Education, 10*(3), 359–388.

O'Halloran, K.L. (2011). Multimodal discourse analysis. In K. Hyland, & B. Paltridge (Eds.), *Companion to discourse analysis* (pp. 120–137). London: Continuum.

O'Halloran, K.L., & Smith, B.A. (2013). Multimodal text analysis. In C.A. Chapelle (Ed.), *The encyclopedia of applied linguistics* (pp. 1–6). Oxford, UK: Wiley-Blackwell. Retrieved from http://onlinelibrary.wiley.com/doi/10.1002/9781405198431.wbeal0817/full.

O'Halloran, K.L., E, M.K.L. & Tan, S. (2014). Multimodal analytics: Software and visualization techniques for analyzing and interpreting multimodal data. In C. Jewitt (Ed.), *The Routledge handbook of multimodal analysis* (2nd edition) (pp. 386–396). London: Routledge.

O'Halloran, K.L., Podlasov, A., Chua, A., Tisse, C.-L., Lim, F.V., & Smith, B.A. (2014). Challenges and solutions for multimodal analysis: Technology, theory and practice. In F. Yan, & J. Webster (Eds.), *Developing systemic functional linguistics: Theory and application* (pp. 271–297). London: Equinox.

Poyatos, F. (2002). *Nonverbal communication across disciplines, Volume 1: Culture, sensory interaction, speech, conversation*. Amsterdam: John Benjamins.

Pozzer-Ardenghi, L., & Roth, W.-M. (2005). Photographs in lectures: Gestures as meaning-making resources. *Linguistics and Education, 15*(3), 275–293.

Querol-Julián, M. (2011). *Evaluation in discussion sessions of conference paper presentation: A multimodal approach*. Saarbrücken: LAP Lambert Academic Publishing.

Rayson, P. (2008). From key words to key semantic domains. *International Journal of Corpus Linguistics, 13*(4), 519–549. Doi:10.1075/ijcl.13.4.06ray.

Sbisá, M. (1987). Acts of explanation: A speech act analysis. In F.H. van Eemeren, R. Grootendorst, J.A. Blair, & C.A. Willard (Eds.), *Argumentation: Perspectives and approaches* (pp. 7–17). Dordrecht: Foris Publications Holland.

Silipo, R., & Greenburg, S. (2000, May 16–19). Prosodic stress revisited: Reassessing the role of fundamental frequency. Proceedings of the NIST Speech Transcription Workshop, College Park, MD. Retrieved from http://www1.icsi.berkeley.edu/~steveng/2000/PDF/Prosody.pdf.

Thibault, P.J. (2000). The multimodal transcription of a television advertisement: Theory and practice. In A. Baldry (Ed.), *Multimodality and multimediality in the distance learning age* (pp. 311–385). Campobasso: Palladino Editore.

Tognini-Bonelli, E. (2001). *Corpus linguistics at work*. Amsterdam: John Benjamins.

van Eemeren, F.H., Grootendorst, R., & Snoeck Henkemans, F. (1996). *Fundamentals of argumentation theory: A handbook of historical backgrounds and contemporary developments*. Mahwah, NJ: Lawrence Erlbaum Associates, Inc.

von Wright, G.H. (1971). *Explanation and understanding*. Ithaca: Cornell University Press.

Wagner, E. (2010). The effect of the use of video texts on ESL listening test-taker performance *Language Testing, 27*(4), 493–513.

Weimer, W.B. (1997). Science as a rhetorical transaction: Toward a nonjustificational conception of rhetoric. *Philosophy and Rhetoric, 10*(1), 1–29.

Weinberg, A., Fukawa-Connelly, T., & Wiesner, E. (2013). Instructor gestures in proof-based mathematics lectures. In M. Martinez, & A. Castro Superfine (Eds.), *Proceedings of the 35th annual meeting of the North American chapter of the International Group for the Psychology of Mathematics Education* (p. 1119). Chicago: University of Illinois at Chicago.

White, G. (2011). Interactive lecturing. *The Clinical Teacher, 8*(4), 230–235.

Wittenburg, P., Brugman, H., Russel, A., Klassmann, A., & Sloetjes, H. (2006). ELAN: A professional framework for multimodality research. Proceedings of LREC 2006, Fifth International Conference on Language Resources and Evaluation. Retrieved from http://www.lrec-conf.org/proceedings/lrec2006/pdf/153_pdf.pdf.

Young, L. (1990). *Language as behaviour, language as code: A study of academic English*. Amsterdam: John Benjamins.

8 Multimodality in Business Communication

Body Language as a Visual Aid in Student Presentations

Juan Carlos Palmer-Silveira

8.1 BUSINESS COMMUNICATION

Business communication has become an increasingly relevant field of study all over the world in recent years, as companies find it of high interest for their work force (Bargiela-Chiappini, 2004; Evans, 2010; Rogerson-Revell, 2007, 2008; Varner & Beamer, 2005). It is almost impossible to find a job posting nowadays without an explicit mention of excellent oral and written communication skills (Guffey & Loewy, 2010), and companies devote great efforts to get the best possible training in this sense for their sales force. In fact, together with teamwork, critical thinking and analytical reasoning, oral and written communication skills appear as a factor that most employers consider as an essential asset in order to perform successfully in a business environment. Many authors have pointed out the importance of these skills in professional settings (DeLange et al., 2006; Deppe et al., 1991; Kavanagh & Drennan, 2008; Morgan, 1997; Nelson et al., 1996; Novin & Tucker, 1993; Stevens, 2005), considering that companies are often multinational corporations that need to communicate accurately in different intercultural situations.

Most academic institutions around the world have recognized that they should provide good business communication courses to students, and these have become basic to later finding good professional positions in economically sound corporations. Most firms look for people who can communicate their image in an appropriate way. As Amutha (2010, p. 30) aptly points out, "the companies seem to demand from the universities to give them students with people-related skills. They needed people who could work in a team, sharing their inventive and creative ideas." Modern companies need people who can work together in a multinational environment. This is because today's market can be defined as a multicultural space, where a deep knowledge of the fine nuances of heterogeneous audiences would help any sales person to enhance his/her professional expectations (Barker & Gower, 2010; Oliveira, 2013). Firms need people who can communicate the company's image professionally, sell a product and endorse a service. In short, they need good communicators.

Most corporations are showing great interest in solving communication problems, as they are now clinching deals with firms from all over the world. International business communication aims to address any problem that may arise in this new multinational environment. The concept of a national company is somehow disappearing, and firms are trying to adapt themselves to a new global market. This also implies that multiculturality can be seen as a way to solve communication problems with other companies. Most corporations are now formed by workers coming from different countries and/or regions, showing different educational backgrounds, as well as different religious beliefs, ethnic groups or social classes, a fact that can help firms to understand and overcome possible communication problems with foreign counterparts (Dowling & Welch, 2004; Palmer-Silveira, 2013; Varner & Beamer, 2005). As a response to this need, universities offer specific communication courses to their students, also trying to help them to minimize the impact of nerves and apprehension, aspects that often jeopardize their ability to find a good job (Gardner et al., 2005). Additionally, there has been great interest in analyzing the use of simulation techniques to enhance students' ability to communicate in business settings (Kolb & Kolb, 2009; Russ, 2009).

Many authors have pointed out that business communication can be enhanced through the involvement of students across the business curriculum (e.g., Cyphert, 2002; Drury-Grogan & Russ, 2013; Hunt 2003). Additionally, it is the sharing of the cultural features of all the different people who take part in a business venture that increases the opportunities to enhance communication among firms, or even between headquarters and subsidiaries (Lauring, 2011). However, it is a challenge for international companies, formed by nonnative speakers of English, to start using this language in order to endorse their products and services on an international scale, where English has become the lingua franca of business communication worldwide. Needless to say, linguistic competence plays an important role in the communication process. Nevertheless, as the following section will show, language is not the only element to be considered.

8.2 SHARING INFORMATION WITH THE AUDIENCE

Many scholars have analyzed the way professionals behave when sharing information with their audiences (Cicala et al., 2012; Evans, 2013; Pan et al., 2002; Querol-Julián & Fortanet, 2012), also pointing out that language, though obviously crucial, is not the only feature to be considered. Some people do not behave as they would normally when having to face some specific situations. Indeed, having to deliver a message in front of an audience is often construed as a fairly stressful activity. Facing an audience may cause doubts and hesitation to many students and/or professionals, as they often know that their success (and, in turn, their companies' success in selling a product or service) quite often depends on their ability to carry out a presentation in a professional way. This is not a simple task for a number of reasons. For instance, words sometimes do not come easy. In many situations, people fail to communicate effectively because of a mixture of lack of confidence and weak preparation. Sometimes both problems appear together, but they can be overcome by receiving the appropriate training. In fact, students often take part in courses where they are taught how to share information in front of an audience, and how to use linguistic structures and paralinguistic devices to overcome pressure (Hincks & Edlund, 2009; Otoshi & Heffernen, 2008). Getting the right training can help both students and professionals to deliver a good oral presentation. This is what many companies ask academic authorities to accomplish, as they have noticed that their prospective employees often lack these abilities. All in all, most public and private institutions have recognized this need and are offering students/professionals specific instruction on how to become better presenters.

In business settings, one important way to achieve any commercial goal is through the right use of verbal communication. People speak in order to send a message, and those words have to be chosen properly to succeed in that communicative purpose. Many companies post job listings stating that the chosen candidate should have 'good oral abilities.' Nevertheless, some businesspeople do not understand what is hidden behind this skill: They can speak fast and fluently, but they may not be able to communicate effectively. Employees who utter concepts clumsily can jeopardize their company's possibilities to clinch good deals. The use of the right word or expression in the appropriate context and in a clear way can help any speaker achieve a predefined goal; if this is basic in any communicative situation, it can be even more relevant when dealing with business-related situations, where success is often identified with making a profit. However, it is important to consider other modes of communication beyond verbal language, i.e., the role of multimodality in human-to-human interaction (Norris, 2004). Good communicators realize that the importance of the message is not only the message itself, but also the way it is interpreted by an audience. It is the connection between speaker and audience—i.e. human-to-human interaction—that results in successful communication (Gallo, 2009). As we suggested above, language itself cannot be defined as the only element conveying a message in an oral framework: All interactions are multimodal. Thousands of years ago people could not speak, but they were still able to communicate through body language and primitive sounds, something that animals and babies still do. Emotions are often shown by a smile, a frown or a teardrop. There is much more to communication than language itself, and a good business professional should be able to understand all the possibilities that a multimodal approach can offer. To communicate, we have to consider the right choice of semiotic elements (words, gestures, body language, images, even the spatial arrangement of objects) that may imply a meaning to the message delivered (Nelson & Johnson, 2014). Any possible combination of these elements can be studied in order to see new possibilities that could improve the way a message is sent (Kress, 2003, 2010). This has a lot to do with the dynamics of persuasion, in which the main goal is to show that a message is both positive and relevant for others (Bamford, 2007; Perloff, 2003).

With a multimodal approach, we can easily understand why misunderstandings can arise not because of the use of a specific word or phrase, but by the way these are uttered. The way we move, they way we look at the audience, the clothes we wear, the tone of our voice and many other aspects all contribute to how our message is interpreted, and can be consciously used to communicate more effectively. The gestures that a person uses imply subtle nuances that increase his/her communicative abilities (Tabensky, 2008, 2012). Companies know this and they look for well-trained professionals capable of conveying their corporate image through business presentations. As Tomsett and Trott (2014, p. 50) point out, "Multimodal teaching methods lend strength to the desire of business to employ graduates with the ability to integrate an understanding of commerce and business with creative and innovative ways of solving problems." Thus, given a specific problem (for instance, a firm's interest in increasing its sales), multimodality can be used as an asset to deliver that message more successfully.

Multimodal communication also involves new technologies that offer different possibilities to presenters to convey their messages in a more accurate way. The use of PowerPoint presentations and other similar software products help students and professionals to enrich their speech with visual modes of communication (images, audiovisual materials), integrating technical devices into spoken discourse (Bucher & Niemann, 2012). This integration of technology in presentations can be defined as a new visual rhetoric (Stark & Paravel, 2008). In fact, traditional overhead projectors have been replaced by light laptop computers and small beam projectors used by presenters to improve the communication process.

8.3 THE WAY PRESENTERS BEHAVE: BODY LANGUAGE

As we know, all human beings are different, behave in a different way in specific situations, and show some specific characteristics that can help them to communicate properly. Thus, two people do not act exactly the same way when facing similar situations, despite having received similar training. We are all different, and we have to learn which are our positive features, as well as our most important weaknesses. Becoming aware of these pros and cons can maximize communicative competence. With particular reference to nonverbal elements, Jurin et al. (2010) point out that a large component of meaning transferred in a communication system (ranging from 60 to 95%) is accomplished through nonverbal communication. A detailed study of nonverbal aspects of business communication can help students/professionals to succeed in the business world. In short, good nonverbal communication can help them deliver a message successfully, whereas a clumsy effort may sabotage a possible sale. Among the features that can jeopardize students' communicative abilities are nerves, which often affect presenters. In natural conditions, many students get quite nervous when asked to present a product or service in front of their classmates. This is often experienced as very stressful. However, a sufficient amount of practicing will help them to know their weaknesses and learn how to improve. They learn by performing, by doing it better each time, by analyzing what they do and by acting on the comments and suggestions that other students and teachers offer as feedback (Campbell et al., 2001; De Grez et al., 2012).

In many cases, students know what to say and how to say it, but their body language betrays them. Goman (2008, p. 3) points out that "a thorough understanding of the role that body language plays in our day-to-day business activities is vital." Learning to deliver a message in front of an audience should also be based on observing how our body can help us to enhance our communicative abilities. Body language is an important feature of non-verbal communication, as it transmits both attitudes and emotions. Some authors have focused on how body language is used in order to convey messages in different communicative contexts (Borg, 2008; Busso et al., 2005, 2007; Chartrand & Bargh, 1999). In business contexts, Goman (2008) indicates that those people who understand body language (not only to decode the silent signals of others, but also to use it when trying to project a specific attitude) may gain a competitive advantage.

8.4 THE ANALYSIS: STUDENT BUSINESS PRESENTATIONS

In this study, we analyze student business presentations in a compulsory course, Persuasive Language and Business Presentations, that is part of the professional itinerary of the one-year master's degree in English Language for International Trade (ELIT). It is a 4-credit course and students have one 120-minute session a week. We are currently engaged in the tenth edition of this program, and with an average of 20–25 students per year, we have already taught well over 200 students. Our aim has been to offer a practice-based methodology, teaching them how to design, create and deliver an oral message to enhance the corporate image of the firm they may work for. A good amount of sessions allow the students to perform their business presentations and work on how to improve both their linguistic and paralinguistic abilities when performing this type of task. Students are required to learn both the linguistic skills necessary to deliver a formal business presentation, as well as the paralinguistic features that could enhance the overall aim of a professional presentation, typically the promotion of a product or service.

For our current analysis, we used three video-recorded samples of the students' final presentation, all of them taken from the same edition of the master's program (2012/2013). We should point out that students are video-recorded four times during the semester in order to observe the way they improve their linguistic and paralinguistic abilities in their presentations.[1] The analysis aims to describe and evaluate body language used by students in short 10–15-minute presentations. We also analyze differences between effective body language that enhances their communicative abilities, as well as less effective body language that can distract the audience and jeopardize the success of their presentations.

8.4.1 Participants

The three examples taken for this study have not been chosen at random. The students share some common features to start with. All of them originally studied the English philology degree before taking part in our master's program, were 24 years old at the time of the recordings,[2] shared the same professional expectations and could well be defined as active students. Additional information about the participants is provided in Table 8.1, followed by short narratives that highlight their individual abilities so that we are better able to understand their behavior and progress during the whole learning process.

8.4.1.1 Student A

Student A was totally determined to take part in this process, something that he shares with the other two students selected for this study. Initially, he did not have the ability to present a product or service, and could be described as a fairly static presenter. He improvised information that he added to his main storyline, thus creating digressions. He could not maintain eye contact with his audience, though he tried hard to do so. His use of body language was basically nonexistent, and limited to moving his left arm up and down quite often. In any case, he could be described as an active student, terribly eager to improve and always asking for advice.

8.4.1.2 Student B

Student B could be clearly considered an active student, becoming a leader figure for the group. When she had to initially face the presentation activity in front of the classroom, she seemed to get blocked and her body movements were almost nonexistent or rather awkward. She could not maintain her back straight, and her physical position was rather unnatural. She seemed to lose control and her natural abilities to perform a presentation

Table 8.1 General features of the recordings analyzed

Student	Gender	Language competence level in English	Topic of presentation	Duration (including discussion session)
A	Male	C1/C2	Porsche 911	12:56
B	Female	C1/C2	EducaPoker	11:22
C	Female	C1/C2	MacBook Air	10:55

were jeopardized by her nervousness. Essentially, her difficulties appeared to be caused by a lack of training and practice.

8.4.1.3 Student C

Student C was also an active student, an aspect she shares with the other two students, even if she did not show it as often as her two colleagues. She did a relatively good job in her initial presentation, but was still fairly static in her body movements. She did not smile during the presentation, and kept some distance towards her classmates. However, she appeared to be in control of the situation, implementing excellent organizational skills that allowed her to go through her presentation without digressions. Her fluency in English also allowed her to appear less nervous than her fellow students. In any case, her initial presentation could be clearly improved, and she was willing to do so.

The three participants were members of a class of approximately 25 students and the presentations were delivered in front of the class. They had all performed their prepared presentations 48 hours earlier in a final rehearsal. Thus, the audience was able to have a preview of the different topics so that they could effectively ask questions in the final part of the presentation (discussion session).[3]

8.4.2 Conditions

As common elements, based on the specific instruction all the students had received in the classroom, the three presentations were based on a similar layout. Students started with a simple introduction, in which they stated their name and position in the company, the purpose of the presentation, the expected length and the different parts of its structure. In all cases, the students had divided the body of the presentation in three or four sections, clearly signaling the section transitions both linguistic and paralinguistically. They wrapped up by introducing the basic conclusions of their presentations in a final summary, before giving the audience the opportunity to ask questions, or request necessary clarifications they might need before deciding whether to use the product or service endorsed. In addition, the time allocated for each presentation could range from 10 to 15 minutes. Finally, because the aim was to replicate real-life business presentations, the students were required to dress appropriately and they could use supporting materials (samples, business cards, tags) for their PowerPoint presentations to help them convey a global message.

8.4.3 Nonverbal Features Analyzed

The analysis focused on how presenters use body language to transmit some specific aspects of their message. We analyzed the following nonverbal features: a) use of the physical space *(stage)*, b) use of their hands *(hands)*, c) eye contact with the audience *(eyes)* and d) head movements *(head)*. These were identified on the basis of the problems observed during the year, as well as in our experience during the previous editions of the master's program. Each feature is described in further detail below.

Stage: whether students remain static, basically establishing a position during their presentation and sticking to it, or if they decide to use the space available, moving along the stage and getting closer to the audience. In order to do so, we have distinguished different possibilities:

- SP (static position): The student does not move from one specific position where s/he can be seen by the audience. In the three cases analyzed in this study, this was their original basic position in the initial presentation performed during week 1.
- SW (slow walker): The student walks along the stage slowly and is always aware of the audience. In some specific cases, the student moves slowly from one side of the classroom to the other (SWS = slow walker, side to side). In other cases, the student moves back and forth, going from the screen to the front tables (SWF = slow walker, back and forth).
- AA (active attitude): The student moves along freely, getting closer to the audience, trying to maintain as much eye contact as possible. In some cases, the student demonstrates this active attitude while walking quickly from one side of the classroom to the other (AAS = active attitude, side to side), whereas in others the student moves back and forth, walking from the screen to the front tables (AAF = active attitude, back and forth).

Within these two final options, we also observe whether the student moved from side to side of the classroom (SWS/AAS) or if s/he preferred to move back and forth (SWF/AAF), getting physically closer to the audience during specific moments.

Hands: how the students used their hands to emphasize ideas or concepts. We distinguished these possibilities:

- CF (closed fists): The student closes her/his hands to show strength or relevance of an idea or concept s/he is trying to highlight.
- OH (open hands): The student tries to offer a clear image about a specific concept s/he is dealing with during the presentation (a clarifying movement).
- PF (pointing finger): The student uses a finger to point out a relevant concept, something s/he does not want the audience to miss (an emphatic movement).
- EF (enumerating fingers): The student uses three or four fingers to indicate that a part of her/his message is divided into as many parts as the fingers that are shown.

Alongside these common possibilities, the students' hands often moved in other ways that revealed nervousness and other problems, which were also taken into account. In any case, the use of PowerPoint to add information visually implies that the students had a wireless laser presenter device in one of their hands, thus minimizing the possibilities to move their hands.

Eyes: whether students looked constantly at their audience during the presentation to convey eagerness to endorse a product or service. However, having a screen behind them, where the information they were offering was highlighted, sometimes forced them to turn their back to the audience, thus losing eye contact. This was one of the most typical problems during our initial sessions. Eye contact was analyzed as follows:

- EA (eye contact with the audience): The student keeps eye contact with their classmates/customers as taught.
- ES (student looks at the screen): The student occasionally has a quick look at the screen to be sure that the message can also be observed on screen. It is a short and fast movement, coming back to the EA position almost immediately.
- EU (student looks up): In some situations, in order to remember ideas or concepts to share with the audience, the student looks up, trying to visualize the information. This gives an impression of forgetfulness and lack of security that students should avoid.
- ED (student looks down): This tends to happen when the student is nervous and unable to keep eye contact with the audience. Needless to say, students should avoid this situation.

Head: movements of the head to reinforce an idea or a specific concept appearing in their presentation. Random head movements seem to indicate lack of control during a communicative performance. Students were taught not to move their heads without control, something that they do in their one-on-one communicative interactions fairly often. Nevertheless, presenting in front of an audience requires a higher level of body control. The kind of head movements most often observed in our students' presentations were the following:

- HA (head agreement or "ducking"): The student swiftly moves the head up and downward, trying to reinforce the positive aspects of the point commented.
- HD (head disagreement): The student swiftly moves the head left and rightward, trying to reinforce the negative aspects of the point commented.
- HT (head tilting): This is used quite often in the discussion session at the end of the presentation. The student often bends the head slightly

to either side to show that s/he is paying attention to the questions asked by a member of the audience.

Additionally, we analyzed any other body movements that could offer any additional information to the audience. After completing the analysis, we elicited feedback from the three participating students. In these sessions, we asked them about all the different body language movements that we were able to observe in order to better understand underlying motivations for their nonverbal behaviors during their presentations. In this way, the results of the analysis were ratified.

8.5 RESULTS AND DISCUSSION

In the following paragraphs, we describe and discuss the most salient nonverbal features used by the three students, as they were observed from the video recordings.

8.5.1 Stage

8.5.1.1 Student A

This student starts his presentation in the center of the stage, smiles at the audience and welcomes them to the presentation. He then starts moving slowly back and forth (SW). He is clearly controlling the space, always in movement but trying to place himself away from the screen, in such a way that his message is often enhanced by the visuals shown to his audience. He invades the *safety zone* (the space between the audience and the screen) only twice during the presentation. Nevertheless, he has learned some different strategies to get closer to the audience and he uses them. For example, he steps forward and places his hands on the front table, getting quite close to the people sitting in the front row, as shown in Figure 8.1. He moves his chest forward, somehow invading the space where the audience is, but he does so smiling and looking at them directly. It is a rehearsed movement, something that the students have learned during the year, which can be quite complicated if not properly executed. However, student A does it very naturally, and it works quite well. He does it again during the discussion session when two of the students ask him questions. Again, it works well and enhances the impression of his concern for his classmates' doubts.

8.5.1.2 Student B

This student also moves nicely (SW) during her presentation. She works hard at opening her chest and arms and keeping her back straight, one of our recommendations during the early stages of the course. She invades the *safety zone* as Student A did, but she is clever enough not to stop there: She walks in front of the screen, but stays towards the side without blocking it.

Figure 8.1 Student A stepping forward and leaning on front table

She then she walks back to the initial center position of the stage. She repeats this same movement twice, while projecting images of famous people who are supporting her service. She never blocks the image when an important concept appears on screen. A difference with Student A appears during the discussion with the audience. Student B simply stands in front of the student who asks her a question, looking at her, motionless. She does not lean on the table as Student A did, but just listens and nods as a signal of understanding. She then moves again when answering the question, though this time she minimizes the walking area, staying close to the questioner and maintaining eye contact.

8.5.1.3 Student C

Here we can see some differences in this student's approach to stage management. She starts from the same position, in the center of the stage, but then she moves slightly to her right side in a position where the audience can see her, without hiding the screen with her body. She initially assumes a static position (SP), though she moves every now and then back and forth in a very natural way, sometimes assuming an SW approach. Her body control is excellent, and body, eyes, hands and gestures all work together to reinforce the message. Additionally, considering the type of product endorsed (a lightweight laptop computer), her movements help her to make it more relevant to the audience. She shows the computer to the audience, keeping it high so that no visual contact is lost. Her ability to control her position on the stage can only be defined as excellent. Only once does she block the screen, but moves quickly out of that position. Regarding the discussion session, Student C simply gets as close to the front row as possible, always facing the person asking the question. Once again, she is aware of the space she is using in order to communicate her information more professionally. None of the three students analyzed used the AA approach, but their movements still show complete control of their presentations.

8.5.2 Hands

Hand movements tend to be used to emphasize ideas or concepts that the students understand as particularly important. All our students are using a laser pointer device in one of their hands, forcing them somehow to start with a CF position. From that initial moment onwards, the use of their hands is different.

8.5.2.1 Student A

He starts by placing his left hand on top of his right one, and placing them both in front of his chest. This is his natural position, only altered in few occasions. For instance, when he enumerates the different sections of his presentation, he starts using EF, though he tries hard not to do so too obviously. Instead of showing his hand clearly to the audience, he just opens his palm and uses the fingers without moving his arm at all. In general, we can say that he tends to overuse this movement and repeats it constantly, though the fact that his presentation is based on the use of a digit (number 4) is somehow leading him to this overuse.

Apart from the EF movement, Student A seems to be always in control of his hands. Among the different types of movements we have been able to notice, there are a few that we would like to point out. For instance, he moves his left hand in a fairly peculiar gesture, as if spreading butter on bread, in order to show the audience that he is planning to move from one section to another. He also opens his hands (OH) to show that the presentation will only take ten minutes of their time, trying to seem sincere and natural. He repeats this movement often to reinforce an idea, so the OH movement can be understood as a way to strengthen the message. In addition, in order to emphasize a concept, he uses his right hand (with the laser pointer) and moves it gently up and down. Although he does not open his hand to do so, this hand movement communicates to the audience that this concept is an important one. Later, he points at the screen, something that he has not done so far; this is a movement he has been working hard to avoid since his initial presentation. Probably his most shocking movement is when he steps forward and places both hands on the front table. As we commented above, this position can be invasive for members of the audience sitting in the front row, but he shows great control. He leans his body on both hands, showing an attempt to get as close to the audience as possible. He does so twice again in the discussion session, at the end of his presentation.

8.5.2.2 Student B

She starts with a fairly different approach, holding the laser pointer in her left hand, and simply letting her left arm remain loose. Then she starts moving that arm to support the meaning implied by the words and images she is using. In addition, both hands touch each other and then are separated to specify concepts. Once, she also uses EF movements, clearly showing her fingers. However, several times, she repeats gestures, such as raising two or three fingers to illustrate the corresponding numbers. She also uses a wide range of additional movements. For instance, she closes her fist (CF) to express the concept of refunding money, as shown in Figure 8.2. In order to imply a sequence, she places her open hand in front of her chest and gently rotates her wrist. Additionally, to show a reversal of the sequence, she uses both index fingers and rotates them as if moving a wheel mechanism.

Another movement that Student B does is to open her arms and hands, trying to show her audience that they all are part of the company she is endorsing, accompanied by a small nod. This OH movement seems to aim to let everyone understand the relevance of the product endorsed for their daily lives. We must remember that the presenter is introducing an online gambling website, something that may be viewed negatively by some people, and she tries hard to offer a trustworthy message. She does this same movement quite often afterwards, always accompanied by slight head movements and gentle smiles, offering a positive message. Suddenly, mimicking the physical representation of getting a trophy, she raises her hand and opens it wide, while the image of a person getting an award appears on screen. Interestingly, she also opens her arms wide while showing the images

Figure 8.2 Student B's CF movement

of some well-known people, implying that they would appreciate the service endorsed. This OH movement is repeated, introducing a rhetorical question and offering an example. She also points at the screen (PF) a few times in the middle part of her presentation in order to clarify concepts.

8.5.2.3 *Student C*

She starts by placing both hands together and then begins to introduce some numbers, reinforcing them by using EF movements. This is repeated during the whole presentation every time a number is mentioned. To clarify concepts to the audience, she opens her left hand and moves it gently, introducing a simple concept. She introduces important terms by highlighting them with her little finger, in a rather peculiar movement, or directly moves her left open hand, while completing an HA movement, ducking her head as an emphatic device. In order to deny an action *(we did not remove anything),* she places her left hand open and facing downwards, then moves it laterally. She also points at the audience (PF) when explaining the use of one of the computer's features. Nevertheless, as a follow-up, she places all five fingertips together, implying the fact that they can touch the product, opening it in a very fast movement. The most striking feature of this presentation is when the student shows a video in which a hand shows different finger movements to use the computer. At the same time, Student C places herself by the screen and replicates all the movements with her left hand. Then, to stress the simplicity of use, she faces the audience opening both arms and showing the palm of her hands.

In this specific case, Student C also uses her hands to introduce props to the audience. For example, she shows a mobile phone to the audience to talk about how thin her product is. In addition, she shows a laptop computer, placing it high to be seen by the whole audience. The act of holding the computer with both hands minimizes her possibilities to use any other hand movement during the discussion session.

8.5.3 Eyes

Regarding eye movements, we stressed in the classroom that presenters should keep eye contact with their audience continuously. All three students provide good examples of learning to maintain eye contact.

8.5.3.1 *Student A*

He looks at the audience all the time (EA), and forces himself to pay attention to every single classmate. While walking along the stage he stops in front of some colleagues and takes time to look at them closely. He does not look directly at the camera, one of the main mistakes that many students made in prior presentations. He is aware that the images appearing on screen are reflected in the window at the back of the room and, instead of turning his back to the audience to see what is on the screen, he maintains some visual contact by looking at this window that acts as a mirror for the presenter. This allows him to project a more professional approach. He looks at the screen directly only three times during his whole presentation, and always to point out concepts displayed there (ES). He never looks up or down (EU/ED), something that he did a lot in his initial presentation.

8.5.3.2 Student B

She also tries to maintain continuous eye contact (EA) with her audience and usually succeeds, though she also looks at the screen (ES) every now and then, thus losing eye contact for a moment. She has a natural tendency to look at the classmates sitting at her left side, but she still manages to look at the rest of the audience, especially in the second half of her presentation. She also has a tendency to close her eyes for a moment during her talk, as if resting, probably because of the natural pressure involved in this activity. It seems that this allows her to relax and feel better. She only looks at the floor (ED) once during her whole presentation, during the section where she seems to be more nervous. At a certain point, she looks closely at the camera and from then on, she appears to feel a bit more comfortable. She looks at the camera again twice, though very briefly in both cases.

8.5.3.3 Student C

She maintains continuous eye contact with her audience (EA), paying attention to everyone and gazing at all areas in the classroom. She is seemingly unaware of the camera, and looks only at the operator every now and then, as at any other member of the audience. She loses eye contact in two specific situations: first, when she holds props high and looks at them, also encouraging

Figure 8.3 Student C's continuous eye contact with her audience

the audience to look at them as well. Then, she looks at the screen (ES) in order to replicate the movements that can be seen in the video. However, even during this action, she still forces herself to maintain some degree of eye contact with her classmates. She never looks up or down (EU or ED movements). Figure 8.3 illustrates Student C's effective use of eye contact.

8.5.4 Head

8.5.4.1 Student A

He generally stays in control of this aspect and chooses among some options. We can see some purposeful reinforcing nods, when he is trying to offer a positive image of the product endorsed. He also nods to the audience when asking them a rhetorical question, placing his hands on the front table and moving his chest forward. Interestingly, he also nods after pronouncing problematic words correctly. This seems to be a natural movement that he would have probably replicated if he had had the same problem in his native language. He also briefly tilts his head to the left when trying to clarify a concept. This movement seems to be natural and unaffected; nevertheless, it is quite surprising considering that there is nothing similar in the rest of his presentation. In any case, he accompanies it with a smile, something that offers an even more natural sense to the movement. Finally, he frowns when asking another rhetorical question, accompanying this facial expression with a brief HD movement to the left and to the right, showing disagreement.

8.5.4.2 Student B

She begins by accompanying a slight hand movement and a head nod when she talks about her prior business experience, perhaps to increase her credibility with the audience. During her open hand movements, she also nods, holding her head slightly forward in an attempt to make the message more relevant for her classmates. She also has a natural tendency to tilt her head to both sides while speaking, though it is not an exaggerated movement. When positive aspects of the presentation message appear (this presentation focuses on winning at gambling), the presenter often nods, moving her head (HA) up and down gently and repeatedly. In fact, the use of the word *money* tends to be accompanied by a slight nod or a series of brief ones. However, one of the problems observed in the initial part of her presentation is that the student does not smile while introducing some concepts, probably because of her nervousness. Her attitude appeared too stiff at first, but fortunately she then began to smile when introducing some ideas and concepts, which improved her overall performance.

8.5.4.3 Student C

She also has a natural tendency to nod at the start of her presentation, though this seems to be connected to natural stress and, in fact, disappears very soon. From then on, she nods slightly only when she introduces a concept that may be of interest to her classmates, in an attempt to offer a positive image. Her nodding is more pronounced in other moments: when a certain word does not come easy, when she tries to stress one action that can be done with the computer she is endorsing, or when she reinforces an idea or concept by asking the audience a question. Nevertheless, when introducing a rhetorical question, she also moves her head gently from left to right, or just to the left, a movement that is fairly different from what we have seen with the other two students analyzed. She also uses that HD movement when disagreeing, when uttering a negative statement or when in doubt. Finally, she tilts her head to the right, to signal the beginning of the final section of her presentation.

8.6 CONCLUSIONS

As the analysis performed in this study suggests, these students who were initially unaware of their lack of nonverbal communicative abilities while presenting a product or service have improved considerably after receiving specific training. Practice was a necessary asset to evaluate their strengths and weaknesses and, in turn, to overcome problems observed. The opportunity to receive all kinds of feedback, especially from their classmates, has helped them to understand those aspects that can enhance their communicative efforts to effectively convey a corporate message. In any case, we should keep in mind that this study has just focused on three students and in a specific classroom context. In fact, different results could be observed in different settings or with a larger number of participants. In any case, our purpose has been to offer a more complete vision on presentation techniques than what tends to be found in many textbooks devoted to the teaching of presentation skills, where aspects like body movement, use of space or eye contact are often dealt with superficially or even neglected.

Based on our analysis, we can now make some recommendations concerning different aspects of nonverbal communication that need to be addressed and reinforced in the classroom. Students should be taught to be aware of the space they can use for their presentations, starting from the center of the stage where they welcome the audience. This position allows them to be seen by everyone and capture the audience's attention. Then they can use that space for their own benefit, moving slowly and always facing their classmates/customers. They should also be aware that, if they are using a PowerPoint presentation, they should not step between the projector and the screen. Moreover, student presenters need to learn how to get closer to the audience, how to lean on the front tables as a way to project an image of control and, even more importantly, how to stop and look at the audience in order to stress a specific part of their message. Learning how to move in this way creates more dynamism during the presentation. To convey an image of self-confidence, students should assume an open position, showing chest and arms to the audience. An additional tip that can be recommended in some specific cases is to use props during the presentation, showing them to the audience by holding them with one hand, though never covering the presenter's face.

Hand movements will always depend on the possible use of a laser pointer. If so, the student should be aware of the kind of movements s/he will have to perform with the other hand. Opening our hands from an initially controlled position, with closed fists, offers an image of trustfulness, whereas moving them slowly and gently marks a rhythm in the presentation that can later be used to stress some ideas or concepts. Students should try to avoid pointing at the audience with a finger or overusing fingers for enumeration. Moving hands to imply dynamism is a positive feature, as long as the presenter is aware of the image s/he is trying to offer to the listeners. Hands convey messages but, without adequate control, they can distract the audience from what is being said.

Eye contact is one of the most important features that every single presenter should be aware of. We talk to people, trying to engage them in our message, and we have to be sure that we have their attention if we want to succeed. In fact, it is hard not to pay attention to someone who is looking at you closely. Therefore, it is important for students to learn to smile and look at every member of the audience during a presentation. When using PowerPoint, students should check images very briefly and, if possible, try to direct attention towards themselves and not only to the screen. They should always keep in mind that the visual presentation should be a device used to help enhance the message, but it cannot be the most important element. Needless to say, looking at the floor or at the ceiling must be avoided.

A reinforcing nod is probably the most common resource used to convey the positive nature of a message. Gentle and forward head movements done while smiling can reinforce the positive aspects of the product/service endorsed. Nods are also helpful to introduce key words that are repeated throughout the presentation. In addition, moving the head to the left and to the right reinforces disagreement. Students should also be keenly aware of the gestures they use during the discussion session. Bending the head slightly to either side shows that they are paying attention to the person asking a question. Finally, frowning should be avoided, and a glass of water should be always at hand to avoid dry mouth problems that can lead to distracting mouth or lip movements.

As a final remark, we must recognize that personal characteristics can sometimes bias the overall success of the presentation. Some people have problems smiling, others keeping eye contact, and still others keeping a straight posture. Training is important, but enhancing students' self-confidence should be a must. Students should realize that speaking in public is a demanding activity, but also a fulfilling one in which they will be able to do their best to achieve a goal. Presentation techniques should always be accompanied by a thorough analysis of every student's own features, and it will be up to us, as teachers, to teach them to give their best, to minimize any problems and to maximize their possibilities to express themselves successfully. Every single rehearsal will help them to become better professional presenters.

ACKNOWLEDGMENTS

I would like to thank Felipe Carceller-Bono, Mihaela Andra Alecsandru and Elena Veronica Nita, who kindly granted permission to use their presentations and reproduce their images for this study.

NOTES

1. The students are recorded during their initial presentation during the first week, when we analyze their presentations delivered on a natural basis, without having received any kind of feedback. After basic instruction on presentation skills, seven to eight weeks later, they are video-recorded again and receive specific feedback. Finally, they are video-recorded again during the final rehearsal and in their final presentation during the last week of the course.
2. The students' age is a key feature in understanding their ability to use communication devices. These students can be defined as *millennials,* individuals born between 1980 and 2000 (Hartman & McCambridge, 2011), characterized by being technologically sophisticated, capable of working in teams and reluctant to make decisions independently.
3. This time allocated to the audience in the final part of the presentation is known as Q&A (question and answer) time, and is often used to clarify aspects of the presentations that might not have been clearly communicated. This is also defined as a *discussion session* in academic settings (Querol-Julián, 2010; Wulff et al., 2009).

REFERENCES

Amutha, M.M. (2010). Oral and written communication skills. *Journal of Literature, Culture and Media Studies, 2*(3), 30–38.

Bamford, J. (2007). Accentuating the positive: Evaluation and persuasive discourse in business presentations. In R. Salvi, & J. Bamford (Eds.), *Business discourse: Language at work* (pp. 135–155). Roma: Aracne Editrice.

Bargiela-Chiappini, F. (2004). Intercultural business discourse. In C.N. Candlin, & M. Gotti (Eds.), *Intercultural aspects of specialized communication* (pp. 29–51). Bern: Peter Lang.

Barker, R.T., & Gower, K. (2010). Strategic application of storytelling in organizations: Toward effective communication in a diverse world. *Journal of Business Communication, 47*(3), 295–312.

Borg, J. (2008). *Body language: Seven easy lessons to master the silent language.* Upper Saddle River, NJ: Pearson.

Bucher, H.J., & Niemann, P. (2012). Visualizing science: The reception of PowerPoint presentations. *Visual Communication, 11*(3), 283–306.

Busso, C., Deng, Z., Grimm, M., Neumann, U., & Narayanan, S. (2007). Rigid head motion in expressive speech animation: Analysis and synthesis. *IEEE Transactions on Audio, Speech, and Language Processing, 1*(3), 1075–1086.

Busso, C., Deng, Z., Neumann, U., & Narayanan, S. (2005). Natural head motion synthesis driven by acoustic prosodic features. *Journal of Computer Animation and Virtual Worlds, 16*(3–4), 283–290.

Campbell, K.S., Mothersbaugh, D.L., Brammer, C., & Taylor, T. (2001). Peer versus self assessment of oral business presentation performance. *Business Communication Quarterly, 64*(3), 23–42.

Chartrand, T.L., & Bargh, J.A. (1999). The chameleon effect: The perception-behavior link and social interaction. *Journal of Personality and Social Psychology, 76*(6), 893–910.

Cicala, J.E., Smith, R., & Bush, A.J. (2012). What makes sales presentations effective—a buyer-seller perspective. *Journal of Business and International Marketing, 27(*2), 78–88.

Cyphert, D. (2002). Integrating communication across the MBA curriculum. *Business Communication Quarterly, 65*(3), 81–86.

De Grez, L., Valcke, M., & Roozen, I. (2012). How effective are self- and peer assessment of oral presentation skills compared with teachers' assessments? *Active Learning in Higher Education, 13*(2), 129–142.

DeLange, P., Jackling, B., & Gut, A. (2006). Accounting graduates' perceptions of skills emphasis in Australian undergraduate accounting courses: An investigation from two Victorian universities. *Accounting and Finance, 46*(3), 365–386.

Deppe, L.A., Sonderegger, E.O., Stice, J.D., Clark, D. C., & Streuling, G.F. (1991). Emerging competencies for the practice of accountancy. *Journal of Accounting Education, 9*(2), 257–290.

Dowling, P.J., & Welch, D.E. (2004). *International human resource management: Managing people in a multinational environment.* London: Thomson Learning.

Drury-Grogan, M.L., & Russ, T.L. (2013). A contemporary simulation infused in the business communication curriculum: A case study. *Business Communication Quarterly, 76*(3), 304–321.

Evans, S. (2010). Business as usual: The use of English in the professional world in Hong Kong. *English for Specific Purposes, 29*(3), 153–167.

Evans, S. (2013). "Just wanna give you guys a bit of an update": Insider perspectives of business presentations in Hong Kong. *English for Specific Purposes, 32*(4), 195–207.

Gallo, C. (2009). *The presentation secrets of Steve Jobs: How to be insanely great in front of any audience.* New York: McGraw-Hill.

Gardner, C.T., Milne, M.J., Stringer, C.P., & Whiting, R.H. (2005). Oral and written communication apprehension in accounting students: Curriculum impacts and impacts in academic performance. *Accounting Education: An International Journal, 14*(3), 313–336.

Goman, C.K. (2008). *The nonverbal advantage: Secrets and science of body language at work.* San Francisco: Berrett-Koehler.

Guffey, M.E., & Loewy, D. (2010). *Essentials of business communication.* Mason, OH: South-Western.

Hartman, J.L., & McCambridge, J. (2011). Optimizing millennials' communication styles. *Business Communication Quarterly, 74*(1), 22–44.

Hincks, R., & Edlund, J. (2009). Promoting increased pitch variation in oral presentations with transient visual feedback. *Language Learning and Technology, 13*(3), 32–50.

Hunt, S.K. (2003). Encouraging student involvement: An approach to teaching communication. *Communication Studies, 54*(2), 133–136.

Jurin, R.R., Roush, D., & Danter, J. (2010). *Environmental communication: Skills and principles for natural resource managers, scientists and engineers*. London: Springer.

Kavanagh, M.H., & Drennan, L. (2008). What skills and attributes does an accounting graduate need? Evidence from student perceptions and employer expectations. *Accounting and Finance, 48*(2), 279–300.

Kolb, A.Y., & Kolb, D.A. (2009). The learning way: Meta-cognitive aspects of experiential learning. *Simulation and Gaming, 40*(3), 297–327.

Kress, G. (2003). *Literacy in the new media age*. London: Routledge.

Kress, G. (2010). *Multimodality: A social semiotic approach to contemporary communication*. London: Routledge.

Lauring, J. (2011). Intercultural organizational communication: The social organizing of interaction in international encounters. *Journal of Business Communication, 48*(3), 231–255.

Morgan, G.J. (1997). Communication skills required by accounting graduates: Practitioner and academic perceptions. *Accounting Education, 6*(2), 93–107.

Nelson, M.E., & Johnson, N.H. (2014). Editors' introduction: Multimodality, creativity and language and literacy education. *Pedagogies: An International Journal, 9*(1), 1–6.

Nelson, S.J., Moncada, S., & Smith, D. C. (1996). Written language skills of entry-level accountants as assessed by experienced CPAs. *Business Communication Quarterly, 59*(4), 22–27.

Norris, S. (2004). *Analyzing multimodal interaction: A methodological framework*. London: Routledge.

Novin, A. M., & Tucker, J.M. (1993). The composition of 150-hour accounting programs: An empirical investigation. *Issues in Accounting Education, 8*(2), 273–291.

Oliveira, M.F. (2013). Multicultural environments and their challenge to crisis communication. *Journal of Business Communication, 50*(3), 253–277.

Otoshi, J., & Heffernen, N. (2008). Factors predicting effective oral presentations in EFL classrooms. *The Asian EFL Journal, 10*(1), 65–78.

Palmer-Silveira, J.C. (2013). The need for successful communication in intercultural and international business settings: Analytic and comparative studies, new trends and methodologies. *Ibérica, 26*(1), 9–16.

Pan, Y., Wong, S., & Scollon, R. (2002). *Professional communication in international settings*. Oxford: Blackwell.

Perloff, R. (2003). *The dynamics of persuasion*. London: Lawrence Erlbaum Associates, Inc.

Querol-Julián, M. (2010). *Discussion sessions in specialised conference paper presentations: A multimodal approach to analyse evaluation* (Unpublished PhD dissertation). Universitat Jaume I, Castellón (Spain).

Querol-Julián, M., & Fortanet, I. (2012). Multimodal evaluation in academic discussion sessions: How do presenters act and react? *English for Specific Purposes, 31*(4), 271–283.

Rogerson-Revell, P. (2007). Using English for international business: A European case study. *English for Specific Purposes, 26*(1), 103–120.

Rogerson-Revell, P. (2008). Participation and performance in international business meetings. *English for Specific Purposes, 27*(3), 338–360.

Russ, T.L. (2009). The status of the business communication course at U.S. colleges and universities. *Business Communication Quarterly, 72*(4), 395–413.

Stark, D., & Paravel, V. (2008). PowerPoint in public: Digital technologies and the new morphology of demonstration. *Theory, Culture and Society, 25*(5), 30–55.

Stevens, B. (2005). What communication skills do employers want? Silicon Valley recruiters respond. *Journal of Employment Counseling, 42*(1), 2–9.

Tabensky, A. (2008). Expository discourse in a second language classroom: How learners use gesture. In S.G. McCafferty, & G. Stam (Eds.), *Gesture: Second language acquisition and classroom research* (pp. 298–320). New York: Routledge.
Tabensky, A. (2012). Non-verbal resources and storytelling in second language classroom interaction. *Journal of Applied Linguistics, 5*(3), 321–348.
Tomsett, P. M., & Trott, D. C. (2014). Multimodal pedagogy in international business education. *International Journal of Research in Social Sciences, 4*(2), 50–56.
Varner, I., & Beamer, L. (2005). *Intercultural communication in the global workplace.* New York: McGraw-Hill.
Wulff, S., Swales, J.M., & Keller, K. (2009). "We have seven minutes for questions": The discussion sessions from a specialized conference. *English for Specific Purposes, 28*(2), 79–92.

9 Assessing Multimodal Listening

Mari Carmen Campoy-Cubillo and Mercedes Querol-Julián

9.1 INTRODUCTION

This chapter studies the use of multimodal texts as input for listening comprehension assessment. It is oriented towards the analysis of criteria of multimodal listening tasks that should be met in the use of videotexts and other multimedia tools for assessing listening in foreign language teaching.

The majority of the studies investigating the use of video and audio-only resources in Second Language/Foreign Language listening focus on the comparison of students' performance when using one input or the other to understand a text (Brett, 1997; Gruba, 1993; Coniam, 2001; Wagner, 2008, 2010b). However, this type of comparison cannot determine whether one mode is better than another to enhance performance. In fact, students are responding to different means of information and different informational contents when using one or the other. Moreover, results could also vary according to the kinds of questions or output that are elicited from the tasks that are used. A correct answer to these questions may or may not be enhanced by one mode (audio recordings), or by the use of co-occurring modes (video recordings, i.e., audio and dynamic visual elements/nonverbal information), depending on whether the data provided by the mode(s) contains qualitative information for the requested answer. For instance, if we choose to include a video, does the nonverbal information aid comprehension? Are the questions clearly related to this nonverbal information? Besides, most studies on the use of video in the classroom also lack well-defined assessment criteria, which are an essential aspect in the learning process.

Regarding text type and nonverbal item testing, Brett (1997), for instance, compared different formats (audio, video, multimedia) with the same or similar text. However, the task type in this study mainly focused on form (understanding phrases and sentences, or deleted words to be written while listening) and paid no attention to nonverbal information. The results of this study showed that students performed better when a multimedia environment was used. This suggested that a media input was better for the tasks assigned. However, if no attention is paid to other modes different from speech, then questions related to gestures, contextual images, etc. are not considered and therefore not tested. Thus, in this case, the use of video does not make any sense and it can be considered distracting.

The point is that the use of aural-only texts or videotexts should be determined by the aims of the listening activity. Thus, if our main aim is for our students to listen in order to recognize words and insert them in a fill-in-the-gap exercise, and we want them to exercise their ability to recognize specific phonemes (phonemic discrimination), then audio-only texts might prove better than videos. In this case, we are not as interested in text comprehension as in phoneme and word recognition, and the students will not have any visual distraction (though this may not always be the case: Lip movement for instance may also help listeners, as observed in McGurk and MacDonald, 1976). However, if we aim at fostering multimodal comprehension skills, a broader perspective needs to be considered. Our students should be trained to understand and interpret situations where both linguistic and nonlinguistic features (gestures, facial expression, intonation, word stress, pauses, hesitations, etc.) co-occur and interact to create meaningful messages. For example, students may be asked to figure out how facial expressions or gestures can influence the linguistic message or even convey additional meaning.

This chapter intends to put forward a theoretical framework for the description of the kind of information that is relevant in each mode (e.g., gestures, facial expression, images, etc.), and the relationship between their linguistic and nonlinguistic features from a pedagogical point of view. It is by offering this theoretical description, while considering Rost's (2011) general map of listening ability, that we may provide the necessary foundation for understanding how to assess multimodal listening tasks.

9.2 RESEARCH ON LISTENING: PAVING THE WAY TOWARDS MULTIMODALITY

Listening is an essential skill in many areas of our lives. As Shellenbarger (2014) explained, "the failure to listen well not only prolongs meetings and discussions but also can hurt relationships and damage careers." In an academic context, listening also has a key function since understanding information transmitted in the classroom is of paramount importance. Two main listening types can be distinguished: transactional or one-way listening, and interactional or two-way listening (see Lynch, 2011). The same event may contain both types of listening situations, as in many university lectures where this academic genre is understood as "a relatively informal conversational style of speech with no overt interaction between lecturer and audience" (Sueyoshi & Hardison, 2005, pp. 68–69). Research on interactional listening plays an essential role in higher education, for instance in tutorials or seminars, and in conversational-style lectures (interactive), where empirical evidence has supported the benefits of interaction for listening comprehension in FL students (Morell, 2004, 2007). Research on transactional listening (e.g., listening to noninteractive lectures) has paid special attention to the way learners cope with taking notes (Badger et al., 2001) and understand discourse structure (Tauroza & Allison, 1994), or how they recall information (Jung, 2003). However, even in more noninteractive listening situations, when the students can access the speaker, there may be a degree of interaction. It is transactional listening that we pay most attention to in this chapter, as we discuss the use of multimodal tools, and specifically videotexts, for teaching and assessing listening where there is no verbal interaction with the speaker.

The target groups that can benefit from this approach are FL students. It could also be of interest to SL students, though we place more emphasis on the needs of FL because the experience that they have with the new language and culture is much lower. This position is justified by the experimental study done by Sueyoshi and Hardison (2005), who claimed that the experience in the SL dramatically influences the students' awareness and inclusion of visual cues in listening strategies.

There is no question that oral communication is multimodal, that is, speech is just one component part of the great amount of oral and visual information that is conveyed and perceived when we construct meaning (Jewitt, 2013), e.g., sound, music, background noise, gestures, facial expression, body posture, gaze, text, images, figures, etc. With this in mind, when teaching "a" FL, and particularly when teaching listening skills, it seems obvious that multimodal communication, and thus multimodal resources, should play a significant role. If we train our students to be communicatively competent in the FL, we need to give them the opportunity to learn from real-life situations. Though the issue of authenticity is quite controversial in language learning, we cannot deny that "authentic language is the target of virtually all language learners" (Rost, 2011, p. 165). Authenticity in language learning refers to many aspects and has many faces, e.g., the situation, the task, the language or the input. Thus far, authentic input has been generally characterized by spontaneous spoken discourse. Our stance in the definition of genuine listening input takes a broader perspective to embrace not only oral features, but also visual ones. Nowadays, the Internet facilitates access to resources for the FL classroom, authentic multimodal input among them. The acknowledgment of the important role of this type of input leads to a (re)definition of what is understood by listening.

The International Listening Association defines listening as "the process of receiving, constructing meaning from and responding to spoken and/or nonverbal messages" (ILA, 1995, p. 4). As can be seen in the definition, the nonverbal part of the listening process is included. However, tradition in language teaching has always put more emphasis on grammar and lexis than on the interactional and nonverbal aspects of communication. Likewise, more importance is given to understanding specific words or specific information than to being able to understand the message as a whole. This is reflected in the fact that most listening tasks do not include questions on meaning inference, or on the understanding of interactional, nonverbal or contextual information.

From a historical point of view (Ariza & Hancock, 2003; Buck, 2001), the different approaches to teaching and assessing listening have evolved in relation to how the listening process was understood within the language learning process. In the environmentalist approach, the role of the listener was to simply listen for structures; learners were required to repeat, imitate and memorize isolated words and phrases. This role was broadened in the innatist approach where the listener should participate in the listening process to understand what is being said. The importance here lies in the reception of the message. Participation became a more important part of the listening construct from the perspective of the interactionalist approach. In this case, participation is more active since students are required to listen with a purpose, thus the listener's role is to listen both for content and meaning. The listener is asked to process the information and to construct meaning, as well as to activate content (cultural knowledge, topic familiarity, previous experience, etc.) and formal schemata (rhetorical conventions, discourse forms, and text types). Other components of the listening construct became more visible in the interpretive approach, such as pragmatic or sociolinguistic issues, which focused not only on processing information, but also on being able to interpret it within a communicative context. Thus, information is constructed alongside the listening situation and is modified as more information is revealed and (re)interpreted. Likewise, a quest for input authenticity was encouraged. Top-down and bottom-up approaches to listening (Buck, 2001) focus on the learners' prior knowledge to make predictions and on the recognition of linguistic elements, respectively. In many cases, both are used in a language classroom as they also are in real life.

However, to include all the aspects that have been incorporated as part of a listening event over the years, the interpretation of both verbal and nonverbal information is also needed. This is where the multimodal approach we propose comes in. This approach requires being aware of the modes that are activated in a communicative event to generate meaning. It requires the learner to develop an ability to observe how verbal and nonverbal cues co-construct meaning. It means teaching and learning how these modes operate, and designing models of possible mode interaction or co-occurrence. When designing materials for the classroom and assessment tasks, the multimodal approach needs to consider the inclusion of audio material, but also other communicative modes. The nonverbal part of the construct is given or should be given its own specific value in language learning and testing, as it becomes an essential part of the construct.

In the past few decades, research on FL listening skills has considered the type of input that is employed both in classroom teaching and for assessment purposes. Notably, the work of Gruba (1993, 1997, 2004, 2006), Vandergrift (1999, 2003, 2007, 2010, 2012), Vandergrift and Goh (2009, 2012) and Wagner (2007, 2008, 2010a, 2010b) examined how learners react to audio vs. video and/or multimedia sources, and the benefits and limitations of including one or more modes in listening tasks designed to learn or test this skill. While some studies investigating the use of different input modes concluded that no difference was observed in the use of one mode (audio) as opposed to another (video listening) (Gruba, 1993; Coniam, 2001), other studies observed that learners showed better results when watching video or multimedia material as opposed to listening to audio-only versions of a listening test (Brett, 1997; Sueyoshi & Hardison, 2005; Wagner, 2010b). Learner performance in these tests is directly related to how we understand and interpret the listening text: only its verbal information, the nonverbal part of the text or both. Analyzing performance in multimodal tests without considering the types of nonverbal information implied in the listening process is basing experimental research on a theory that does not correspond to the listening construct. Gruba (1997) rightly pointed out that language comprehension tests must incorporate nonverbal communication aspects (e.g. culture or kinesics), which make test developers consider modes of presentations that include verbal, visual elements and also situational information provided by those elements. This will offer listening comprehension support to those test takers who are not particularly skillful in one single domain.

This author advocates for the importance of video input in academic listening assessment and urges further research on this topic. A similar conclusion was reached in Feak and Salehzadeh's (2001) study where they developed and validated an EAP (English for Academic Purposes) video listening placement test. It could be said that all speakers make use or can make use of "visual symbol systems" to gather and interpret situational information in their L1, L2 or Ln, though it is true that the more information modes we may access, the more comprehension opportunities to understand a message we may have.

As Gruba (1997, p. 338) went on to state, "Problems that may arise related to the influence of video on language proficiency assessment can be tackled within a larger perspective which sees visual elements as a key, not incidental, part of comprehending the world." It is this view of the "visual elements as a key" that needs to be taken into account for a more adequate approach to the multimodal listening construct. Thus, although the studies discussed in this section have contributed to the understanding of language learner listening skills and the use of different input media, in most cases some or all of the aspects below were not considered and need to be targeted in future studies, namely:

1. No pretests were carried out to determine students' overall proficiency level.
2. No listening pretest was carried out to determine students' listening proficiency level.

3. In most cases, no specific audio/video material and/or the questions used for the listening test employed in the study were included as part of the information provided by authors.
4. Little importance was given to nonverbal communication in the listening input materials (i.e., whether there were significant intonation shifts, gestures, facial expressions, etc. in the text that could be related to the test questions). An exception is Wagner (2010b) who briefly addressed this issue, and Vandergrift's (2011) analysis in interactive listening.
5. No information was given about whether any nonverbal skill was explicitly tested.

9.3 MULTIMODAL LISTENING SITUATIONS IN FORMAL LEARNING SETTINGS

This section presents a classification of the main situations or contexts in which listening can occur in formal learning settings at the university. Thus far, we have broadly distinguished two types of listening situations, transactional and interactional, attending to the level of interaction with the speaker. However, the complex construct of listening makes us consider other features that may shed some light on the demands of each academic listening situation to construct meaning, as well as their benefits in the multimodal listening learning process: a) the type of setting, face-to-face or virtual and b) if communication takes place mediated by some kind of technology, e.g., Massive Online Open Courses (MOOCs), Open Course Ware (OCW) platforms, Multimedia Educational Pills (MEPs), or/and by a lecturer in real time (via lectures or webinars). Indeed, the situation that provides us with a variety of modes will, in turn, determine how the micro and macrostructure of the listening situation is organized. We will have to deal with different types of listening tasks and, accordingly, different assessment methods and purposes, depending on:

1. Whether we find ourselves in an interactional or transactional situation
2. The number of speakers participating and the kind of role they play (from more active to less active or passive)
3. The relationship among speakers (relative power among participants, social distance, etc.)
4. The kind of information we may need to elicit from this situation

In Figure 9.1, we summarize how we envisage the most significant listening situations that students may find in higher education, drawing on the level of interaction the students may have with the speaker in formal learning settings. As argued by Delanty (2001), the university has to play a new and crucial role in the 21st-century knowledge society, though the adaptation to this changing scenario seems to be moving at slow pace. One step forward to fulfill part of the knowledge society's needs is represented by the growing offer of online undergraduate and postgraduate courses in both online and traditional universities. Moreover, the presence of ICTs (Information and Communication Technologies) in face-to-face learning, as well as in blending learning courses, also demands special consideration since a multimodal nature is inherent to these resources.

Let us consider each of the elements reflected in Figure 9.1. Formal learning may occur in a live setting (traditional, face-to-face setting) or in a virtual one. The e-learning setting varies in terms of how concerned the institution is in maintaining the lecturer's presence in a distance learning context. Regarding our main interest in this study, this is of special relevance for multimodal listening skills development. Whereas some universities with online courses choose to restrict interaction with the students to written communicative modes (emails, forums or chats), others attempt to be closer to classroom learning, and conferencing software is used to give lectures, seminars or tutorials (what is called live streaming). This is what we understand about an e-learning setting; there are clear differences from the classroom. However, the students also have the opportunity to listen to and watch the lecturers and PowerPoint presentations, or any other visual aid, in real time. In a virtual delivery format, the visual input is commonly more reduced and focused on the speaker. Tutorials, seminars and lectures are the most frequent listening encounters in formal learning settings, and the degree of interaction is expected to decrease from tutorials to seminars and from seminars to lectures.

Regarding two-way interaction situations, we cannot ignore webinars and their important presence, both in formal and informal educational settings. This live stream resource serves, among others, the purpose of

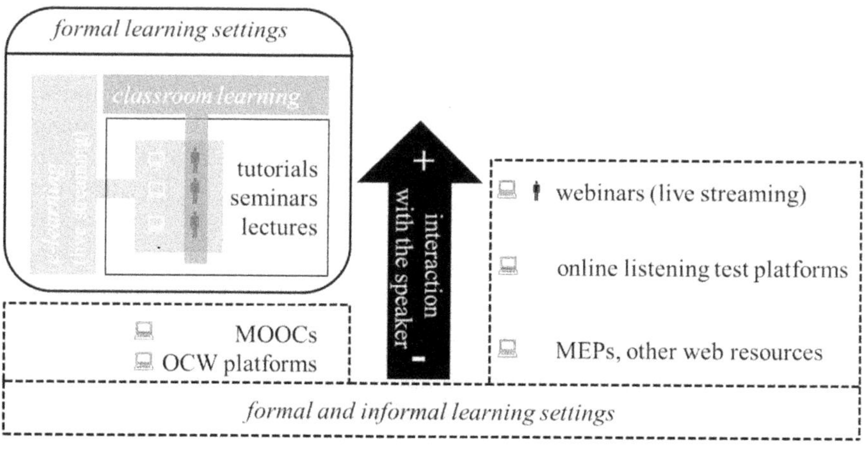

Figure 9.1 Multimodal listening situations in formal learning settings

increasing international academic cooperation among universities. This gives students the opportunity to complete their learning by attending lectures from all around the world with minimum effort in terms of expenses and time. Students attending traditional courses find in webinars a different listening situation with different interaction patterns. Though online students are familiar with this virtual listening context, usually they do not know the speaker. As a consequence, the aural and visual context and other features that will be discussed later are of paramount importance to decode the message and to construct the meaning in this situation.

Both listening and speaking skills can be used in two-way listening situations and assessment can also be done online. Using media like Skype teleconferencing would yield a more natural interpersonal context. Speaking skills are usually assessed in these situations, but there is less emphasis on listening ability with respect to what the student is able to comprehend when another speaker(s) is talking to him/her. Both or all speakers may use nonverbal communication devices. In this case, the speaker should not only be able to communicate nonverbally (encode nonverbal communication), but also to decode nonverbal communication conveyed by other speakers.

One-way listening situations are events where one person is giving some kind of public speech—for instance live academic lectures, or videoconferences that are increasing in popularity in graduate courses—and where participation of the listener is usually much lower than that of the main speaker of the event. Here multimodality applies most of all when the main speaker is a good communicator and makes ample usage of nonverbal communication. Likewise, MOOCs and OCW platforms give free access to video lectures, which are commonly used in informal learning, and can also be used in class as a videotext resource. Similarly, MEPs are mainly materials for transactional listening situations and can be embedded with a considerable amount of nonverbal information.

In the different situations explained above, one or more modes may be salient. Listening sources may be the teacher's or a speaker's voice, an audio text, a videotext or multimedia texts. Audio and video input modes are defined by their main nature, that is, by whether the information conveyed is mostly auditory or visual. Thus, even though videotexts used in language teaching all include audio recording, it is the visual input that first comes to mind when we think of using videotexts. If the added communication modes in videos as opposed to audios are the visual modes, when considering the use of videotexts in the language classroom the nonverbal visual information should be analyzed. This means that teachers need training in the interpretation of nonverbal cues that can be taught to students. When we talk about multimedia software, we intend the combination of different modes or media to express a message (Kress & van Leeuwen, 2001). The interest in finding out whether audio, video or multimedia resources are more suitable pedagogical devices for teaching listening skills lies in the assumption that user interaction with more than one communication mode may result in a more meaningful learning experience. Since an important feature of multimedia resources is their interactive nature, their use in language learning is essential when we want to pay attention to learner participation in the process. In this sense, it is not so much the teacher who decides the path a learner should follow, but it is the learner who may choose from a variety of paths offered by the teacher or by a specific multimedia product. One drawback for multimedia use in language learning is that all learners need to have and be able to use a computer, while for watching a video or listening to a recording, only one electronic device is required and may be shared by all students. However, in this case intelligibility may be lower when a number of students listen or watch from a screen with loudspeakers (as opposed to using headphones or personal computers).

In most of these situations, listening implies watching. For most cases, events in which listening occurs are interactive and are therefore combined with speaking skills. For these two reasons, the teaching and assessment of listening skills should also include the evaluation of other skills (i.e., multiskill tasks should be fostered). Combining listening skills with other language skills may yield tasks that are more natural or similar to real-life events and may thus be more meaningful for students who, in turn, could obtain better results. Imagine, for example, that we design a test that starts with a listening task in which learners pay attention to a video, including meaningful nonverbal information, and are later asked to perform an oral task that is similar to the video. Will students recall intonation patterns accompanied by gestures, and be able to reproduce them better when speaking in a parallel speaking task (i.e., parallel to the event they listened to)? The answer to this question demands further research on the benefits of using mixed skills tasks where one of the skills is multimodal listening. To a certain extent, this could be considered nonverbal information transfer/interpretation and application, i.e., listening with a purpose beyond (linguistic) comprehension that would lead to the design of meaningful learning situations for our students.

9.4 MULTIMODAL LISTENING INSTRUCTION AND ASSESSMENT

9.4.1 Monitoring Listening and Giving Listening Instructions

Systematic and purposeful observation of listening practice is part of the monitoring process. Monitoring listening also considers the way activities progress towards specific listening aims. Thus, the way instructions are given is important in the sense that task sequencing should be adequate both for classroom tasks and for assessment situations. Also of importance in these situations is the person who controls the listening task. The following is a list of possible instructional and monitoring situations:

1. Teachers decide when, for how long and how many times an oral text is reproduced.
2. Students interact with the audio or video recording by controlling it to achieve comprehension outcomes in a listening exercise. Students decide on the amount of time needed to achieve a goal within the given range of time for a task.
3. Students interact with multimedia materials for listening comprehension practice in an autonomous manner with no time constraints and no testing on the part of the teacher.

In a multimedia environment, the last two are employed, while in the classroom or in some testing situations, the first option is frequently used. Nowadays, most students feel comfortable with a multimedia environment since they are quite familiar with it; it may even result in a calming effect as the students already have the images to rely on, so they can guess meanings even when they do not understand the words they hear.

Monitoring is an important piece of the listening task when trying to define how listening is taught and assessed within the listening construct. Monitoring takes place most of the time during classroom hours, especially for productive skills tasks. In multimodal listening assessment, being aware of the multiple sources of information is a complex task in which the teacher must help to clarify how to utilize the different modes and how these may combine. When teaching listening, careful monitoring of the students' progress in understanding multimodal patterns is necessary. Once these patterns are understood, students can monitor their multimodal pattern understanding. In fact, learners should be involved in comprehending the listening situation, interpreting the information and trying to construct meaning from the various modes that are active in the multimodal listening. When students are assessed, the amount of control that they may have over the listening task may vary depending on how we understand the task. Thus, in a multimodal environment, the degree of control and the interactional patterns need to be defined.

As indicated above, a difference is observed in the testing procedure regarding whether questions are answered while listening with no pauses, while listening with pauses or after listening. This is important particularly in multimodal environments. For example, if students are taking a test in a multimedia format, the second option, i.e., listening and watching part one in an event and having some time to answer before the task continues to the second part, seems to be a more adequate administration procedure. The listener/watcher needs to process information in several modes, so keeping all that information in mind for all the questions until the end of the task is just not feasible, especially in an exam with all the stress that may be added in that situation.

Some of the research on listening tests that compare audio and video input criticizes the use of video resources because students sometimes feel distracted by the video or they do not use it as frequently as expected to accomplish the listening activity (Coniam, 2001; Ockey, 2007; Wagner, 2007, 2010b). This is not surprising, but in this case, it is the design of the listening task that should be questioned: If the video does not provide useful information and the students are asked to answer questions while the video is on, then of course they will focus on the verbal information alone, or will find the video distracting. This aspect is also related to the issue of listening text types, which may refer to a specific presentation format and to a particular choice of mode (audio, video, multimedia), as well as the genre selected (lecture, interview, radio recording, etc.). Wagner (2010b), for instance, compared the effect of nonverbal information on test performance across different genres and concluded that nonverbal information affects performance. However, this study did not focus on when this nonverbal information is valuable per se, or in which cases the information enhances or clarifies the verbal information. Research is needed not only on whether visual information has a positive impact on performance, but also on how and when learners benefit from the inclusion of nonverbal information while listening.

9.4.2 Listening Purpose and Task Format

Before deciding which listening format is the best, it is important to have a very clear idea of what we want to assess and how. Thus, task design and purpose should be thought out very carefully. There are three main questions here that are relevant to reach a balanced proposal for multimodal learning objectives and assessment criteria:

1. The relationship between question type and modes employed in the listening test
2. The complexity of the listening task in terms of verbal and nonverbal information processing
3. The way test administration procedures are aligned with the question type and to the complexity of the test (e-testing vs. paper)

The types of questions we decide to use in a listening test depend on the purpose of the listening task. The listening purpose may be contemplated from two perspectives: One is the kind of information that we want our students to retrieve from the listening test (context, verbal, gestural, etc.), and the other is what we want to ask them to do with that information.

Generally speaking, we listen to other people for a variety of purposes: to obtain information; to enjoy a conversation or someone's speech; to learn something in educational, professional or everyday contexts; or to try to simply understand someone or something. In the context of learning languages, the educational purposes may be summarized as follows (Nation & Newton, 2009; Weir & Vidaković, 2013):

1. Listening for accuracy: word or phrase comprehension
2. Listening to understand the main message or important information bits within a recording
3. Listening to understand complex information
4. Listening to understand detailed information or to find specific data; information transfer (fill in a chart or table while listening)
5. Listening to understand the context and to infer information

And in our multimodal proposal we would add:

6. Listening and *watching* to understand information from other modes different from verbal input

The purpose of listening should determine the types of questions or tasks that are used and the administration procedures that are the most appropriate to answer those questions (i.e., while listening or after listening). There are different question formats that may be used for listening tasks (open with long or short answers, true/false, multiple choice, etc.). We need to consider how adequate each of these question formats can be for a listening task or test. Each format has its own advantages and disadvantages. For instance, multiple choice questions can be quite misleading since students are not asked if something they heard was true or false, but which option within several possibilities is true. This may be quite confusing for students since they are given more (misleading/complex) information. However, because multiple choice tests are easier to mark, they are a favored option. Designing true/false questions for a listening test is an arduous task. In fact, many times deciding whether something is totally or partially true does not depend so much on understanding the message (more precisely, the words they hear), but on how we as individuals interpret that message. It is for this reason that answers that give a space for students to write a more or less long answer where they can really express their point of view are sometimes preferred. Written answers, however, are time-consuming when marking exams and not cost effective, which is a drawback. At the same time, both multiple choice and true/false questions can be answered quickly in an exam situation, which brings us to our next reflection.

As we have seen in the previous section, we may use different text formats and different question types to assess listening skills. Yet if we include the ability to process more than one mode as part of the listening construct, the issue of purpose and question type becomes even more complicated. Each format may include one or more communicative modes. When just one mode is present, or when we want to focus on only one mode, we are working within a monomodal approach. When two or more modes are active, we can talk about multimodality. Thus, depending on what we want to assess, we need to ask ourselves the following basic questions:

1. How do we assess listening comprehension, using individual or combined modes? That is, are we using a video to formulate:
   a. questions to assess the comprehension of audio/verbal information only,
   b. questions to assess visual information only,
   c. a combination of both question types, or
   d. questions using the combination of audio and video when they join to generate a cohesive message?
2. If several features belonging both to verbal and nonverbal communication are used at a specific point in a communicative event, what kind of assessment questions can we ask?
3. How can we formulate those questions so as not to confuse students?

Listening tasks may also be formulated so that more than one skill is used. Thus, the purpose of the listening activity may be to use a mixed-mode assessment question leading to the integration of two skills (Nation & Newton, 2009). For example, students may be asked to watch and listen to a video about a topic and then be required to write an essay on that topic. In this case, we can talk about a mixed assessment mode, i.e., listening to retrieve information that will lead to a written task. Students may also be asked to listen to an audio recording of part of a telephone conversation in which a person is giving information on the different ways to reach a place. Then the student can be asked to inform a friend about how to reach that place. The second task focuses on the verbal message, while the first one allows for processing, interpreting and evaluating verbal and nonverbal information to produce an outcome. In the task using multimodal input, students can use verbal input, but also image input, to create their written text. Imagine, for example, a video talking about a place: For this task students may use their own interpretation of images or the verbal information provided in the video to describe that place. Similar tasks may be designed in combination with those involving speaking skills.

For either type of task (involving an individual mode or mixed modes), very clear assessment criteria need to be defined for the students (and also for the teachers and test raters so that they may discern whether the student has understood the input or part of it). Defining listening sub-skills is an important issue, particularly in the type of task where more than one main skill is required.

9.5 A FRAMEWORK FOR MULTIMODAL LISTENING ASSESSMENT

Our discussion on listening assessment, and particularly on using videotexts as the listening source, will focus on how students construct meaning using this multimodal input. We have developed our proposal for multimodal listening assessment on the basis of Rost's (2011) model for listening assessment. He described the aspects of listening that are part of solid assessments as five types of knowledge: general, pragmatic, syntactic, lexical and phonological. The model we propose is seen from an even broader perspective to bring to the fore the largely ignored nonlinguistic components in listening assessment.

Nevertheless, to design our model it was important to consider the student's perspective in order to understand what components contribute to constructing meaning, and how this meaning is constructed. In Figure 9.2, we provide an overview of 'the what and the how' of meaning construction when videotexts are used.

As can be seen, three types of knowledge should be part of the process of understanding videotexts: a) general knowledge, b) linguistic knowledge (which relates to any information that is decoded from linguistic input) and c) nonlinguistic knowledge. The major change between our model and Rost's (2011) is the status given to extralanguage and paralanguage as components

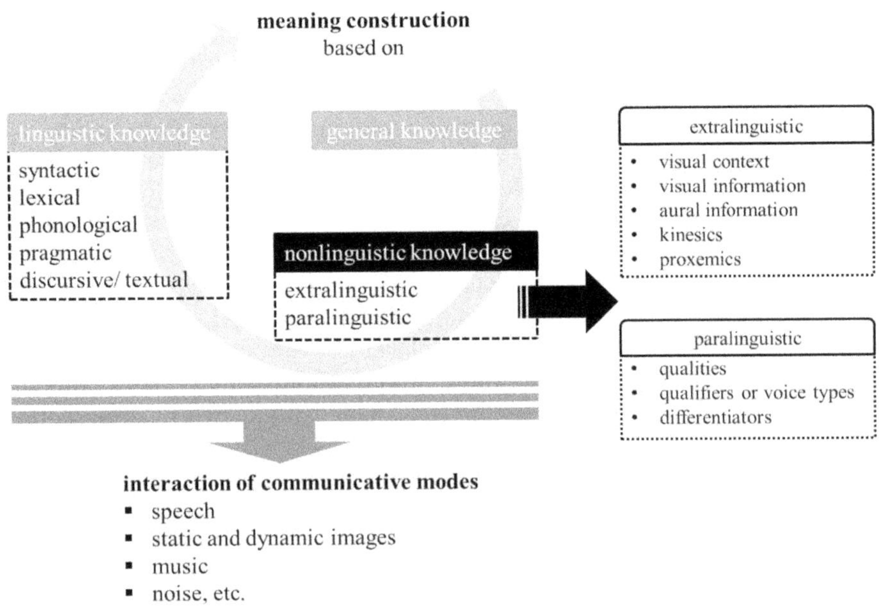

Figure 9.2 Meaning construction using videotexts

of nonlinguistic knowledge, which he considered under the umbrella of general knowledge. Our model also includes a fine-grained description of extralinguistic knowledge, and additionally considers discursive and textual knowledge (inside linguistic knowledge) that serves to recognize genre and discourse patterns or rhetorical conventions.

General and linguistic knowledge are commonplace in the description of listening skills and general language skills. In contrast, nonlinguistic knowledge needs further discussion in these contexts. As mentioned above, we understand this type of knowledge as articulated in extralinguistic and paralinguistic information. By extralinguistic knowledge, we refer to all the input the students receive from the videotext that has a visual or aural nature. Here we find five kinds of input: a) visual context or visual background, b) visual information (figures, tables, etc.), c) aural information (music, background noise, etc.), d) kinesics (gestures of hands and arms, head movement, facial expression, gaze and body posture) and e) proxemics, that is, interpersonal distance (Hall, 1959). With regard to paralinguistic knowledge, we follow Poyatos's (2002) definition of paralanguage that distinguishes three categories: a) qualities (e.g., loudness, intonation rage, syllabic duration, etc.), b) qualifiers or voice types and c) differentiators (e.g., laughter, throat-clearing, yawning, etc.).

Linguistic and nonlinguistic knowledge are ways of communication. Bara, Cutica and Tirassa (2001, p. 73) claimed that there are "superficial manifestations of a single communicative competence whose nature is neither linguistic nor extralinguistic, but mental." Even so, these are expressed physically with different modes to enable communication. The modes students find in videotexts can be speech, static and dynamic images, music and noise, among others. Speech is primarily related to linguistic knowledge, but also to nonlinguistic knowledge. In this respect, aural information (extralinguistic input), such as a background conversation, is speech, as is paralanguage. Static and dynamic images are part of nonlinguistic knowledge. Static images are visual information, whereas dynamic images refer to kinesics and proxemics. Finally, music appears in many videotexts and its contribution to meaning has also been studied (Jewitt, 2003). Music, like noise, is another mode to express aural information.

If we acknowledge that all these features interact in multimodal listening, we should clearly describe them for students and include these items in the syllabus, as well as in test specifications within the listening construct. When working with a multimodal listening task, we should ask students to interpret not only verbal information, but also to be able to identify, analyze and interpret all nonverbal modes of information. The study of gestures is one of the kinesic sub-modes that has received considerable attention from scholars (see Bavelas et al., 1992; Kendon, 2004; McNeill, 1992), together with facial expressions (see Ekman, 2007). Gullberg (2006) discussed cross-cultural and cross-linguistic repertoires of gestures that should be considered as part of the acquisition of a language, in what she called *SLA (Second*

Language Acquisition) of gestures, similar to Raffler-Engel's (1980) *second kinesic acquisition*.

In short, the construction of meaning in videotexts relies on understanding the complexity of the interaction of the modes that define them. Thus, the implementation of a multimodal listening assessment, understood also as part of students' training for the development of their listening comprehension skills, could also consider some of the expected difficulties students may find because of the nature of videotexts. Among these, information density might be especially problematic, not only in terms of lexical density (as would occur in audio-only listening), but also modal density (the linguistic and nonlinguistic interweaving of modes). Accordingly, in a situation in which there is a strong coherence and cohesion within and among modes, students would find fewer comprehension difficulties. But this is something that does not always occur in real-life events. For example, Figure 9.3 depicts a complaint speech act in a video sequence.[1] The woman had asked her nephews to buy some bread while she was finishing lunch at home, but they found no bread at the bakery and simply went to the beach with friends. At lunch time there was no bread and she complains because they did not even let her know there was no bread earlier in the morning. She says: "Why didn't you tell me?"

The meaning she conveys goes beyond her words: They should have phoned her so she could have gone to the bakery later. The utterance employed does not mention any telephone use, a piece of information that is exclusively understood if attention is paid to visual cues. The metaphoric gesture (a pictorial gesture that encodes an abstract idea, "phoning") shows she is reproaching them. Additionally, her feelings are also revealed by facial expression (raising eyebrows) and shoulder movement (raising shoulders slightly). This example illustrates important information conveyed by nonverbal input, which should also be considered when assessing listening comprehension, thus pushing students to focus on the whole input they receive in the videotext, rather than just on oral information. One question that

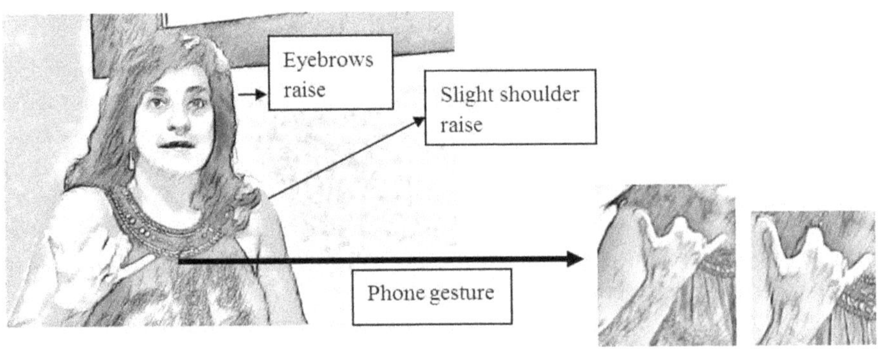

Figure 9.3 "Why didn't you tell me?"

could be asked in a listening activity could be "When they found no bread was left in the bakery, what should they have done?" a) phone their aunt, b) go back home, c) go to the beach.

One of the problems of testing listening is that, in many cases, there is no teaching practice as such, but rather the time devoted to listening skills in the classroom is basically also testing the skill, with little or no reflection on what the students listen to, why they listen or how they can manage and improve their listening skills. Multimodal listening comprehension instruction should include comprehensible multimodal input. Likewise, practice in classroom listening should be parallel to the testing of this skill. For this reason, students should be given information as to the kinds of modes they should pay attention to, and classroom discussion should focus on all the available modes that come into action in the particular listening event to be practiced. At the same time, some instruction should appear in listening tests as to the modes the students should pay attention to before the listening starts.

It becomes obvious that both teacher and student training are needed in order to develop a multimodal working pedagogy. Figure 9.4 is a possible factsheet guide that students and teachers could work with in order to understand and evaluate multimodal texts in listening practice. It entails recognizing the multimodal video sequences or meaning units that comprise a specific event (the videotext listening comprehension). Here, listening sequences are understood as communicative units in multimodal discourse and for this reason become comprehension units when teaching multimodal listening skills.

In a testing situation, an important part of test design should be the presentation of a guiding set of questions, or brief information, to situate the listener in the event in terms of general sociocultural information. This should be done before the listening takes place in order to reduce the cognitive burden. Expecting students to reach so many and varied knowledge types, as well as to follow the content of a listening activity in an exam setting, is perhaps putting too heavy a burden on them. In most formal listening tests, virtually no time is given for students to react to complex issues unless these are well rooted in the students' previous knowledge, both cultural and pragmatic.

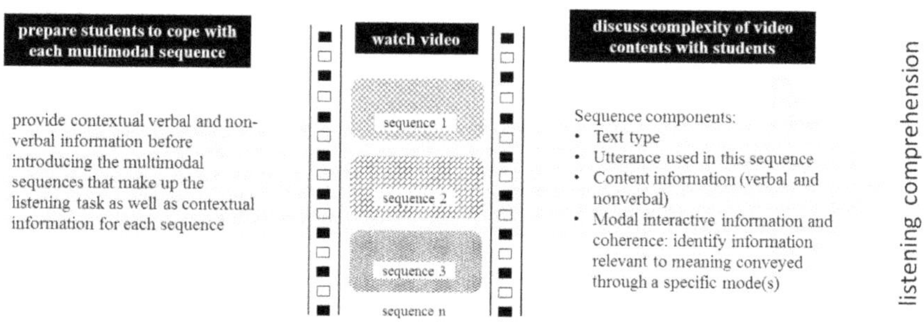

Figure 9.4 Information organization factsheet to address listening tasks

Presenting context visuals—i.e., visual elements that provide information about the context (Ginther, 2002)—as part of the pretest questions could be considered not only a means to help students situate the event from a socio-cultural point of view, but also to prepare them for the listening test.

9.6 CONCLUDING REMARKS

Multimodal listening comprehension assessment should be able to measure the student's ability to identify, interpret and evaluate verbal and nonverbal information in multimodal texts in order to answer a set of questions or resolve a task. Nevertheless, interpreting nonverbal communication is not always an easy task as it typically depends on the context. Interpreting gestures on their own is not feasible; most gestures are polysemous and context-dependent.

Multimodal listening comprehension assessment should define criteria for evaluating the nonverbal aspects of multimodal listening. However, before that, relevant nonverbal communication modes should be analyzed, synthesized and organized in a user-friendly way for students to be able to understand and deal with them in a coherent and productive way. The study of nonverbal communication and its specific importance in language learning must occur prior to multimodal language assessment. Multimodal listening comprehension assessment also implies that teachers need to have clear principles upon which to support their teaching practices.

Throughout this chapter, we have seen how analyzing and understanding the multimodal nature of listening to videos is a complex task that demands a great deal of effort from both students and teachers. The listening task per se becomes intricate. For this reason, further research into defining a difficulty threshold in multimodal listening would be useful. This could provide the grounds to enable the teacher or test rater to ascribe difficulty levels to language proficiency levels, thus helping teachers and test developers to select videotexts and design suitable tasks and activities accordingly.

NOTE

1. The example illustrated by Figure 9.3 was a real conversation that the authors witnessed and have reproduced for this chapter.

REFERENCES

Ariza, E.N., & Hancock, S. (2003). Second language acquisition theories as a framework for creating distance learning courses. *The International Review of Research in Open Distance Learning, 4*(2). Retrieved from http://www.irrodl.org/index.php/irrodl/article/viewArticle/142/222.

Badger, R., Sutherland, P., White, G., & Haggis, T. (2001). Note perfect: An investigation of how students view taking notes in lectures. *System, 29*(3), 405–417.

Bara, B., Cutica, I., & Tirassa, M. (2001). Neuropragmatics: Extralinguistic communication after closed head injury. *Brain and Language, 77*(1), 72–94.

Bavelas, J.B., Chovil, N., Lawrie, D., & Wade, A. (1992). Interactive gestures. *Discourse Processes, 15*(4), 469–489.

Brett, P. (1997). A comparative study of the effects of the use of multimedia on listening comprehension. *System, 25*(1), 39–53.

Buck, G. (2001). *Assessing listening*. New York: Cambridge University Press.

Coniam, D. (2001). The use of audio or video comprehension as an assessment instrument in the certification of English language teachers: A case study. *System, 29*(1), 1–14.

Delanty, G. (2001). *Challenging knowledge: The university in the knowledge society*. Buckingham: Society for Research into Higher Education & Open University Press.

Ekman, P. (2007). *Emotions revealed: Recognizing faces and feelings to improve communication and emotional life* (2nd edition). New York: Owl Books.

Feak, C., & Salehzadeh, J. (2001). Challenges and issues in developing an EAP video listening placement assessment. *English for Specific Purposes, 20*(Supplement 1), 477–493.

Ginther, A. (2002). Context and content visuals and performance on listening comprehension stimuli. *Language Testing, 19*(2), 133–167.

Gruba, P. (1993). A comparison study of audio and video in language testing. *JALT Journal, 15*(1), 85–88.

Gruba, P. (1997). The role of video media in listening assessment. *System, 25*(3), 335–345.

Gruba, P. (2004). Understanding digitalized second language videotext. *Computer Assisted Language Learning, 17*(1), 51–82.

Gruba, P. (2006). Playing the videotext: A media literacy perspective on video-mediated L2 listening. *Language Learning and Technology, 10*(2), 77–92.

Gullberg, M. (2006). Some reasons for studying gesture and second language acquisition (Hommage à Adam Kendon). *IRAL, 44*(2), 103–124.

Hall, E. (1959). *The silence language*. Garden City, NY: Doubleday and Co.

ILA. (1995). A ILA Definition of Listening. *The Listening Post, 53*(1), 4–5.

Jewitt, C. (2003). Re-thinking assessment: Multimodality, literacy and computer-mediated learning. *Assessment in Education, 10*(1), 83–102.

Jewitt, C. (2013). Multimodal teaching and learning. In C.A. Chapelle (Ed.), *The encyclopedia of applied linguistics* (pp. 4109–4114). Oxford: Blackwell.

Jung, E. (2003). The role of discourse signaling cues in second language listening comprehension. *Modern Language Journal, 87*(4), 562–577.

Kendon, A. (2004). *Gesture: Visible action as utterance*. Cambridge: Cambridge University Press.

Kress, G., & van Leeuwen, T. (2001). *Multimodal discourse: The modes and media of contemporary communication*. London: Edward Arnold.

Lynch, T. (2011). Academic listening in the 21st century: Reviewing a decade of research. *Journal of English for Academic Purposes, 10*(2), 79–88.

McGurk, H., & MacDonald, J. (1976). Hearing lips and seeing voices. *Nature, 976*(264), 746–748.

McNeill, D. (1992). *Hand and mind: What gestures reveal about thought*. Chicago: The University of Chicago Press.

Morell, T. (2004). Interactive lecture discourse for university EFL students. *English for Specific Purposes, 23*(3), 325–338.

Morell, T. (2007). What enhances EFL students' participation in lecture discourse? Student, lecturer and discourse perspectives. *Journal of English for Academic Purposes, 6*(3), 222–237.

Nation, I.S.P., & Newton, J. (2009). *Teaching ESL/EFL listening and speaking.* Routledge: New York.
Ockey, G. (2007). Construct implications of including still image or video in computer-based listening tests. *Language Testing 24*(4), 517–537.
Poyatos, F. (2002). *Nonverbal communication across disciplines: Volume II. Paralanguage, kinesics, silence, personal and environmental interaction.* Amsterdam: John Benjamins.
Raffler-Engel, W. V. (1980). Kinesics and second language acquisition. In B. Kettemann, & R.N. St. Clair (Eds.), *New approaches to language acquisition* (pp. 101–109). Tübingen: Gunter Narr Verlag.
Rost, M. (2011). *Teaching and researching listening.* Edinburgh: Pearson Education Limited.
Shellenbarger, S. (2014, July 22). Tuning in: Improving your listening skills. How to get the most out of a conversation. *The Wall Street Journal.* Retrieved from http://online.wsj.com/articles/tuning-in-how-to-listen-better-1406070727?tesla=y&mg=reno64-wsj&url=http://online.wsj.com/article/SB10001424052702304058404580045441119703492.html.
Sueyoshi, A., & Hardison, D.M. (2005). The role of gestures and facial cues in second language listening comprehension. *Language Learning, 55*(4), 661–699.
Tauroza, S., & Allison, D. (1994). Expectation-driven understanding in information systems lecture comprehension. In J. Flowerdew (Ed.), *Academic listening: Research perspectives* (pp. 35–54). Cambridge: Cambridge University Press.
Vandergrift, L. (1999). Facilitating second language listening comprehension: Acquiring successful strategies. *ELT Journal, 53*(3), 168–176.
Vandergrift, L. (2003). Orchestrating strategy use: Toward a model of the skilled second language listener. *Language Learning, 5*(3), 463–496.
Vandergrift, L. (2007). Recent developments in second and foreign language listening and comprehension research. *Language Teaching, 40*(3), 191–210.
Vandergrift, L. (2010). Researching listening in applied linguistics. In B. Paltridge, & A. Phakiti (Eds.), *Companion to research methods in applied linguistics* (pp. 160–173). London: Continuum.
Vandergrift, L. (2011). L2 listening: Presage, process, product and pedagogy. In E. Hinkel (Ed.), *Handbook of research in second language teaching and learning* (Volume II, pp. 455–471). New York: Routledge.
Vandergrift, L. (2012). Teaching interactive listening. In H.P. Widodo, & A. Cirocki (Eds.), *Innovation and creativity in ELT methodology* (pp. 1–14). New York: Nova Science Publishers.
Vandergrift, L., & Goh, C. (2009). Teaching and testing listening comprehension. In M. Long, & C. Doughty (Eds.), *Handbook of language teaching.* Malden, MA: Blackwell.
Vandergrift, L., & Goh, C. (2012). *Teaching and learning second language listening: Metacognition in action.* New York: Routledge.
Wagner, E. (2007). Are they watching? Test taker viewing behavior during an L2 video listening test. *System, 11*(1), 67–88.
Wagner, E. (2008). Video listening tests: What are they measuring? *Language Assessment Quarterly, 5*(3), 218–243.
Wagner, E. (2010a). Test-takers' interaction with an L2 video listening test. *System, 38*(2), 280–291.
Wagner, E. (2010b). The effect of the use of video texts on ESL listening test-taker performance. *Language Testing, 27*(4), 493–513.
Weir, C., & Vidaković, I. (2013). The measurement of listening ability 1913–2012. In C. Weir, I. Vidaković, & E. Galaczi (Eds.), *Measured constructs* (pp. 347–419). Cambridge: Cambridge University Press.

10 Teaching Learners How to Use Pragmatic Routines Through Audiovisual Material

Silvia Bruti

10.1 INTRODUCTION

In this chapter, I aim to show the benefits of using film clips and film language as multimodal resources in the foreign language classroom, especially for the teaching of pragmatic features of conversational interaction by taking the case of conversational routines as a paradigmatic example. I will start by reviewing some of the merits of using audiovisual material in language teaching and defending the authenticity of film language in a pedagogical context (sections 10.2 and 10.3). Then I will describe conversational routines in more detail in both spoken and film dialogue (section 10.4), before showing how to exploit film clips to teach these conversational features in the language classroom (section 10.5). In the latter part of section 10.5, I will show some practical examples of multimodal transcription and analysis of some clips from the Berkeley Language Center's Library of Foreign Language Film Clips (LFLFC). Some conclusions will follow in section 10.6.

10.2 AUDIOVISUAL MATERIAL IN THE LANGUAGE CLASSROOM

It is undeniable that we live in a world where images are pervasive in any moment and in any situation, be it formal or informal, private or public. We can access distant sites or reach people far removed from us on our computer screen or mobile phone very simply by a mere click of a finger. As many scholars advocate (e.g., Ballarin, 2007; Celentin, 2007), given the impressive power that media and visual images have, they should and are in fact more and more often introduced in the foreign language curriculum as a way of enhancing learners' proficiency in the foreign language and, at the same time, entertaining them by creating a relaxed atmosphere and offering a change from the routine activities of the classroom.

Until recently, however, at least in Italy, the use of film in foreign language teaching has not, for the most part, been very frequent for two reasons. First of all, schools were usually poorly equipped, with difficult access to multimedia rooms, which were shared by many classes and therefore not always available. I am here referring to TV sets and video-recorders initially and DVD players later on. Now that films are available both on DVD and also as digital files, the situation is somewhat better, as personal computers, laptops, tablets and even mobile phones provide available screens. Furthermore, the introduction of interactive white boards, which has strongly been favored over the last few years, allows teachers to access a whole wealth of multimedia resources.[1] The second reason is linked to lesson preparation when video material is involved: Teachers, until a few years ago, felt discouraged and thus avoided using films or video material in general because they thought they were time-consuming and too challenging to deal with. It is certainly true that a lesson involving video material needs to be prepared in advance and is more time-consuming for the teacher than merely following the textbook, as previewing, selecting and careful lesson planning are all necessary steps (see, for instance, Stoller, 1995, p. 68). However, it is also incomparably more challenging for learners, as it stimulates their sensitivity and encourages them to broaden their imagination and creativity. In addition, these lessons are most of the time more rewarding in terms of results.

This chapter explores the viability of audiovisual material in teaching students how to use conversational routines. As the literature on the subject has shown, the advantages of the pedagogic exploitation of films in the ELT classroom are manifold (Rodríguez Martín, 2006).[2] Films or audiovisual texts in general help nonnative speakers to acquire more natural-sounding pronunciation; they can be used to introduce students to a vast array of linguistic varieties in context (Stoller, 1995; Shawback & Terhune, 2002), exploiting the communication of various semiotic codes at the same time (paralinguistic features, kinesics, oculesics, proxemics); they provide learners with information, both linguistic and factual, that they can strategically reuse on other occasions; they are a first-rate vehicle for the teaching of any structural (i.e., morphological, syntactic) or communicative aspect (i.e., semantic and pragmatic features of spoken interaction) (Massi & Merino, 1996); and they allow for the design of multifaceted and varied activities that can be put into practice in the language classroom (Stoller, 1995; Canning-Wilson, 2000). Nevertheless, media should be considered as a means to an end, that is, instruments that trigger further language use and broaden interests, and not as ends in themselves.

As Kaiser (2011) convincingly contends, the instances in which the watching of a whole film is preferable over that of a clip are few. Usually, students have numerous difficulties in following and understanding a whole audiovisual text. Maintaining concentration for so long might prove to be a real effort, especially when students do not understand a good percentage of the text and therefore get discouraged. The shortcomings of seeing a decontextualized extract can be easily overcome if the teacher explains the context of the scene, or if more scenes from the same film are shown. In general, the use of clips from films, commercials, documentaries or any other genre makes it easier for students to focus on one piece at a time and to "explore the language of the clip and the various components of visual semiotics (dress, setting, gesture, facial expressions, color palette, etc.)" (Kaiser, 2011, p. 234). To this end, at the Berkeley Language Center, a group of researchers set out to compile an Internet-based database of film clips, i.e., the Library of Foreign Language Film Clips (hereinafter LFLFC), which allows authorized instructors and students to access the clips, either from the classroom or from home. Clips are first cut from audiovisual texts and then variously tagged (e.g., linguistically and culturally; see Kaiser, 2011 for more details), so that they can be retrieved according to the user's interests and needs. The project has grown into a huge collaborative network that involves several institutions that have been granted authorization to access and share their materials.[3]

10.3 THE 'AUTHENTICITY' OF AUDIOVISUAL DIALOGUE

In what follows, I will discuss some of the objections that are often raised against the authenticity of film language, because of its planned and scripted nature, i.e., "written-to-be-spoken-as-if not-written" (Gregory & Carroll, 1978, p. 42) or its "prefabricated orality" (Baños-Piñero & Chaume, 2009; Chaume, 2012). Gregory and Carroll (1978) paved the way for the debate on the authenticity of film language when they argued that this is a peculiar register, in that it aims to sound natural, but is in fact carefully planned to appear so. Several studies on scripted texts (see, inter alia, Baños-Piñero & Chaume, 2009; Baños-Piñero, 2013) have pointed out that scriptwriters—and subsequently audiovisual translators—pick specific features of speech that are widely accepted and identified as such by the audience. This selection plays a crucial role, as credibility is singled out by professional operators and scholars alike as one of the most important ingredients for a successful audiovisual product. Abstracting from the differences that depend on each culture's norms, Chaume (2012, p. 81) argues that the language of audiovisual texts can best be described as "a combination of features deriving from both oral and written texts." This is because, on the one hand, it encourages creativity and spontaneity, while on the other, it is ruled by a complex set of norms, i.e., the constraints of the media, the conventions of the genre, the stylistic rules dictated by television authorities (for example standardization, censorship, patronage) and broadcasting companies, as well as the strong link that exists between visual images and words. For these reasons, in the analysis of audiovisual dialogue and its translation, Chaume (2012, p. 82) suggests using an integrated approach that takes into account the "multiple semiotic codes operating simultaneously." However, other works that aim to ascertain the comparability of fictional dialogue with spontaneous conversation have achieved partially contrasting results. Specialized studies like those by Quaglio (2009a; 2009b) and Forchini (2012), both adopting

Biber's (1988) multidimensional analysis, highlight rather similar uses and patterning in both registers, for example, in dealing with the so-called *interpersonal dimension* (Biber, 1988). The analysis of more specific features, such as vague language (Quaglio, 2009b), shows however that changes may affect frequency but undoubtedly go beyond it, as they are dictated by the need for clarity in the audiovisual text and the requirement to attract an audience. Other corpus-based studies comparing screen dialogue (by using a small corpora of film transcripts) and real-life conversation in the British National Corpus (Rodríguez Martín & Moreno Jaén, 2009; Rodríguez Martín, 2010) have similarly concluded that movies employ a wide range of conversational strategies and devices. Consequently, they can be very useful for raising awareness of key conversational processes among language learners.

Kaiser (2011) is in favor of the deployment of film material in the language classroom and maintains that film is itself "an authentic source material (that is, created for native speakers and not learners of the language), a cultural artifact as worthy of study in foreign language classrooms as canonical texts of literature." Although admitting that speech in films is performed, Kaiser contends that this performance is one in which "native speakers suspend disbelief and accept the dialogue as 'real'" (2011, p. 233). Furthermore, another valuable asset is that it often portrays a vast array of sociolects, that is, speech that can be distinguished on the basis of several sociolinguistic parameters, such as age, gender, social class, provenance and level of education, thus exposing learners to many of the varieties they will encounter in real-life interactions in the L2.

Engaged in finding 'authentic' material for the language class, Tatsuki and some of her collaborators set out to evaluate the genuineness of various pedagogical materials, such as textbooks, films and other broadcast media (Kite & Tatsuki, 2005; Tatsuki & Nishizawa, 2005; Tatsuki & Kite, 2006). As pointed out above, the comparability of film language to naturally occurring language is an open-ended debate, with few studies providing empirical data and validation of the feasibility of the operation, although many recommend using films in foreign language teaching (see, inter alia, Stoller, 1995). Tatsuki and her coworkers also aimed at determining if in the case of differences, these were relevant, or even beneficial for learners. Results for compliments, for example, showed consistent similarities with natural conversation in the syntactic patterns used, in the way compliments are responded to and in the topics of the compliments themselves. Similar results were found for apologies, which likewise show the same syntactic and semantic patterns as ethnographically collected data. For both speech acts some differences were also evidenced: They mainly affect gender distribution as women tend to compliment each other the most, whereas in films the pattern is reversed and men compliment women and other men significantly more than they do in 'real life,' at least from what emerges from ethnographic studies of naturally occurring speech (Manes & Wolfson, 1981; Holmes, 1988, 1989,

1990). Tatsuki therefore underlines that this could in part be attributed to the way men are portrayed in Hollywood films, but also to some limitations of the ethnographic studies on compliments, in which the data were collected by graduate students, mostly women, in women-centered situations. As for the differences, Tatsuki (2006) provides an interesting example: Research on compliments (Manes & Wolfson, 1981) has shown that five adjectives account for the majority of compliments exchanged; however, if learners encounter a more varied range of adjectives in films, they are likely to retain more useful vocabulary to be used later in everyday interactions.

10.3.1 Multimodality in Audiovisual Texts

As O'Halloran (2004, p. 1) points out, there has recently been a "shift in linguistic enquiry where language use is no longer theorized as an isolated phenomenon" but is explored in connection with visual codes. The analysis of talk in audiovisual products, although prioritized, is thus complemented by an examination of actors' gestures and costumes, camera movements and lighting, as shown, for example, in Piazza's (2010) study of the interrelationships between the verbal and visual codes in a short film by Antonioni. She illustrates how the complex narrative discourse of the film can be explained by combining a linguistic analysis with a semiotic analysis of the nonverbal elements, for example elements of the *mise-en-scène*. Drawing mostly on Kress and van Leeuwen's (1996) multimodal model, the author transcribes extracts of the film juxtaposing the verbal and visual text. The former contains the dialogues, whereas the latter details the camera angle, the composition of the frame, costumes, movements and gestures.

Despite this recognized shift in interest towards multimodality, in a recent comprehensive work devoted to film discourse interpretation, Wildfeuer (2013, p. 1) argues that "contemporary approaches to film analysis have not yet succeeded in systematically defining and describing how filmic devices are intersemiotically combined to narrative structures." In her book, Wildfeuer explores exactly how the meaning-making process takes place, highlighting not only the contribution of various modalities tied together by film editing, but also the "active participation of the spectator" (2013, p. 1). Although she draws on a plurality of models, Wildfeuer elaborates her personal analytical framework for meaning interpretation and applies it to different films. The multimodal transcription, which is the first necessary step in the analysis, includes a shot of the scene, followed by a shot description, the audio track (specifying sounds and noises), the spoken language and the music.

10.3.2 Teaching Multimodality Through Audiovisual Texts

One of the strengths of using audiovisual texts in the EFL classroom is that they offer a contextualized representation of communication in which the verbal code is paralleled and complemented by other semiotic codes. The importance of teaching students how to make meaning through different semiotic modalities should therefore not be underestimated.

Alongside language, gestures also play a pivotal role in both spontaneous interaction and in audiovisual dialogue. Gullberg (2006) discusses some reasons for teaching the meaning potential of gestures to language students: First of all, since they have a specific cross-linguistic and cross-cultural repertoire, learners should be made aware of the set of gestures available in the target language; second, given that gestures may be acquired along with language but are nonetheless independent from it, they can shed light on the acquisition process and its pitfalls (e.g., L1 interference, transfer, etc.). Finally, and most importantly, gestures favor comprehension and learning (e.g., retention of vocabulary) and facilitate interaction, by integrating or 'scaffolding' language. Such a view is also supported by Sueyoshi and Hardison (2005), who conducted an experimental study to establish the contribution of gestures and facial cues to second language listening comprehension. Campoy-Cubillo and Querol-Julián (this volume) also focus on the use of multimodal texts as input for listening comprehension tasks, suggesting that the purpose of listening tasks should be more clearly defined (e.g., indicating if comprehension includes aspects of nonverbal information) and that students should be taught how to interpret nonverbal cues. On the basis of these premises, listening comprehension activities should be redesigned so that all modes of communication can be assessed for their contribution to the construction of meaning.

One final aspect that is particularly relevant in teaching multimodal analysis of audiovisual texts is related to how visual shots are built, how they are sequenced, which perspective is adopted (e.g., where the camera is positioned in relation to the characters) and the distance between the viewer and the depicted world of the image. All these aspects are described in a very detailed way by Baldry and Thibault (2006) in a chapter dedicated to the analysis of TV ads, which also provided a coding scheme for multimodal transcription. Simpler coding schemes, which could be successfully implemented to teach meaning interpretation in the language classroom, are those used in the multimodal analyses by Piazza (2010) and Wildfeuer (2013) (see also Bateman & Schmidt, 2012 and Bateman, 2014).

10.4 CONVERSATIONAL ROUTINES IN SPONTANEOUS AND FILM DIALOGUE

In this chapter, I decided to focus on the multimodal dimension of a small number of conversational routines. According to Florian Coulmas (1981), these consist of a whole series of speech acts that convey a vast array of sociopragmatic meanings, including greetings, leave-takings, compliments, thanks, apologies and the like. They are rather repetitive in form and despite their somewhat predictable nature, these expressions actually turn out to be quite complex in that they presuppose practices and habits that change across cultures. As Laver (1981, p. 304) puts it, "Routines of greeting and parting, far from being relatively meaningless and mechanical social behaviour, can thus be understood as extremely important strategies for the negotiation and control of social identity and social relationships between participants in a conversation."

Speech and the management of conversational features are very often marginalized in syllabi, and reduced to few simplified and far-fetched dialogues in textbooks, at best accompanied by audio recordings. It is only quite recently that conversation has begun to be considered for its own sake and as a separate register: In *The Longman Grammar of Spoken and Written English* (Biber et al., 1999), a comprehensive chapter is devoted to the so-called features of conversations, which are compared with those of other registers. Carter and McCarthy (2006) also allocate a chapter to grammar and spoken language, maintaining that features of speech have not been systematically illustrated until recently because of the strong bias that most grammars of English have had towards the written language. As Moreno Jaén and Pérez Basanta (2009, p. 288) rightfully claim, "Teachers cannot teach conversation, which is by nature multimodal, with monomodal materials." Rodríguez Martín & Moreno Jaén (2009), who also rely on films in order to teach conversation, investigate some paradigmatic conversational processes by calling upon Rühlemann's situational framework (2007). In Rühlemann's (2007, p. 385) words, conversation is "the major situationally defined variety of the spoken language" and it can only be described on the basis of the situational factors that rule and define conversational exchanges.

The growing number of studies devoted to the type of formulaic language found in conversational routines is a tangible sign of the role that it plays in language learning and use. Formulae are in fact studied from at least three different perspectives: the cognitive, the pedagogical and the social. The best evidence of the importance of formulaic language is also, and more importantly, to be ascribed to its ubiquity in human communication. As Conklin and Schmitt (2012, p. 46) report, "Normal discourse, both written and spoken, contains large (but not yet fully determined) percentages of formulaic language." Linguists who calculated its recursiveness in different corpora using different methods came to similar conclusions, i.e., that "overall . . . formulaic language makes up between one third and one half of discourse" (Conklin & Schmitt, 2012, p. 469). One further consideration is yet in order: The processing of formulaic language is shown to be faster than that of nonformulaic language, and thus both perception and understanding of the dialogues might take advantage of this feature. In addition, when such chunks of language are learned, they can be successfully reused in appropriate situational contexts, as they are prefabricated routines that can be recalled as if they were a single word, thus saving on precious elaborating time when involved in online production.

Conversational routine is only one among various labels that are used to refer to a set of speech acts: routines, formulae or formulaic expressions (Bardovi-Harlig, 2012, 2013). Within this group, requests and apologies have perhaps been granted more attention. Quite recently greetings have also been focused upon, in that they betray different attitudes associated with different politeness requirements in lingua-cultures. As Coulmas (1979, p. 239) makes clear, the pragmatic conditions of their appropriate use can be accounted for "in terms of cognitive systems of beliefs, wants, wishes, preferences, norms, and values." Greetings, good wishes and introductions share a common purpose: the exchange of expressions and pleasantries between two people or a group interacting for the purpose of fulfilling social duties or creating and consolidating rapport. In most cases, greetings are used as a prelude to making a proper conversation or introducing the topic of a talk. Their specular counterpart, i.e., leave-takings, appear instead in closing sequences when people part, and they neatly round off a conversation (Eisenstein-Ebsworth, Bodman & Carpenter, 1996; Laver, 1981).

In general, greetings and leave-taking formulae 'proper' are used to open and close communication (phatic function), to express feelings and attitudes towards interlocutors (expressive function) and, more specifically, to indicate the relation between speaker and interlocutor in terms of power (superiority/inferiority) and solidarity (nearness/remoteness) (see Brown & Gilman, 1960). A special type of greeting may be 'inscribed' in an introduction (see Eisenstein-Ebsworth, Bodman & Carpenter, 1996), which may involve more or less ritualized exchanges with the specific function of allowing the parties to find a connection for the first time. Likewise, terms of direct address also express and codify social meaning along the scalar dimensions of power and vicinity. Finally, what counts as utterances of phatic communion varies a great deal across social groups and generations, and notably across cultures (Coupland, Coupland & Robinson, 1992, p. 213). Utterances of phatic communion can perform different functions depending on their position: When they occur in the opening phase of an exchange, they defuse the potential hostility of silence (e.g., talk about the weather and/or inquiries about health), and have initiatory and exploratory functions; when they occur in the closing phase, they typically bring about effects of mitigation (e.g., *I must leave*) and consolidation (e.g., *See you next Saturday*) of social relationships (Coupland, Coupland & Robinson, 1992).

The genre of the text also has a direct bearing on the use of social rituals: If in spontaneous conversation much time is granted to phatic talk, i.e., talk that is conducive to solidarity but does not achieve other discursive aims, in other genres social chit-chat might be far less employed. This is, for example, the case of cinematic language: Both films and television employ language that is planned to sound natural (see Section 10.3). Furthermore, an audiovisual text is severely limited in time and thus needs to squeeze the narrative into the time boundaries imposed by the format. Consequently, phatic talk and sequences that do not favor plot progression are only used when they are instrumental to the current situation. Sometimes the first meeting between two people is not shown onscreen, to save precious showing time, but the introduction is 'reabsorbed' in the departure formula that these people use, e.g., "It has been a pleasure meeting you" (for more details, see Bonsignori & Bruti, forthcoming).

Audiovisual texts prove to be quite a useful instrument for the teaching of pragmatics in that they are representative of naturally occurring speech from a pragmalinguistic perspective, although perhaps less so from a sociopragmatic perspective, as the scenarios that are presented are in some cases stereotypical. Moreover, these resources may offer students a global and visual representation that includes crucial interactional modes, i.e., kinesics, proxemics, oculesics and paralinguistic features (e.g., tone, volume, pitch and other voice qualities). Through the analysis of all these aspects, students can be made aware of key conversational practices and learn to deal with features of conversational grammar in context. They can also widen their awareness of the importance of being familiar with the grammar of conversation in order to improve their conversational competence. The feasibility of this method was shown to be successful for the teaching of compliments by Rose (2001), who compared a corpus of compliments extracted from American films with natural-occurring data, thus demonstrating that film language is a good representation of conversation. Similarly, the ADELEX research group (2007), which is devoted to the evaluation and development of lexical competence, has a research thread that addresses the teaching of conversational features through films.[4]

10.5 USING FILM CLIPS TO TEACH CONVERSATIONAL ROUTINES

In the teaching of conversation, especially to classes of postgraduate students whose command of the language is already quite good and who mainly need to be taught more subtle aspects of interaction in the foreign language, film data is extremely valuable. In class, it is essential to use material that is appropriate to the students' skills and that does not overburden them. For this reason, selected extracts—for example, scenes from DVDs, or cut clips from the digital version of the film—are to be preferred. The advantages of this method are numerous because only part of the time in class is devoted to watching the clips, which can be preceded and followed by *ad hoc* learning activities.

One of the assets of the previously described LFLFC—a project in which my university participates thanks to an institutional agreement—is that the film database can be queried through different search terms: descriptive tags, clip title, clip description, pedagogical comments, user comments and vocabulary. The most important ones for the teaching of conversational routines are descriptive tags, which in turn are divided into three broad areas: linguistics, speech acts and culture. Linguistic tags mainly refer to the act of locution (in the sense of Austin, 1962) and include grammatical features, lexicon, sociolects, genre and other tags (see Kaiser 2011 for more details). Speech acts point to the functional use of language and refer to both the illocutionary and perlocutionary aspects. Most conversational routines belong to this group, e.g., greetings, introductions and well-wishing, but also advice, interruptions and permissions. Finally, cultural tags include the setting where an exchange takes place (e.g., bank, school), actions that characters are engaged in (eating, grooming), and topics of discussion (education, marriage, elections, etc.; see Kaiser, 2011).

As Kaiser (2011) explains, tagging is sometimes a matter of individual choice, but the risk of inconsistency has been reduced by the methodical training of the taggers; furthermore, it is always possible for instructors who use clips to add their comments, for example, pinpointing a certain tag that is scarcely relevant. Also useful are the clip title and description: The former allows instructors to distinguish between different clips from the same film, whereas the latter helps students in particular to correctly locate the clip within the plot of a film that they might not have watched. This information may be kept hidden when showing the clip, in case the instructor thinks it unnecessary or conflicting with the kind of activities s/he has planned, for example, inferring from the visuals. Finally, some activities to be carried out with specific clips may be suggested by taggers. Likewise, instructors may comment on these activities or suggest others they have devised, or also suggest further tags. This obviously contributes to the dynamic quality of the database.

One further element that is tagged is the language of the clip: The main vocabulary items used in the clip are tagged so that they can offer a kind of reference framework to better understand the spoken exchange of the clip (it is important to keep in mind that clips are not 'simplified' excerpts, so the language employed may contain a number of difficulties and the speech pace is often quite rapid). Among more refined heuristic tools, there are subtitles, either in the language of the clip or interlingual, that is, in the target language, or both. The implications of using subtitles in language teaching are manifold, but it is up to the instructor to judge if and how to use them in certain activities. Subtitles in general are useful to bridge the gap between reading and listening skills and to improve rapid reading to keep up with the subtitles that accompany the dialogues (there are many studies that show their contribution to increased literacy; see, for example, Kothari 2001). Subtitles also facilitate correct pronunciation of words/expressions (consciously or not); make it easier to follow the plot; develop recognition skills; reinforce understanding of context-bound expressions, new vocabulary or idioms; as well as help students understand humor and motivate them to watch films on their own. In particular, subtitles in the language of the original are certainly helpful for understanding or clarifying expressions that otherwise learners would not recognize and thus retain; on the contrary, subtitles in the target language are instead particularly beneficial in establishing correct lexical mappings between lexemes in the two languages involved. Yet, there are also some shortcomings, as learners often concentrate so much on reading that they do not pay enough attention to the dialogues (even though the teacher may prepare tasks that induce them to do so). In any case, at a certain point subtitles need to be removed so that students get used to watching clips or films exploiting their own resources (see, inter alia, Danan, 2004; Vanderplank, 1988, 1990).

10.5.1 A Multimodal Analysis of Two Film Clips

Given the centrality of formulaic language in conversation, in what follows I propose an analysis—based on a multimodal transcription—of two clips from the LFLFC where greetings and leave-takings are crucial.

The audiovisual material on routines in the LFLFC is not extensive and it is not enriched with pedagogical material, although it would be possible to develop activities in the future.[5] The search across the film database for greetings returned 12 clips distributed in four films, *A Beautiful Mind, Up in the Air, 50 First Dates* and *The Devil Wears Prada*. All of them, except *A Beautiful Mind,* portray contemporary life.

The clip that I have chosen as a possible exemplification of greetings is entitled "Honeymoon through pictures," lasts 3:00 minutes and is taken from *Up in the Air* (Reitman, 2009). Subtitles are available in English. Apart from showing several examples of greetings, it also includes other interactional features, such as compliments and informal chat. The descriptors assigned to the clip are 'compliment,' 'greeting,' 'introduction,' 'professions' and 'wedding.' The interaction revolves around a family reunion to celebrate an engagement and a future wedding, so people greet each other, some new acquaintances are made and the future brothers-in-law discuss their jobs.

For reasons of space, I will report only some parts of the multimodal transcription of the clip, focusing, in particular, on two topical moments. As can be seen from the table below, the first column describes the consecutive shots, including the shot composition and the distance between the intended viewer and the depicted world. One aspect that is worth taking into account is what framing position (i.e., understanding the aesthetic and communicative effects that different shots have, i.e., close-ups, medium close-ups, medium shots, medium long shots, long shots and extreme long shots—see Lacey, 2005) and editing (i.e., the way the various shots are joined together) mean in the clip narrative. The second column is devoted to a description of kinesic and proxemic aspects. Kinesics encompasses hand and arm gestures, head movements, facial expressions, gaze and body posture (Kendon, 2004; McNeill, 1992; Ekman, 2007), while proxemics is concerned with interpersonal distance between the characters. The third column accommodates the audio track, comprising both noises and sounds other than music, which is included in the fourth column. The last column contains the names of the characters and the spoken dialogues. This multimodal transcription model is similar to that adopted by Wildfeuer (2013).

Table 10.1 "Honeymoon through pictures"—greeting

	Shot description	Kinesics and proxemics	Audio track	Music	Spoken language	
1	Medium shot of two people.	A man and a woman enter a restaurant room from the left, moving towards the camera.	Hubbub of voices, clattering of tableware.	Background music.		
2	Long shot of the crowded restaurant room. The two people enter the frame from the left.			Background music.		
3	Medium long shot of a woman sitting at the table seen from behind.	The woman at the table turns to look at the man who addresses her. She gets up and moves towards the new comers from right to left.		Background music.	RYAN JULIE	Hey, look who's here! Oh my God!
4	Medium close-up of the man, Ryan, and the woman, his girlfriend, Alex.	Ryan and Alex smile.		Background music.		
5	Medium close-up of another woman, Julie.	Julie enters the frame from the left and hugs Ryan. She pats him on the back with her right hand.		Background music.	JULIE RYAN	Oh my God! Ryan! Hey!

6	Medium close-up of Ryan and Julie.	Ryan and Julie smile.	Background music.	JULIE	Hi.
7	Medium close-up of Julie, seen from behind, facing Ryan and Alex.	Ryan and Alex smile.	Background music.		
8	Medium close-up of Julie; Ryan also seen on the left.	Julie raises her right arm, almost parallel to the floor.	Background music.	JULIE	You must be Alex.
9	Medium close-up of Julie, seen from behind, facing Ryan and Alex.	Julie and Alex shake hands.	Background music.	ALEX	Yes, I am. Hi. How are you?
10	Medium close-up of Julie looking at Alex; Ryan is partially seen on the left.	Alex turns towards Ryan.	Background music.	JULIE	You are so beautiful. Kara was right.
				ALEX	Thank you.

The most interesting part of the clip for the teaching of routines is obviously the first one, when Ryan and his girlfriend Alex arrive at Julie and Jim's rehearsal dinner: Here the various greetings mesh with introductions, as often happens in real life, and in cinematic language in particular (people have to be introduced not just because of the plot, but also to let the audience know who they are). The framing position and the editing in this clip both deserve attention. Apart from the first shot, which is a long shot of the room, serving the purpose of showing the setting, the majority are either medium close-ups or medium shots, insisting respectively on the characters' heads and shoulders or on most of their bodies. As can be seen from the transcription, their head movements, facial expressions and gestures accompany and complement their verbal exchange. The main type of edit in this extract is the shot/reverse-shot pattern, i.e., when character A is shown looking at character B, and then character B is shown looking back at character A. Since they are shown facing in opposite directions, the audience supposes that they are looking at each other. This strategy is typical of conversation and emphasizes the rapid succession of the turns, at the same time smoothing out the transition between shots so that the viewer perceives one continuous action that unfolds linearly. The only interesting instance of hand gesture in the extract above occurs when Julie raises her right arm, almost parallel to the floor, while turning to Alex for a proper introduction (shot 8), as reproduced in Figure 10.1.[6]

As Ferré (2011) contends, gestures are complex to interpret because they perform several functions at the same time: Here the arm raised in a horizontal position parses the speech and ushers in the introduction, but it also plays an interactional function, that of welcoming the newly-met woman.

Figure 10.1 "Honeymoon through pictures"—greeting and introduction, shot 8

The search for leave-takings returned five clips distributed in an equal number of films, *A Beautiful Mind, American Beauty, Up in the Air, 50 First Dates* and *The Devil Wears Prada*. Again, they all portray contemporary life, except for *A Beautiful Mind*.

The clip that I have chosen as an exemplification for leave-takings is entitled "Hitting on a girl, part 2," lasts 2:20 minutes and is taken from *50 First Dates* (Segal, 2004). Subtitles are available in English. The descriptors provided for the clip are 'animals,' 'dating,' 'flirtation,' 'leave-taking' and 'restaurant.' The reason why I have chosen this clip is that, apart from nicely showing how people often find it difficult to take leave, it is very humorous and lively. Furthermore, since I had not seen the film before, I was able to test whether the clip was comprehensible in itself. The two protagonists, Lucy and Henry, engage in conversation and talk about different sea creatures, and Henry shares some peculiar details about walruses. Lucy invites Henry for breakfast the following day and he accepts. The most important tags turn out to be 'flirtation' and 'leave-taking,' which, as shall be seen from the multimodal transcript below, mesh in interesting ways. Again, for reasons of space, I will comment on the ending of the clip, although it has been completely transcribed.

As the two young people get along well and enjoy each other's company, when it is time to part, they find it difficult and make up excuses to restart the conversation. This is why the extract is especially useful for understanding the logic of turn-taking, with its topic closings and re-openings, and the various departing techniques that are used. After Lucy says she has to go, Henry asks her why, gaining some more time. These conversational management devices (Rodríguez Martín & Moreno Jaén, 2009) are reflected in the framing position, which mostly exploits medium close-ups or medium shots of the two interactants, apart from a long shot that helps situate them in the setting. The kinesic and proxemic elements in this part are numerous and meaningful, and perform different functions: When Henry turns to go, Lucy points with her right thumb towards the café and draws nearer to Henry, uttering the following words, "Would you like to have breakfast again?" (shot 6), as reproduced in Figure 10.2.

In this case, Lucy's pointing at the café qualifies as a substantive gesture (Kendon, 1995), as it provides necessary content information. In contrast, all the other features variously contribute to expressing pragmatic information, ranging from the signaling of discourse boundaries (when they both stretch out their hands to shake them) to the expression of emotional states. For the latter, this first occurs when they agree to meet again the following day and then go their separate ways—they can finally release the tension that has built up, so both of them, independently of one another, begin to dance to express their excitement. It occurs again when the van parked between their cars drives away and they catch sight of each other dancing. They are first paralyzed with embarrassment, then Henry rushes to his car to rapidly disappear and Lucy covers her face with both hands. It

Table 10.2 "Hitting on a girl, part 2"—leave-taking

	Shot description	Kinesics and proxemics	Audio track	Music	Spoken language	
1	Medium shot of Lucy and Henry.	Lucy touches her watch and bends her knees slightly.	Lucy and Henry laugh.		LUCY	I have to go.
2	Medium shot of Henry, Lucy seen from behind.				HENRY	Where you going?
3	Medium shot of Lucy, Henry seen from behind.	Lucy makes a circular movement with her right arm. Then she moves her right forearm towards her body and slightly bends her head to the right.			LUCY	It's my dad's birthday and we go every year and pick a pineapple. It's a tradition.
4	Medium close-up of Henry, Lucy seen from behind.	Henry rocks from side to side.		Background music.	HENRY	That sounds nice. Okay, well . . . I had a great time. . . .
5	Medium close-up of Lucy, Henry seen from behind.			Background music.	LUCY	Me too.
					HENRY	Okay.
6	Medium shot of both.	Henry turns to go. Lucy points with her right thumb towards the café and draws nearer to Henry.		Background music.	LUCY	Would you like to have breakfast again?

7	Medium close-up of Henry, Lucy seen from behind.	Henry continues moving, this time back and forth.		Background music.	LUCY	Tomorrow morning, same time, as I teach an art class at 10.
					HENRY	Oh, really?
					LUCY	Yeah.
					HENRY	I wish I could make it, but . . . yes, I will be there.
8	Medium shot of both of them.	Lucy stretches out her right hand. Henry does the same. Lucy slightly bends her knees. They shake hands. She bows and kisses Henry's hand.	Lucy giggles.	Background music.	LUCY	Take care.
					HENRY	Okay.
					HENRY	Oh.
					LUCY	One for the road. It is fishy.
9	Long shot of Lucy and Henry.	Lucy and Henry approach their cars.		Background music.	HENRY	Got you good. Aloha.
					LUCY	Aloha.
10	Medium close-up of Henry.	Henry walks between a car and a van, smiling.		Background music.	HENRY	See you tomorrow. Oh my God.
11	Medium close-up of Lucy's back. Then she turns towards the camera, smiling.	Lucy is next to her car. She starts dancing, shaking her arms in the air. She turns while the van parked between her car and Henry's drives away. Henry dances, his back to the camera. Each turns around and they see each other dancing. Lucy is agape.		Music is louder. A new rhythm starts.	LUCY	Oh my goodness.

(*Continued*)

Table 10.2 (Continued)

	Shot description	Kinesics and proxemics	Audio track	Music	Spoken language	
12				Music stops.	HENRY	Oh . . .
13	Medium close-up of Lucy, Henry's back is to the camera.					
14	Medium close-up of Henry turning his back to the camera.	Henry rushes to his car and opens the door.			HENRY	Shit.
15	Medium close-up of Lucy.	Lucy smiles. She covers her face with her hands and gets in her car.				
16	Medium close-up of Henry, inside his pick-up.		Sound of the engine of Henry's car.		HENRY	I had a . . . bee on me.
17	Medium close-up of Lucy, in her car.	Lucy smiles.	Lucy giggles. Sound of the engine of Lucy's car.		LUCY HENRY (VOICE-OVER)	All right. He was a big one.
18	Medium close-up of an old, Hawaiian man.	After completing his turn, the man disappears to the right.	He says something in the local language.		HAWAIIAN MAN	. . . which means "look at those two shitheads."

Figure 10.2 "Hitting on a girl, part 2"—leave-taking, shot 6

is quite interesting to observe which verbal elements complement the kinesic ones: Henry, in fact, cannot avoid cursing and invents the most banal of excuses to justify his dancing, while Lucy smiles and seems to accept Henry's excuse.

10.5.2 Some Reflections on Using Multimodal Transcription to Teach Conversational Routines

The multimodal analysis of two film clips that I have proposed in this chapter shows how these resources can be effectively used to teach conversational routines from a holistic perspective, focusing not only on language, but also on key nonlinguistic aspects of interaction. More specifically, film clips can also be exploited to reflect on cultural values, behaviors and traditions of the lingua-culture portrayed in the clip as an instrument to enrich students' intercultural competence. Finally, as the analysis has demonstrated, they can be employed to explore the meaning-making potential of the several semiotic systems working together in audiovisual texts (Kaiser, 2011).

In the classroom, multiple viewings of clips may be exploited, for example, starting with a first 'dumb' viewing, which allows learners to understand the context, identify the main characters and notice the kinesic and proxemic aspects of the interactions. This is essential to form some expectations on the story world and the plot, which will enable them to later concentrate on the phonetic and semantic components of the dialogue, in a second and third viewing. The addition of subtitles, when available, or also when prepared by the instructor for a particular purpose, may be a bonus because they provide learners with confirmatory/nonconfirmatory evidence of what they understood. In addition, they allow them to reflect on some of the formal properties of the language in the dialogues and to connect auditory to visual input (Garza, 1991). Utilizing different input modes and connecting them with one another helps learners with form-meaning mapping, a vital step for foreign language acquisition (Doughty, 2004). Research on the use of captioning—an alternative label for subtitling, found especially in SLA literature (Danan, 2004; Vanderplank, 1988, 1990; Winke, Gass & Sydorenko, 2010)—shows that subtitles help learners notice and parse "structural patterns or chunks in the videos, which may assist them in remembering and learning from the patterns presented" (Winke, Gass & Sydorenko, 2010, p. 81). The role of chunks has strongly been supported in the SLA literature (see Section 10.4 and Conklin & Schmitt, 2012, inter alia), because information processing in chunks is less costly than processing individual bits and then linking form and meaning. As for the processing of formulaic sequences, Conklin and Schmitt (2012) recognize that they are easier to process than matched nonformulaic sequences.

After the showing phase, with the audio and video combinations indicated above, the instructor may present a grid for multimodal transcription such as the one used in Tables 10.1 and 10.2 above, and show students how to apply it to the clip. In this way, students will pay attention to the contribution of any element to the expression of interpersonal meaning, but also to important cultural correlates, such as the gestures or body postures that are used when greeting someone, or when being introduced to a stranger in a different culture. To go one step further in the analysis of audiovisual data, ELAN (*E*UDICO—European Distributed Corpora—*L*inguistic *An*notator), "an annotation tool that allows you to create, edit, visualize and search annotations for video and audio data" (Austin, 2013), could be adopted.[7] One of the strengths of this tool is that it can find elements in the data and analyze multimodal texts in a fine-grained way, as each level of analysis has a specific "tier," but all of them can be visualized at the same time. However, since the manual annotation requires extended time, a sample analysis could be carried out by the instructor and shown in class to enhance students' sensitivity towards the interplay of the various semiotic levels.

10.6 CONCLUSIONS

The purpose of this study was to endorse the use of audiovisual texts (mainly clips for the reasons explained previously) for teaching aspects of interactional dynamics and fostering multimodal awareness in the foreign language class. After establishing the feasibility of using film dialogue as a model for face-to-face conversation, I have considered the case of conversational routines. In particular, I have suggested ways of exploiting film clips, such as those contained in the Berkeley LFLFC database, by means of a multimodal transcription that integrates linguistic analysis with information encoded in nonlinguistic channels (e.g., the technical aspects related to framing and editing, and the nonverbal signals of communication expressed through kinesics and proxemics). Afterwards, I suggested possible uses of film clips in the language classroom for the teaching of linguistic and cultural aspects of conversational routines in the target language, relying on different audio and video combinations that also highlight their multimodal dimension.

The model proposed for using film clips in language instruction is a starting point that could be extended to include other interesting aspects of face-to-face interaction, such as oculesics and paralanguage. An analysis of oculesics (Ekman, Friesen & Ellsworth, 1982) would make it possible to evaluate how and to what extent people hold eye contact and what they convey through it (e.g., paying attention, showing respect, expressing a variety of emotions). It must be noted that culture plays a relevant role in this respect, as the necessity for eye contact differs radically across cultures, and learners could thus be made aware of different requirements. Likewise, it would be worthwhile to investigate the paralinguistic features of speech (Poyatos, 2002). These include loudness, rate, pitch, pitch contour and voice qualities, that is, "the permanently present, background, person-identifying feature[s] of speech" (Crystal, 1991, p. 376), such as nasality, breathiness, and idiosyncratic features (e.g., 'strangled' or 'throaty' voice). This type of analysis would be extremely useful for understanding characterization and for fathoming the attitudinal and emotional qualities of an utterance.

NOTES

1. Interactive white boards (known in Italian as LIM, i.e., Lavagne Interattive Multimediali) became popular in Italy—although somewhat later than in other European countries, in particular the UK—and began to be used in schools in 2006, after Giuseppe Fioroni, minister of education at the time, announced their introduction (see Veltri, 2006). The initiative was also supported by his successor, Maria Stella Gelmini, who revamped the project with the clear objective of supplying Italian schools with 10,000 interactive white boards (see Dotta, 2008).
2. For a review of some possible limitations, see Canning-Wilson (2000).
3. The University of Pisa joined the project in 2014. I wish to thank Mark Kaiser, associate director of the Berkeley Language Center and manager of the LFLFC project, for granting me permission to utilize the LFLFC database for my research purposes.
4. The project of the ADELEX (Assessing and Developing Lexical Competence through the Internet) research group is based at the University of Granada and is coordinated by Pérez Basanta.
5. The number of clips in English is also lower in comparison with the material available in other languages, as the interest of the Berkeley group is primarily in the teaching of foreign languages, i.e., languages other than English.

6. The two illustrative images reproduced in this chapter were captured from film DVDs owned by the Language Center of the University of Pisa.
7. ELAN was developed at the Max Planck Institute for Psycholinguistics, the Language Archive, Nijmegen, the Netherlands. It is freely available at http://tla.mpi.nl/tools/tla-tools/elan/.

REFERENCES

ADELEX Research Group. (2007). Exploring conversational grammar through films. Retrieved from http://www.ugr.es/~inped/exploringnewpaths/conversationalgrammar/introduction.htm.

Austin, J. L. (1962). *How to do things with words*. Oxford: Clarendon Press.

Austin, P. K. (2013). Software tools for language documentation (PowerPoint presentation). Retrieved from www.hrelp.org/events/workshops/aaken2013/assets/pka_software.ppt.

Baldry, A., & Thibault, P. J. (2006). *Multimodal transcription and text analysis: A multimedia toolkit and coursebook*. London: Equinox.

Ballarin, E. (2007). Materiale audiovisivo e glottodidattica. In G. Cardona (Ed.), *Vedere per capire e parlare: Il testo audiovisivo nella didattica delle lingue* (pp. 7–25). Torino: UTET.

Baños-Piñero, R. (2013). 'That is cool': Investigating the translation of adverbial intensifiers in English-Spanish dubbing through a parallel corpus of sitcoms. *Perspectives: Studies in Translatology, 21*(4), 526–542. Special issue: Corpus linguistics and audiovisual translation: In search of an integrated approach, edited by R. Baños-Piñero, S. Bruti, & S. Zanotti.

Baños-Piñero, R., & Chaume, F. (2009). Prefabricated orality: A challenge in audiovisual translation. *InTRAlinea*. Special issue: The translation of dialects in multimedia. Retrieved from http://www.intralinea.org/specials/article/1714.

Bardovi-Harlig, K. (2012). Formulas, routines, and conventional expressions in pragmatics research. *Annual Review of Applied Linguistics, 32*, 206–227.

Bardovi-Harlig, K. (2013). Pragmatic routines. In C. A. Chapelle (Ed.), *The encyclopedia of applied linguistics* (pp. 1–7). London: Wiley-Blackwell.

Bateman, J. (2014). Looking for what counts in film analysis: A program of empirical research. In D. Machin (Ed.), *Visual communication* (pp. 310–329). Berlin: De Gruyter Mouton.

Bateman, J., & Schmidt, K.-H. (2012). *Multimodal film analysis: How films mean*. New York: Routledge.

Biber, D. (1988). *Variation across speech and writing*. Cambridge: Cambridge University Press.

Biber, D., Johansson, S., Leech, G., Conrad, S., & Finegan, E. (1999). *Longman grammar of spoken and written English*. Essex: Pearson Education Limited.

Bonsignori, V., & Bruti, S. (forthcoming). Translating introductions and wishes in audiovisual dialogue: Evidence from a corpus. In M. Ji (Ed.), *Empirical translation studies: Interdisciplinary methods explored*. London: Equinox.

Brown, R., & Gilman, A. (1960). The pronouns of power and solidarity. In T. Sebeok (Ed.), *Style in language* (pp. 253–276). Cambridge, MA: MIT Press.

Canning-Wilson, C. (2000). Practical aspects of using video in the foreign language classroom. *The Internet TESL Journal*, 6(11). Retrieved from http://iteslj.org/Articles/Canning- Video.html.

Carter, R., & McCarthy, M. (2006). *Cambridge grammar of English*. Cambridge: Cambridge University Press.

Celentin, P. (2007). Applicazioni didattiche del video. In G. Cardona (Ed.), *Vedere per capire e parlare: Il testo audiovisivo nella didattica delle lingue* (pp. 27–51). Milano: UTET.

Chaume, F. (2012). *Audiovisual translation: Dubbing*. Manchester, UK: St. Jerome.

Conklin, K., & Schmitt, N. (2012). The processing of formulaic language. *Annual Review of Applied Linguistics, 32*, 45–61.

Coulmas, F. (1979). On the sociolinguistic relevance of routine formula. *Journal of Pragmatics, 3*(3/4), 239–266.

Coulmas, F. (Ed.). (1981). *Conversational routine: Explorations in standardized communication situations and prepatterned speech*. The Hague: Mouton.

Coupland, J., Coupland, N. & Robinson, J. D. (1992). 'How are you?': Negotiating phatic communion. *Language in Society, 21*(2), 207–230.

Crystal, D. (1991). *A dictionary of linguistics and phonetics* (3rd edition). Oxford: Blackwell.

Danan, M. (2004). Captioning and subtitling: Undervalued language learning strategies. *Meta: Translators' Journal, 49*(1), 67–77.

Dotta, G. (2008, October 3). Nelle scuole arriva la lavagna interattiva. *Webnews*. Retrieved from http://www.webnews.it/2008/10/03/nelle-scuole-arriva-la-lavagna-interattiva.

Doughty, C. J. (2004). Effect of instruction on learning a second language: A critique of instructed SLA research. In B. VanPatten, J. Williams, & S. Rott (Eds.), *Form-meaning connections in second language acquisition* (pp. 181–202). Mahwah, NJ: Lawrence Erlbaum Associates, Inc.

Eisenstein-Ebsworth, M., Bodman, J.W., & Carpenter M. (1996). Cross-cultural realization of greetings in American English. In S.M. Gass, & J. Neu (Eds.), *Speech acts across cultures: Challenges to communication in a second language* (pp. 89–107). Berlin: Mouton de Gruyter.

Ekman, P. (2007). *Emotions revealed: Recognizing faces and feelings to improve communication and emotional life* (2nd edition). New York: Owl Books.

Ekman, P., Friesen, W.V., & Ellsworth, P. (1982). What emotion categories or dimensions can observers judge from facial behavior? In P. Ekman (Ed.), *Emotion in the human face*. New York: Cambridge University Press.

Ferré, G. (2011). Functions of three open palm gestures. *Multimodal communication, 1*(1), 5–20.

Forchini, P. (2012). *Movie language revisited: Evidence from multi-dimensional analysis and corpora*. Bern: Peter Lang.

Garza, T. J. (1991). Evaluating the use of captioned video materials in advanced foreign language learning. *Foreign Language Annals, 24*(3), 239–258.

Gregory, M., & Carroll, S. (1978). *Language and situation: Language varieties and their social contexts*. London: Routledge.

Gullberg, M. (2006). Some reasons for studying gesture and second language acquisition (Hommage à Adam Kendon). *IRAL, 44*(2), 103–124.

Holmes, J. (1988). Paying compliments: A sex-preferential positive politeness strategy. *Journal of Pragmatics, 12*(3), 445–465.

Holmes, J. (1989). Sex differences and apologies: One aspect of communicative competence. *Applied Linguistics, 10*(2), 194–221.

Holmes, J. (1990). Apologies in New Zealand English. *Language in Society, 19*(2), 155–159.

Kaiser, M. (2011). New approaches to exploiting film in the foreign language classroom. *L2 Journal, 3*(2), 232–249.

Kendon, A. (1995). Gestures as illocutionary and discourse markers in Southern Italian conversation. *Journal of Pragmatics, 23*(3), 247–279.

Kendon, A. (2004). *Gesture: Visible action as utterance*. Cambridge: Cambridge University Press.

Kite, Y., & Tatsuki, D. (2005). Remedial interactions in film. In D. Tatsuki (Ed.), *Pragmatics in language learning, theory and practice* (pp. 99–118). Tokyo: Japan Association for Language Teaching Pragmatics Special Interest Group.

Kothari, B. (2001). Same language subtitling: Watch TV "and" read. *Information Technology in Developing Countries, 11*(2). Retrieved from http://www.iimahd.ernet.in/egov/ifip/aug2001/article1.htm.

Kress, G., & van Leeuwen, T. (1996). *Reading images: The grammar of visual design.* London: Routledge.

Lacey, N. (2005). *Introduction to film.* Basingstoke: Palgrave Macmillan.

Laver, J. (1981). Linguistic routines and politeness in greeting and parting. In F. Coulmas (Ed.), *Conversational routine: Explorations in standardized communication situations and prepatterned speech.* (pp. 289–304). The Hague: Mouton.

Manes, J., & Wolfson, N. (1981). The compliment formula. In F. Coulmas (Ed.), *Conversational routine: Explorations in standardized communication situations and prepatterned speech.* (pp. 115–132). The Hague: Mouton.

Massi, M.P., & Merino, A.G. (1996). Films and EFL: What's playing in the language classroom. *Forum, 34*(1), 20–23.

McNeill, D. (1992). *Hand and mind: What gestures reveal about thought.* Chicago: The University of Chicago Press.

Moreno Jaén, M., & Pérez Basanta, C. (2009). Developing conversational competence through language awareness and multimodality: The use of DVDs. *ReCALL 21*(3), 283–301.

O'Halloran, K. (2004) *Multimodal discourse analysis.* London: Continuum.

Piazza, R. (2010). Voice-over and self-narrative in film: A multimodal analysis of Antonioni's *When love fails (Tentato suicidio). Language and Literature, 19*(2), 173–195.

Poyatos, F. (2002). *Nonverbal communication across disciplines: Volume II. Paralanguage, kinesics, silence, personal and environmental interaction.* Amsterdam: Benjamins.

Quaglio, P. (2009a). *Television dialogue: The sitcom* Friends *vs. natural conversation.* Amsterdam: Benjamins.

Quaglio, P. (2009b). Vague language in the situation comedy *Friends* vs. natural conversation. In M. Freddi, & M. Pavesi (Eds.), *Analysing audiovisual dialogue: Linguistic and translational insights* (pp. 75–91). Bologna: CLUEB.

Rodríguez Martín, M.E. (2006). La enseñanza del léxico através del cine en un entorno virtual. In C. Pérez Basanta (Ed.), *Fundamentos teóricos y prácticos de ADELEX: Una investigación sobre la evaluación y el desarrollo de la competencia léxica através delas nuevas tecnologías* (pp. 229–248). Granada: Comares.

Rodríguez Martín, M.E. (2010). Exploring conversational grammar through films in the ELT classroom: A corpus-based approach. In M. Moreno Jaén, F. Serrano Valverde, & M. Calzada Pérez (Eds.), *Exploring new paths in language pedagogy: Lexis and corpus-based language teaching* (pp. 245–258). London: Equinox.

Rodríguez Martín, M.E., & Moreno Jaén, M. (2009). Teaching conversation through films: A comparison of conversational features and collocations in the BNC and a micro-corpus of movies. *International Journal of Learning, 16*(7), 445–458.

Rose, K.R. (2001). Compliments and compliment responses in film: Implications for pragmatics research and language teaching. *IRAL, 39*(4), 309–326.

Rühlemann, C. (2007). *Conversation in context: A corpus-driven approach.* London: Continuum.

Shawback, M.J., & Terhune, N.M. (2002). Online interactive courseware: Using movies to promote cultural understanding in a CALL environment. *ReCALL, 14*(1), 85–95.

Stoller, F. L. (1995). Films and videotapes in the content-based ESL/EFL classroom. In T. Kral (Ed.), *Selected articles from the English forum: Creative class activities 1989–1993* (pp. 62–69). Washington, DC: Office of English Language Programs, United States Department of State.
Sueyoshi, A., & Hardison, D.M. (2005). The role of gestures and facial cues in second language listening comprehension. *Language Learning, 55*(4), 661–699.
Tatsuki, D. (2006, May 13–14). What is authenticity? In *Authentic communication: Proceedings of the 5th Annual JALT—SIG Conference* (pp. 1–15). Shizuoka, Japan: Tokai University College of Marine Science. Retrieved from https://jalt.org/pansig/2006/HTML/Tatsuki.htm.
Tatsuki, D., & Kite, Y. (2006). Comparing film dialogue and ethnographic data cited in pragmatics research. *ATEM Bulletin: Teaching English through Movies, 11*, 26–39.
Tatsuki, D., & Nishizawa, M. (2005). A comparison of compliments and compliment responses in television interviews, film, and naturally occurring data. In D. Tatsuki (Ed.), *Pragmatics in language learning, theory and practice* (pp. 87–98). Tokyo: Japan Association for Language Teaching Pragmatics Special Interest Group.
Vanderplank, R. (1988). The value of teletext sub-titles in language learning. *ELT Journal, 42*(4), 272–281.
Vanderplank, R. (1990). Paying attention to the words: Practical and theoretical problems in watching television programmes with uni-lingual (CEEFAX) sub-titles. *System, 18*(2), 221–234.
Veltri, C. (2006, October 3). Fioroni promuove la Finanziaria "Sicurezza e obbligo a 16 anni." *La Repubblica*. Retrieved from http://www.repubblica.it/2006/07/sezioni/scuola_e_universita/servizi/scuola-2007/fioroni-finanziaria/fioroni-finanziaria.html.
Wildfeuer, J. (2013). *Film discourse interpretation: Towards a new paradigm for multimodal film analysis*. New York: Routledge.
Winke, P., Gass, S., & Sydorenko, T. (2010). The effects of captioning videos used for foreign language listening activities. *Language Learning & Technology, 14*(1), 65–86.

FILMOGRAPHY

A beautiful mind, R. Howard (2001), USA.
The devil wears Prada, D. Frankel (2006), USA.
"Hitting on a girl, part 2" (13:57–16:17), clip from *50 first dates,* P. Segal (2004), USA.
"Honeymoon through pictures" (73:00–76:00), clip from *Up in the air,* J. Reitman (2009), USA.

Contributors

Silvia Bruti, PhD in English from the University of Pisa, is associate professor of English language and linguistics at the University of Pisa. She is currently director of studies of the master in modern Euro-American languages and literatures. Her research interests include topics such as text linguistics, discourse analysis, (historical) pragmatics, corpus linguistics, translation and language teaching. She has published widely in these areas and has co-edited several collections of essays, on reformulation and paraphrase, on lexicography and translation, and on audiovisual translation. She has recently investigated issues in intercultural pragmatics and audiovisual translation. Her most recent work is a monograph on the translation of politeness (Pisa University Press, 2013).

Mari Carmen Campoy-Cubillo is senior lecturer at the Department of English Studies, Universitat Jaume I (Spain). Her main research interests are in the areas of language testing and the application of multimodal corpus linguistics to the teaching of foreign languages. She is a member of GRAPE (Group for Research on Academic and Professional English) and co-editor of the online international journal *Language Value.*

Belinda Crawford Camiciottoli is associate professor of English language and linguistics at the University of Pisa (Italy). Her current research focuses mainly on interpersonal, pragmatic and multimodal features of discourse found in both academic and professional settings, with particular reference to corpus-assisted methodologies. She is the coordinator of the Corpus Research Unit at the University of Pisa Language Center. She has published in leading international journals, including *Discourse & Communication, English for Specific Purposes* and *Business and Professional Communication Quarterly*. In 2013, she published the book *Rhetoric in Financial Discourse: A Linguistic Analysis of ICT-mediated Disclosure Genres* (Rodopi).

Giuliana Diani is a tenured researcher at the University of Modena and Reggio Emilia. She holds an MA in language studies from the University of Lancaster (UK) and a PhD in English linguistics from the University of Pisa (Italy). She has worked on various aspects of discourse analysis and EAP, and language variation across academic genres, disciplines and cultures by analyzing small specialized corpora. Her recent publications include the books *Reviewing Academic Research in the Disciplines: Insights into the Book Review Article in English* (Officine Edizioni, 2012) and *Academic Evaluation: Review Genres in University Settings* (co-edited with Ken Hyland, Palgrave Macmillan, 2009).

Inmaculada Fortanet-Gómez is a senior lecturer and researcher at Universitat Jaume I (Castellón, Spain), where she coordinates the Group for Research on Academic and Professional English. Her research interests are related to academic and professional English and language integrated learning in higher education. She is the author of *CLIL in European Higher Education* (Multilingual Matters, 2013) and has authored chapters and co-edited several internationally published books. She has published articles in *Ibérica, Journal of English for Academic Purposes, Discourse Studies,* and *English for Specific Purposes,* among others.

Juan Carlos Palmer-Silveira, PhD, lectures and carries out research at Universitat Jaume I (Castellón, Spain). He is mainly interested in teaching English for business communication. He has authored and edited several books and articles internationally for over 20 years, mainly related to EAP/ESP. His main research interests are in the fields of academic and professional English, oral English discourse and business presentations in international corporations. He is currently studying how multimodality can help students and professionals to enhance communication in business-related settings.

Mercedes Querol-Julián is a lecturer at the Universidad Internacional de la Rioja (Spain). She is a member of the research group EDEPIG *(Educación Personalizada en la Era Digital).* Her research interests include multimodal analysis of academic spoken discourse and foreign language teaching.

Christine Räisänen is professor of organization and communication at Chalmers University, Gothenburg, Sweden. Her current research areas are organizational change, organizational discourse and leadership. She teaches leadership and communication at the graduate level as well as academic and professional writing for PhD students. She has co-authored a textbook on academic writing and has published in international education and management journals.

Miguel F. Ruiz-Garrido, PhD, member of GRAPE, is an associate professor at Universitat Jaume I (Castellón, Spain). His main research fields are

English for professional and academic purposes. He co-edited *Intercultural and International Business Communication: Theory, Research and Teaching* (Peter Lang, 2006) and *English for Professional and Academic Purposes* (Rodopi, 2010). His latest co-authored article on chairmen's statements was published in 2014 in *Business and Professional Communication Quarterly*.

Noelia Ruiz-Madrid is senior lecturer in the Department of English Studies at Universitat Jaume I (Castellón, Spain), where she teaches both undergraduate and postgraduate courses in the areas of EAP, ESP and EFL methodology. Her research focuses on discourse analysis, genre and integrating technology in the EFL classroom. Her more recent publications have appeared in the *International Journal of English Studies* and *Ibérica*, among others.

Julia Valeiras Jurado holds a degree in English language and literature from the University of Seville and a master's degree in English for international trade from Jaume I University in Castellón. Since 2010 she has worked as a teaching assistant for business and scientific English at University Jaume I and Ghent University in Belgium. She is currently working on a PhD that focuses on a contrastive analysis of the expression of persuasion in different types of oral presentations. Her research interests are oral discourse and genres, intonation and gestures as semiotic modes, and persuasive language.

Zuocheng Zhang holds a PhD from the University of Sydney and is currently a senior lecturer in TESOL education at the University of New England, Australia. His research interests include business English, multimodality, professional discourses and identities, genre studies, university to workplace transition, and pluralingualism and community well-being. He has published extensively on these topics in books and journals such as *English for Specific Purposes* and the *International Journal of Business Communication*.

Index

For Product Safety Concerns and Information please contact our EU
representative GPSR@taylorandfrancis.com
Taylor & Francis Verlag GmbH, Kaufingerstraße 24, 80331 München, Germany

www.ingramcontent.com/pod-product-compliance
Ingram Content Group UK Ltd.
Pitfield, Milton Keynes, MK11 3LW, UK
UKHW022351190926
475702UK00015B/2227
9781138549074